D0754368

choosing to preach

OTHER BOOKS BY KENTON C. ANDERSON

Preaching with Integrity

Preaching with Conviction: Communicating with Postmodern Listeners

choosing to preach

a comprehensive introduction to *sermon options* and *structures*

kenton c. anderson

GRAND RAPIDS, MICHIGAN 49530 USA

ZONDERVAN®

Choosing to Preach

Requests for information should be addressed to:
Zondervan, *Grand Rapids, Michigan 49530*

Library of Congress Cataloging-in-Publication Data

Anderson, Kenton C.
Choosing to preach : a comprehensive introduction to sermon options and structures / Kenton C. Anderson.
p. cm.
Includes bibliographical references and index.
ISBN-10: 0-310-26750-1
ISBN-13: 978-0-310-26750-8
1. Preaching I. Title.
BV4211.3.A535 2006
251—dc22

2006014873

Interior design by Tracey Walker

Printed in the United States of America

---

06 07 08 09 10 11 • 18 17 16 15 14 13 12 11 10 9 8 7 6 5 4 3 2 1

To my students
from every corner of the world,
in celebration of their courageous choice to preach.

contents

list of discussion questions and practical exercises

CHAPTER	DISCUSSION QUESTION	PAGE	PRACTICAL EXERCISE	PAGE
1	1	22	1	31
	2	26		
	3	28		
2	4	34	2	46
	5	38		
	6	42		
	7	44		
3				
Option 3A	8	64	3	53
Option 3B	9	75	4	74
	10	83	5	76
			6	80
4				
Option 4A	11	93	7	91
	12	95		
	13	99		
	14	100		
Option 4B	15	109	8	107
	16	123	9	108
			10	124
5	17	138	11	137
	18	145	12	143
			13	146
6	19	167	14	164
	20	175	15	172
			16	176
7	21	188	17	194
	22	190		
	23	191		
8	24	214	18	221
	25	223		
9	26	246	19	249

preface

I appreciate your taking the time to look at this book. I hope that the title doesn't frighten you. The word *preach* might indicate that this book is for professional preachers or for seminary students. Certainly, that is true. This book aspires to influence the next generation of professional preachers along with those who are long established in their ministries. But this book is not only for the pros.

Preaching takes place whenever and wherever God's people open God's Word with the idea that they might help others hear what God is saying. That can happen anywhere—a small group Bible study in your living room, a ladies' tea on Friday night, a weekend youth retreat at the ski hill, or at the local coffee shop.

Overall, this book affirms expository preaching with a lowercase *e*. It encourages preachers to expose the Word of God but does not demand that a particular form or approach be used. In fact, this book offers a variety of sermon forms in the understanding that God did not create us all alike and we don't all listen the same way. The preacher's job is to help people hear from God. That sometimes means translating the message into languages and forms that the listener is able to hear. The primary concern is that people hear from God as they hear his Word preached.

This book takes a gender-neutral approach, not to take any strong position on the ordination of women but simply to acknowledge that different readers will have different perspectives on the issue. This approach again affirms that preaching, properly defined, can take place in many contexts (Sunday school classes, women's meetings, etc.), some of which present no gender barrier for even the most conservative evangelical denominations.

Throughout the text, I have sprinkled discussion questions, practical exercises, and insights and ideas. As an added feature, the discussion questions can be actively engaged on my website, www.preaching.org. A variety of website tools will allow you to take your study of these themes to a deeper level. Use the sermon-building instrument as a step-by-step guide through the process of preparing to preach. Post your sermons on the sermon forum and offer helpful critique on others' sermons as well. Purchase of this book entitles you to a free six-month subscription to the website. I hope you will take advantage of this opportunity. The CD-ROM accompanying this book gives you a password key to the website, as well as a helpful PowerPoint presentation and audio sermon examples.

Preaching requires making choices. Thousands of choices must be made in the preparation of a sermon—functional choices like whether to use deduction or induction, cognition or affection, and content choices like which story to use or which word to choose. Yet they all begin with one fundamental choice: choosing to preach.

Preaching is a choice. No one demands it of us. Few will be disappointed if we choose to go another way. The only problem is that some of us whom God has chosen can't escape the sense that we have been *called* to preach. This book is for those people—for us—all of us, professional or not. We preach because we have been chosen. We preach because the world needs to hear what preachers have to say. We choose to preach because we cannot do otherwise.

—Kent Anderson
Langley, British Columbia, Canada

acknowledgments

This book was written while the author was on sabbatical at Spurgeon's College in London. Working in the shadow of C. H. Spurgeon was inspiring. Thanks to the good folks at Spurgeon's for the opportunity. Thanks also to the team at Northwest Baptist Seminary and ACTS Seminaries for letting me go and for covering for me in my absence. I appreciate your partnership in the important work of developing godly Christian leaders for kingdom service.

Of course, I am particularly grateful to my family. Thank you, Karen, Kelsey, Kirk, and Katelyn, for sharing the adventure with me. Thanks also to my parents, Rodney and Myrna Anderson, who formed a faith foundation on which I am privileged to build.

I'm also grateful to Paul Engle and Brian Phipps at Zondervan, whose guidance and support has been appreciated. Their vision for this project took me to another level.

Finally, thanks and glory to God for the gift of his Word and for the privilege of preaching it.

introduction

preaching at a crossroads

I sometimes wonder whether preaching is worth the effort. I don't know whether it is any harder to get up a sermon today than it used to be, but it sure feels like it is. In the old days, preachers didn't have so much competition. I suppose I'm not ancient enough to have experienced the "old days," but I imagine that to be the case. Surely there was a time when preachers didn't have to compete with the luminaries of preaching, featured on the radio and television and in MP3 downloads. Surely there was a time when people felt obligated to come to church and listen, whether or not the sermon was any good. There must have been a time when preaching was less complicated, when there was one way to prepare a sermon and everybody knew what it was.

If that day existed, it has passed. If they must preach, preachers today are expected to be as deep as St. Augustine, as practical as Billy Graham, and as entertaining as Jay Leno. If a preacher does not possess all of these qualities, listeners can easily find one who does, if not down the street, then certainly on television or on the Internet. Or they might choose not to listen to preaching anymore at all.

Preaching today is at a crossroads. Changes in church and culture have undone the prior consensus on the importance of biblical exposition as a staple of church life. Local church leaders currently hear from an array of influencial preachers and leaders, some of whom would abandon the sermon, others who would retain the traditional sermon, and yet others who would preserve the sermon but in a much different form.

These different forms are many. A sermon could take numerous paths, each leading to different regions of the human heart and soul. Some sermons appeal to the head and others to the heart. Some emphasize the text of Scripture and others focus on the text of life. Most sermons are somewhere in between, herking and jerking about the homiletic territory, enticing certain listeners and aggravating others. Unfortunately, the territory is not well mapped, and many a preacher feels lost along the way. Many have given up the journey altogether. The truth is there has been change in every age, and the changes that are to come will likely be beyond anything we have so far been able to imagine.

In the meantime, Sunday is coming and the sermon insists itself. Whatever am I going to do? Is preaching really worth the effort? Is there not another choice that I could make?

That is how I feel on Tuesday morning when I return to the office and face the challenge of getting yet another sermon together for the same people who heard me last week, and the week before and the ones before that. Generally, the feeling passes. Sometimes it is the Bible that jump-starts my homiletic engine. Other times it is the people.

People who listen to preaching are special people. The pessimism described above is probably more theoretical than what is actually warranted. At the beginning of one of my classes in preaching, I often ask students for the names of the preachers who have had a profound influence on them. I used to expect to hear the names of famous preachers, the ones on the radio or the ones with the largest number of hits on their websites. I expected that students would tell me about preachers I have heard of, but such is not the case.

My students tell me about their home-church preachers, the ones they grew up listening to, preachers without much reputation beyond their neighborhood. They tell me about preachers who might not be flashy but who are consistent, preachers who might never get invited to present the keynote sermon at the denominational convention but who seldom fail to touch the minds or the hearts of the few and the faithful who rely on them. I find this encouraging.

You never know what God will do when you stand up to preach. I sometimes think about the preachers who spoke the night that Billy Graham or Charles Spurgeon came to Christ. Those preachers were probably up late

Saturday night getting ready, just like the rest of us. Perhaps the sermon was stubborn and the setting depressingly the same—the same as the week before and the week before that. Yet we preachers are a stubborn type. We just keep opening the Bible because it is what we do and because we know that God will do what God will do.

Around the corner from the room in which I am writing is a special pulpit. Spurgeon heard the gospel preached from this pulpit and gave his heart to Jesus. Faithfully preserved, the humble pulpit of the Primitive Methodist Church of Colchester is now engraved with the sermon text "Look unto me and be saved." The teenage Spurgeon who heard that sermon turned into the "Prince of Preachers" and led tens of thousands to faith in Jesus. Of course, nobody could have known then what the results of that sermon would be.

I really do not know what was in the mind of Mordecai Ham when he preached the sermon that led Billy Graham to obedience to Jesus Christ, but I know that the world has never been the same since. How can anyone anticipate what God will do when a preacher speaks God's Word?

It is better that we cannot anticipate the effect of our sermons. If those preachers had known what the result of their evening's sermon would be, they might have made too much of it. They might have pressed too hard or made too much of themselves.

But of course, they didn't know what God was going to do, so they preached like they had always preached—with passion and with conviction. Their choice to preach was settled long before and didn't depend on knowing the details of God's intent. They preached because they were called to preach. They really didn't have a choice.

One never knows what God will do. We preach and God works, and eternity itself is shaped as a result. What a wonder to think that we could share in such a task. What could be greater than to speak and know that God speaks through us? Tremendous things happen when we preach, though we often do not recognize what God is doing. Every now and then, we get a little glimpse—a whispered word at the doorway of the church, a scribbled note, a stammered word of testimony. We realize that our preaching has not been for nothing. We have made our choice. God has spoken through the words that we have preached, and nothing will ever be the same.

PART 1

options

Options are always welcome. Baskin-Robbins offers a different ice cream for every day of the month. I've never found it necessary to sample every kind, but I'm grateful for the opportunity. Something in me bristles a little when I'm asked to decide without an array of options. The local movie theater has eighteen different screens, increasing the possibility that they will offer something worthy of my time and attention. Even then, though, there are times when I feel like Bruce Springsteen, who lamented that his television featured "Fifty-seven Channels and Nothing On."

My introductory homiletic training taught me only one way of preaching. It was a serviceable method, but it clearly was not for everyone. In the years since, I've discovered a number of different options and approaches, beginning with the possibility that we finish with preaching altogether.

It seems best, then, that we don't take anything for granted. We will respect you enough to let you choose your own approach to preaching. We'll start with the question of whether you will preach at all. You're free to say no, but that would render the rest of this book useless to you. Assuming you say yes, you can move to the next group of options. How you respond to those options will lead you to a form of sermon that will be useful to you in your attempt to help people hear from God.

I trust you will say yes to preaching. Perhaps the options offered here will stimulate a new excitement in you for the task. People need preachers who will bring their wisdom, their skills, and their personality to bear so as to help them respond to the God who continues to speak.

It's your choice.

Chapter 1 | FIRST OPTION

are you going to preach?

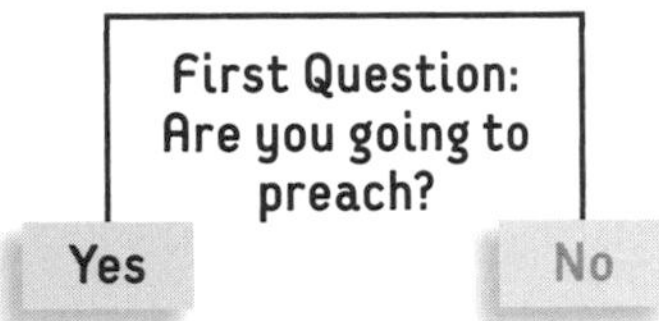
First Question:
Are you going to preach?
Yes
No

Every semester I see it in their faces. Terror. Naked fear.

"What am I doing in a class on preaching? How did it come to this?"

I see them slink into their seats, eyes imploring. "Please be gracious to me," they seem to say. "Please don't make me preach."

I understand their apprehension. It is quite possible that you share it. Some surveys have suggested that people fear public speaking more than anything else — more than getting bitten by a snake or facing financial ruin, even more than death.[1] I am asking a lot when I ask that you would preach.

You may be a raw rookie, reading this as part of your first homiletics class, or you may be a seasoned preacher, a veteran in the pulpit. You may be a youth leader or a Sunday school teacher who is terrified to think that what you do might be called "preaching." No matter how experienced we may or may not be, we all will have to make our choice, renewing our commitment with every opportunity. We have to choose to preach.

Are You Going to Preach?

Yes, I am going to ask you to preach, but you need to know that you don't have to. No one will ever force you to preach, though they may try to force your silence. Silence is always safer. People who keep quiet seldom run into trouble. If you choose not to preach, you will be among the many who have decided not to burden others with the truths they have come to, and you will not come to harm. This is a civilized and tolerant option in a world that prefers to leave well enough alone.

You have to choose to preach. The world conspires to keep us quiet. Inertia stills our tongues. It takes a concerted effort of the will to choose to tell the truth despite the trouble it entails. Proclamation is a choice. You have to choose the road less traveled.

I found a new path near my home this week. Slightly overgrown, the way was not immediately visible. The farther I went, the harder it was to discern the direction. Blackberry bushes were choking the way with prickles and barbs. Small trees and bushes encroached on the trail, making progress difficult. Still, stubbornly, I kept going.

We will do that sometimes. We will put up with the trouble and deliberately take the more difficult road because we think it might convey us to a better place. We know that life is about more than just our comfort. We take our lead from Paul, who knew all about difficult choices and thorny paths. He was hard pressed, perplexed, persecuted, struck down, but not so much that he wouldn't preach (2 Cor. 4:8–9). For Paul, the choice was very simple. "I believed; therefore I have spoken" (2 Cor. 4:13). The matter was never really in question. It didn't matter what might happen or what peril he might face. He believed the gospel was the truth. How then could he keep silent?

It might have been easier all around if he could have kept his mouth shut—easier for him and for his listeners, who would not have had to confront his message and come to terms with their sin. Everyone could have lived at peace if Paul could have left well enough alone. No one begrudged Paul his view of truth. We have no difficulty letting people believe what they want. Everyone is entitled to determine his or her own sense of truth. The problems start when people like Paul decide to be persuasive. The trouble begins when people choose to preach.

Discussion Question 1 | IS PREACHING ARROGANT?

Preachers seem too sure of themselves for these postmodern times. Claiming to understand enough truth for one's own sense of meaning takes courage, but proclaiming the same to others requires a particular sense of hubris, or so the culture thinks.

How can a preacher avoid the charge of arrogance? How do we tell people truth without coming across as if we think we are superior?

The problem with preachers is that they won't let truth remain private. They insist on proclaiming their view of truth to others, and that is what people find so offensive. Some people see preaching as a kind of intellectual rudeness, a violation or rape of the mind and of the soul, beyond excuse.[2] If you seek to persuade me of your view of truth, you are asking me to abandon my view of truth. You are telling me that my way is inadequate or improper, and it is hard not to take that personally. It feels like rejection.

But then, that is the hard reality of making choices, isn't it? The nature of choosing is that selecting one option means rejecting another. It cannot be helped, as much as we might like it to be so. Do you remember standing in the school yard when the captains chose up sides, hoping that they would get around to choosing you, praying that you wouldn't be left out? The problem with choosing is that somebody always gets left out. The problem with preaching is that somebody always feels that his or her views have been rejected.

So maybe we shouldn't preach. Just because we think we know the truth doesn't mean we have to fill the nearest pulpit. Maybe we should just keep our views to ourselves. Most people agree that culture is enriched by a variety of views. Maybe we could be content with that. Maybe we don't need to be so determined to persuade others. Live and let live and leave well enough alone.

Wouldn't it be nice to be able to leave well enough alone? It is not pleasant standing in the school yard when the captains look elsewhere. It is painful to say no to one in order to say yes to another. If we could just leave things be, we could all be at peace. We could tolerate a person's difference instead of trying to change it. Wouldn't it be easier not to make any choice at all?

Yet even that is a choice. Choosing not to preach still requires choosing.

Sometimes a choice is forced on us, leaving us with little option but to look at the situation and decide one way or another. Pilate, for instance, would not have chosen to confront Christ (John 18:28–40). He would have preferred not to have to make the determination, but Jesus and a big crowd of angry people were before Pilate, and none of them were going away. Like it or not, he would have to take a position.

Pilate's problem was political: the people wanted Jesus dead, but the law would not allow it. It would have been convenient if Jesus had killed someone or stolen something, but all he had done was claim to be the Jewish king, which was hardly grounds for a capital conviction, at least by Roman law.

"Are you a king then?" Pilate puts the problem plainly.

"Everyone who is of the truth hears my voice," Jesus answers.

But what did Pilate know about the truth? Pilate was a politician. These questions were beyond his scope of reference. He wasn't trained to tell religious truth.

So Pilate did what people do. He refused to choose. He washed his hands of it and pushed the problem onto someone else's desk.

Many people are like Pilate. When forced to consider questions about God and truth and righteousness—demanding questions that require conviction—the default response is to look for the doorway. People don't know what to do with these kinds of questions, so the easiest thing to do is set them aside; perhaps they will go away.

Which explains why preachers are so unwelcome. Preachers just won't go away. Preachers are far too sure of themselves. They have much too much conviction, and they can be far too convincing. A person might actually have to change his or her behavior, and that would never do. Better to keep a safe distance.

Insight and Ideas | HOW HAS PREACHING HELPED YOU?

Has preaching made a difference in your life? Scroll across your memory and recall those times when a preacher was able to shape your soul. Can you remember what the preacher said or perhaps what text was used? Thank God for those who chose to preach to you.

We recently had a painter in our house. There is no polite way to say it: the man stank. His foul, pungent aroma overwhelmed even the smell of fresh paint. It lingered in the room long after he had vacated it. He was a decent painter, but he smelled terrible.

It struck me that this is what people think about us preachers. We stink. We're nice people and we can put our words together, but a person ought to keep one's distance. People can smell a preacher coming. When we're present, they hold their noses. When we leave, our preacher scent lingers.

That preacher smell is what Paul calls "the aroma of Christ" (2 Cor. 2:15), and a good preacher leaves it everywhere. To some people, the smell is sweet and fragrant, a marvelous aroma of freshness and beauty. To others, it is the smell of death (2 Cor. 2:16). Our perception of this smell depends on what we have a nose for.

When I was young, I owned one of those big, old black Bibles with the maps in the back. I used to look at those maps when the sermon got boring. My favorite was the map of Paul's missionary journeys, the one with the different colored lines heading off in every possible direction, plotting all the places Paul had preached. Paul had traveled that whole map, and everywhere he went, he bore the scent of Jesus.

Paul wasn't always welcome. In some places he was greeted warmly, while in other places he barely escaped with his life. What was the difference? Did he preach well in one city and poorly in another? Maybe he hadn't had a proper time of prayer that morning in Thessalonica. Perhaps he wasn't always on his game.

In fact, Paul's problems had nothing to do with Paul at all. Paul preached the same way in every city. It is just that some people were not prepared to hear. Some were downright angry with the persistence of his preaching.

Still, Paul kept on. He paid a physical and emotional price for his preaching, and that price was dear, yet he never found the cost too high. Paul couldn't choose not to preach. Paul loved the people too much not to preach. He was stubborn that way.

Preachers Love People

Preachers choose to preach because they love their listeners. They care too much about these loved ones to leave them in their sin. Preaching is essentially an act of love.

It takes a lot of conviction to preach, but conviction comes easily to one who is in love. Nothing can dissuade a lover. Love trumps all counterarguments. It puts to rest any uncertainty. For the lover, there is nothing more to be said.

Conviction is, perhaps, the defining characteristic of love. When you love someone, you are so certain of your passions that there isn't anything you wouldn't do to express yourself. You will take your lead from God himself, who was willing to cross the ultimate barrier to love us and to teach us how to love. John wrote, "This is how God showed his love among us: He sent his one and only Son ... as an atoning sacrifice for our sins" (1 John 4:9–10). In so doing, God gave the preacher a model. If you choose to preach, it will be because you love your listeners enough to offer them the truth, no matter what it costs.

It is important that we affirm preaching as an act of love because acts of love aren't generally what we are known for. Preachers haven't always been seen to be very loving. Faced with the prospect of rejection, many preachers have chosen to go to war with their listeners, forcing their ideas on people and lacing their messages with a strong dose of fear. These preachers have conviction, of a sort. They are sure of their ammunition but not so sure of the terrain. They know the truth of what they preach, but they fear the response of the people. Rather than trying to love people into truth, they feel the need to run people over.

But war is the wrong metaphor for preaching. War works when all you want to do is win. If winning is the object, you do not have to care about the loser's person. If preaching is battle, then the listener is the enemy. You do not have to try to convince the enemy. You simply have to beat them.

Discussion Question 2 | CAN PREACHING BE CONFRONTATIONAL?

Is a warlike approach to preaching ever appropriate? Are there some people who can be won only by overpowering them? Are there some times when confrontation is the only way of breaking through?

When the "coalition of the willing" went to Iraq, the armies of Saddam Hussein fell easily. Riddled with corruption, the Iraqi army gave only token opposition. The war was concluded in a matter of days.

Except it wasn't really. Coalition troops won in a physical sense, but the insurgency was not quashed. The coalition held most of the territory, but it failed to win the hearts and minds of those who fought against it.

We might be able to accept that in war, but we can't accept it in preaching. God wants whole people to respond in faith to him. He wants a full commitment from his creatures — body, mind, and soul. It won't happen if we try to bludgeon people into truth. Confrontation has a place. A loving father will confront his son on those rare occasions when it's required, but this is not the normal pattern. Preachers should not try to overpower people. Preachers work to convince people, and nothing is more convincing than our love. The preacher's love might be rejected, but it never goes away. We bring a love that is persistent, not insistent. It is compelling, not combative, and in the end it wins the day.

This is the love that Jesus chose to offer. Like a great romantic figure, he died of love for us (1 John 4:7 – 10).

There is only one way we can learn to love like this. We must let ourselves be loved. Conviction always grows in the soil of knowledge and experience. We need to know that we are loved, and we need to have experienced that love in a way that is tangible and that makes the knowledge meaningful. Sometimes I will hear an argument that is so overwhelming in its logic that there is nothing for it but to submit to its truth. Other times, something will happen that is so emotionally overpowering that I simply know it must be true. It is in the combination of these elements that a profound conviction grows.

You may remember singing, "Jesus loves me, this I know, for the Bible tells me so." We believe that the Bible is an objective record of God's revealed will. Young or old, we have learned that as we study what the Bible says, we become convinced of its truth.

But we also learned to sing, "You ask me how I know he lives. He lives within my heart." This more subjective form of knowledge has been no less important in our faith development. The ever-present experience of Jesus in our lives has profoundly deepened our conviction.

As these pieces are combined, we find the conviction of the lover. Knowledge and experience merge to convince us of the things we know and believe. We learn love, and we feel its impact in our lives. We find we have gained the capacity and the impetus to bless others with that love.

This is the first thing preachers need to do. We need to let God love us. We need to open ourselves to the Word of God and be affected by his love. We need to steep ourselves in this love, head and heart, so that it becomes part of our very nature. We need to receive the forgiveness that is offered in Jesus and make certain that we walk by his grace and not by our own efforts or skills. The more deeply we know the nature of God's love for us, the more we will be compelled to share it with others and the stronger our desire to preach will be.

I have conviction about my faith in Jesus Christ because I know Jesus. I know him through his Word, and I know him through my experience of his love in my life. Having been loved, I sense the need to share that love. I sense the need to preach.

Choosing to Preach

One might think of this compulsion to preach as a calling. Since God has chosen to give me his love, I will choose to share that love. The truth is that before I ever chose to preach, I was chosen for it.

The idea that one could be chosen or called to preach sounds dated to a mind tuned to contemporary ideas about equality of opportunity. Older preachers used to like to challenge young people to consider whether God had called them to preach. Preaching was thought to be a career available only to those who were elected to it by God himself. The pulpit was thus professionalized, but it also was somehow spiritualized through the mysterious concept of divine selection.

The pulpit therefore became a kind of holy ground accessible only to those specially licensed for the task. While this lent authority to the position of the preacher, it also created distance between the pulpit and the pew. Preaching came to lack relevance to the listener unimpressed by claims of special holiness. That distance widened when people discovered that so many of these preachers called to this holy task were living shameful lives in secret, denying their elevated status by their dirty private deeds. Others, who may have offered meaningful careers in service to the Scriptures, found themselves stymied by uncertainty, unsure as to whether they had truly heard "the call," and stayed on the sidelines, never becoming preachers.

Discussion Question 3 | MUST ONE BE CALLED TO PREACH?

Must one be specially called to preach, or does the Bible encourage everyone to go out and preach the Word?

You don't hear so much about "the call" to preach these days. The pulpit has been demystified as less has become expected of its occupants. Education and erudition are optional. Preaching is simply a line item in the job description of those appointed to the task of professional leadership in the church. It can be delegated, diminished, or even dropped in favor of other duties deemed important for the demands of the day. This might be seen as progress, though one can't escape the nagging sense that something wonderful has been lost.

God has always chosen preachers. He chose Ezra to stand above the crowd and open up the Scriptures (Neh. 8:5). He put words into the prophets' mouths (Jer. 1:9). He even chose his very Son to come to earth and carry on a ministry of preaching. "That is why I have come," Jesus said (Mark 1:38). When it was time to establish the first Christian church, God called Peter, and thousands became part of the body through his preaching (Acts 2:41). When the church needed to be encouraged toward spiritual maturity, God chose Paul, who willingly accepted the challenge of proclaiming, admonishing, and teaching so that every listener might be presented perfect in Christ (Col. 1:28).

And now that call extends to us. "Preach the Word," Paul said to Timothy (2 Tim. 4:2), in season and out of season, when it feels convenient and when it feels inconvenient, when we are sure they want to hear and when we are sure they do not want to hear, we must preach. We may not all be professionals, paid to preach from pulpits, but if we are in Christ, we are called to preach in some capacity. In a small group, at a youth gathering, or even at the coffee shop, we can always find people who need us to love them. There will always be those to whom we're called to preach.

Insight and Ideas | WOMEN CALLED TO PREACH

For women, the question of whether one is called to preach can be particularly vexing. Little consensus exists in the church today about whether a woman has the right to preach, at least in a formal sense. Yet however we interpret the contentious texts, we have to come to terms with the fact that the Bible shows us women preaching. Women like Priscilla, Dorcas, and Philip's daughters were involved in opening up the Bible so that people could know God's love in Jesus Christ. Women need to be respectful of their church's position on this matter, but even in the most restrictive congregations, everyone can find opportunities to help others hear from God. To this we are all called, women and men together.

For more assistance with this, see Carol Noren's *The Women in the Pulpit* (Abingdon, 1992).

The world needs preachers. Preaching itself is ready for a renaissance. The church is emerging from a period in which preaching has not been the primary focus of a pastor's ministry. Pastors have come to question the power of the message proclaimed from the pulpit, opting instead to focus on leadership structures and management systems more than on a ministry of God's Word. The pressure not to preach comes from inside and outside the church. People outside the church claim that preaching is an act of arrogance. Who has the right to tell someone else what she or he must believe about God, about truth, about eternity? Yet the pressure from within the church seems no less intense. Church people wonder whether the sermon really works anymore, whether our time might be better spent in small group discussion, or whether we ought to give the preacher's time over to the worship leader.

Part of the problem is that we are tired. The expectations of our lives and ministries are so overwhelming that to preach with excellence seems a burden beyond our ability to bear. Pastors learn to preach just well enough not to get fired, but there isn't a whole lot of heart left in it. We have become so worn out by the "work" of caring for people that we have forgotten that preaching is the work to which we have been called. We have forgotten the long-term benefit preaching can have for the health of a congregation. We have forgotten, but I believe we could remember if we tried.

If preaching were a Dow-Jones company, its stock would be down, but with a strong "buy" recommendation. Preaching is not going away. The future is still bright. A renewed emphasis on preaching, a different kind of preaching, is beginning to be felt among younger leaders in the church.

Insight and Ideas | FIND A MENTOR

Do you have a mentor? Find an experienced preacher whom you trust and spend time reflecting together on your own sense of calling. How has God prepared you to pursue the promise of preaching? What gifts have people recognized in you? Ask your mentor to guide you in a discernment process, utilizing others to recognize God's special calling in your life.

In his book *The Emerging Church*, Dan Kimball devotes two full chapters and a great deal of creative thinking to the subject of preaching. "Preaching is more important and holier than ever as we exercise the sacred privilege of opening the Scriptures and teaching the divine story of God to people who are hearing it for the very first time," he writes. "Woe to us if we take this incredible privilege lightly."[3]

What kind of preaching should we choose? According to Kimball, in "the emerging church," preaching will not necessarily be the focal point of the worship service, but it will be an integrated part of the overall worship experience. The preacher will not serve as a dispenser of biblical truths to help solve personal problems in modern life so much as a teacher of how the ancient wisdom of Scripture applies to kingdom living for a disciple of Jesus Christ. The preacher will not only use words but also communicate the message through a variety of other elements, such as visual images, testimony, story, and the arts.[4] Above all, in the emerging church, preaching will respect the mysteries without abandoning the confidence one needs when approaching Holy Scripture. Such preaching will offer grace as well as truth, knowledge as well as experience. It will love listeners instead of going to war with them. This kind of preaching might have a chance of being heard.

My work with seminary students in the twenty-first century would confirm Kimball's sense that, while the sermon may require rethinking, it will not and must not go away. The death of the sermon has been greatly exaggerated. Students are as anxious as ever to learn how to preach, though they are looking for more authentic forms of preaching.

This "emerging" sense of preaching is not really new. The struggle to keep "dust and divinity" in proper proportion is perennial in preaching. Phillips Brooks, writing in 1877, described the degradation of preaching in the minds of younger people. Even in the late nineteenth century, he felt that the problem had to do with the "slighting of the element of absolute truth." The prevalence of doubt about truth and also "the general eagerness of preachers to find out and meet the people's desires and demands" created the impression that ministry had no definite message but "that the preacher was a promiscuous caterer for men's whims, wishing them well, inspired by a certain general benevolence, but in no sense a prophet uttering positive truth to them ... whether they liked it or hated it."[5]

Brooks's prescription sounds quite a lot like Kimball's. Preaching, Brooks famously suggested, is the presentation of truth through personality.[6] Truth must be embodied. We know truth because it has been told to us (knowledge), and we are convinced of it because we have experienced it. The preacher's challenge, then, is to share our experience with others. People need to know the truth, and they need someone who will tell them the truth. Like Jesus said, they will know that we have told them the truth when they sense that we have loved them (John 13:35). People need preachers who will share the truth with their words and show the truth with their lives.

Practical Exercise 1 | OPPORTUNITIES TO PREACH

Make a list of all of the possible opportunities God has given you to preach. Think not only about the formal opportunities on Sunday mornings but also of all the venues in which and groups to whom you might be able to open the Bible and help people hear from God. Think creatively about new situations God might open up for you.

I have chosen to preach. I have even learned to love it.

I know it isn't cool. Even in church, preachers don't get the respect they once did.

Still, I love it. I love the ants-in-your-pants feeling, when I am internally begging the worship leader, "Stop singing already and let me preach!" because the message burns inside like holy fire. I love the weak-kneed sense of wonder I feel when God surprises me with his Word like a two-by-four across the head.

They say that preaching is past its prime, that proclaiming the Bible is like trying to sell typewriters, that preachers work in the rust belt, and that preaching just doesn't sell like it used to. Maybe they are even right.

It's just that I can't help thinking about the people, all those strange people who keep showing up, who keep listening, and who actually hear and respond to God. I have learned to love them, and therefore I must preach.

Frank sees me at a party. He heard me preach two months ago when I was visiting his church. He had wanted to take his life. He even knew how he was going to do it. It's just that he couldn't quit thinking about the sermon. He couldn't shake the Word of God, and so he called his pastor, found healing, and now he's still here to tell me all about it.

William is a twelve-year-old boy. He has a habit of coming up to me after I've preached to ask if he can have my notes. Not every Sunday, just those

Sundays when he's *really* heard from God and wants to make sure he doesn't forget what he has learned.

Marta tells me she can't count five times in the last five years that she has been bored when I've been preaching. Not because I'm such a captivating preacher but because God has been speaking to her in her life.

You could know what I am talking about.

You could choose to preach.

Chapter 2 | SECOND OPTION

are you going to preach the Bible?

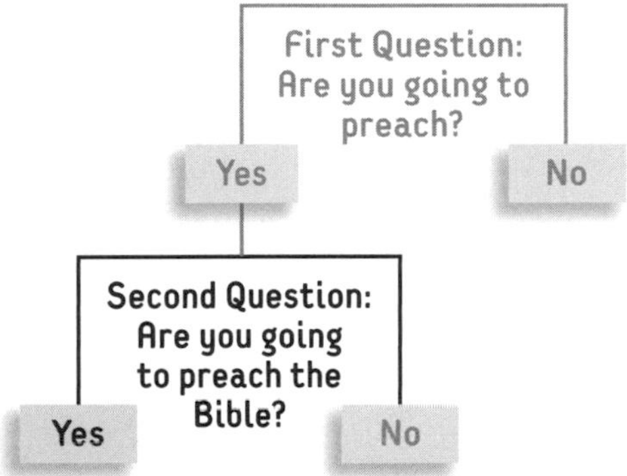
First Question:
Are you going to preach?
Yes
No
Second Question:
Are you going to preach the Bible?
Yes
No

I preached my first sermon at the age of seventeen at a Sunday evening youth service in my home church. The sermon was a team effort featuring my best friend, Jim Overholt, myself, and our pastor, Ian Bowie. Jim preached five minutes on "You are the salt of the earth." I did five minutes on "You are the light of the world," and then Pastor Bowie spent twenty minutes cleaning up the mess.

I cannot recall anything that I said, but I know I was no Spurgeon. I do remember Jim ceremoniously placing a saltshaker on the pulpit as a visual aid for his presentation. I was not nearly so creative. All I know is that I survived the experience.

There is something wonderful about preaching at such a young age, at least the way that I approached the task. A seventeen-year-old knows nothing. What could I possibly say to the people at such a tender age? All I could do was tell them what the Bible said as best I understood it, and it seems that was good enough.

It always is. I might not have been eloquent and I might not have been profound, but at least the people got the Bible. As long as people hear the Bible, there is a chance they will hear from God.

Are You Going to Preach the Bible?

Assuming you have chosen to preach, the next question is whether you will preach the Bible. Preaching the Bible is the traditional choice, but it is not strictly necessary. Most of us are reasonably intelligent, capable of describing all kinds of useful and consequential thoughts. We could preach our personal view of truth, or we could preach the Bible. We could offer our own opinion, or we could preach the wisdom of God.

Christian preachers understand that their task is to offer some kind of spiritual nourishment, but the means of providing that nourishment seems to be a matter still in question. Judging by our practice, one might think that we are embarrassed by our Bibles. Not that we are afraid of the Bible. A little healthy fear might be appropriate. We are afraid, rather, of what listeners might think if we use the Bible too much. We have not entirely abandoned the Bible, but we seem to use it sparingly. Sermons focus on practical themes, with occasional references from the Bible judiciously inserted—only so much as not to be offensive or to otherwise tax the listener's patience. We believe people think the Bible is difficult, irrelevant, or just plain boring and that if we use it, people will quit listening, as if they are going to be scandalized by the fact that we have dared open a Bible—in church of all places!

Discussion Question 4 | CAN YOU PREACH ASTROPHYSICS?

Must one preach the Bible? Could a person preach anything else—astrophysics, supply-side economics, or perhaps the merits of the designated hitter rule? Does preaching have to be biblical to be considered preaching? Why?

Call me crazy, but I just do not believe that anybody is going to get angry or fall over dead if they walk into our church and we open up a Bible. Conversely, I expect that they expect it, just as I would expect to hear readings from the Koran if I walked into a mosque. I think that listeners want to hear the Bible. If a seeker comes into your church, it is because she wants to know what Christians believe and what God has to say. Can you imagine the disappointment you might feel if, having overcome the overwhelming inertia and having actually shown up in church, you didn't hear anything different from what you might have heard on *Oprah*? You didn't have to get off the couch for that. When seekers come to church, somewhere inside they are hoping that they might hear from God.

People will hear from God if we preach the Bible.

Preaching ought to be expository, with a lowercase *e*. It has become common to organize approaches to preaching according to categories related to the sermon's degree of faithfulness to the biblical text. At one end of the scale is the purely *topical* sermon, which is essentially an editorial piece consisting of the preacher's opinion on some broadly spiritual theme deemed to be important or relevant to the listeners' needs. At the other end of the scale is the *expository* sermon, which seeks to replicate the message, form, and impact of the biblical text exactly as they were originally intended.

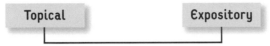

I believe it is the expository form that is necessary. I have opinions—many of them, actually—and some of them might even be worth consideration. I am not, however, arrogant enough to believe that people come to church to hear what I think about anything. That would be more pressure than I am willing to bear. People come to church to hear from God, and that is as it should be. The best way I can ensure that people hear what God is saying is to "expose" them to the Word of God as faithfully and powerfully as possible. This, not surprisingly, requires "expository" preaching.

Unfortunately, however, expository preaching has taken on a capital *E* sense in which Expository not only implies faithfulness to the biblical text but also requires certain formal elements. Such a sermon is thought to consist of a linear series of points (often three) from a limited number of verses, regardless of the genre or form of the text itself. Why it is thought wise to represent a poetic text from the Psalms or a narrative text from the Gospels by means of a didactic, preceptive treatment is not often questioned.

I prefer to use the term *expository* to describe preaching that is faithful to the message, intent, impact, and perhaps even the form of the text. In other words, an expository sermon doesn't require a specific form but rather can take a number of shapes depending on the genre of the text and the needs of the listeners. In short, an expository sermon is one in which the sermon preaches what the text teaches. Perhaps the problem is resolved by excusing the term *expository preaching* in favor of the broader term *biblical preaching.* Arguing for preaching that is deeply biblical only heightens the preacher's responsibility to the text and to the God who speaks the Word.

Whatever term we use to label our preaching, I am going to insist that we preach the Bible. The more we preach the Bible, the more powerful our preaching is going to be. Some of us have heard a lot of boring sermons preached from the Bible, but the answer to this problem is not to abandon the Bible but to improve the quality of our preaching. If we want to make a difference, we ought to preach the Bible.

Let us go back to our theological convictions about Scripture. The conviction of the biblical preacher is that Scripture is the revealed Word of God. We believe, in fact, that God speaks through his Word and that as we faithfully present the Bible, God himself is heard. The Word of God is living and active, and it is mediated through faithful preaching. As Merrill Unger has said, "The authority and power, which the inspired oracles possess, become manifest in the pulpit ministry of the faithful expositor of the Bible. He speaks, yet the thrilling fact is true, God at the same time speaks through him."[1] This conviction is consistent with a lively theology of biblical inspiration. The sermon itself is not inspired, yet God speaks through the sermon, which rightly offers the Word he has inspired.

This emphasizes the need for the preacher to get the Word right. Serious preachers, burdened by the knowledge that they bear the very Word of God, are fastidious about their stewardship of the text. Of course, we have to applaud this concern for exegetical precision. Yet as commendable as this interest in accuracy may be, it should be noted that accuracy is not the end but the means. Preachers exercise care in the study and presentation of the text not to satisfy a pretension for technical merit but because it is critical to our primary task, which is to know and relate to God by hearing what he says.

Exposition with a capital *E* is known for its focus on the technicalities of exegesis. Informational instruction often becomes so much the focus that the relevance of the text disappears.

The problem deepens when preachers, perhaps unintentionally, give the impression that their mediation of the text is required for their listeners to understand it. I wonder about sermons that are so technically erudite that they leave listeners with the impression that they could never get the Bible right without the expert's help.

For example, Robert Thomas writes, "The distinctive characteristic of expository preaching is its instructional function. An explanation of the details of a given text imparts information that is otherwise unavailable to the average untrained parishioner and provides him with a foundation for Christian growth and service."[2] This presentation of the preacher as the expert necessary to the listener's understanding of the mysteries of Scripture leaves me a little cold, both practically and theologically. Practically, it sounds like it is going to be unbearably dull, and theologically, it violates my understanding of the accessibility (perspicacity) of the Bible for every believer. I understand that instruction has always been an essential element in the practice of expository preaching, but man cannot live by instruction alone.

Insight and Ideas | DEVOTIONAL READING OF SCRIPTURE

One reason we have had trouble communicating the power of the Bible is that we have been trained to treat it academically. Perhaps it is time we awoke to a more devotional reading of the passages we preach, along with our exegetical readings. Many have discovered *lectio divina* as a way of reading the Bible for personal growth and spiritual discovery.

Harry Emerson Fosdick famously reminds us that in our attempt to acquaint our listeners with the second-person aorist indicative, we may have lost their attention altogether. "Only the preacher," Fosdick says, "proceeds still upon the idea that folk come to church desperately anxious to discover what happened to the Jebusites. The result is that folk less and less come to church at all."[3] Fosdick's critique of Expository preaching is no less scathing. These preachers "take a passage from Scripture and, proceeding on assumption that the people attending church that morning are deeply concerned about what the passage means, they spend their half hour or more on historical exposition of the verse or chapter, ending with some appended practical application to the auditors. Could any procedure be more surely predestined to dullness and futility?"[4]

That might be a little sharp, but it explains why many preachers seem to be backing away from the Bible. Preachers who choose to preach the Bible do so because they believe that God's voice is heard when his Word is preached. But this does not mean that it has to be boring.

Don't fall into the trap of believing that you have to choose between the Bible and your audience. That is a false and pernicious dichotomy. Too often we hear that if we want to reach unchurched audiences, we have to back away from the Book. We are told that young people have no patience for the Bible. We are encouraged to be creative, to tell stories and to be entertaining, as if being interesting is somehow incompatible with the Bible.

How did we come to believe that the Bible is inherently uninteresting? Maybe we have heard too much uninteresting preaching. Perhaps the problem is with the preachers and not with the Bible. We need to remind ourselves that the Bible is more than just a source of information; the Bible mediates the voice and presence of God himself.

Paul Scott Wilson sees a larger role for the sermon than just imparting knowledge. Preaching, he says, ought to be "more an encounter with God rather than information about God."[5] In fact, this information preachers give to people about God serves to feed the encounter with him, as Haddon

Robinson points out in his widely used definition of biblical preaching. Robinson suggests the expected elements of careful exegetical study and solid hermeneutical practice, but he also includes an emphasis on an encounter with the Holy Spirit. "Preaching," he says, "is the communication of a *biblical* concept derived from and transmitted through a historical, grammatical, and literary study of a passage in its context which the Holy Spirit applies first to the preacher, then through him to his hearers."[6] In Robinson's view, biblical preaching works because God's Holy Spirit uses it to get hold of listeners' lives.

Resource Recommendation | HADDON ROBINSON'S BIG IDEA

Haddon Robinson's *Biblical Preaching* (Baker, 1980, 2001) is worth a careful reading. No book has done more to shape the teaching of preaching among evangelicals over the last twenty-five years. Robinson's emphasis on "the big idea" is particularly important.

The appealing thing about Robinson's definition is that it doesn't set the preacher out as an all-wise expert who has a special pipeline to the voice of God. Put that thought to death right now. We can be of great assistance to our listeners as we apply the insights gained through our education and our expertise, but we must never forget that we are listeners too. We and our listeners come together to the text with the desire to hear from God.

People will welcome our desire to help them hear from God if we do it with humility and sincerity. More than ever before, people today are interested in meeting God. We feed that desire when we preach the Bible. Open the book expectantly with one eye on your text and another on your world. Look for God's hand. See what he is doing and sense where he is moving. Biblical preachers explore what God is saying, and they say what he is doing.

In a nutshell, preaching is *helping people hear from God*. If expositors could see that preaching faithfully is more about people than parsing, we might find that the world is still interested in hearing what we, or rather what God, has to say.

Discussion Question 5 | THE MEDIUM IS THE MESSAGE?

Marshall McLuhan famously said that "the medium is the message." The idea is that the form is more than just a container for the message; it helps to shape the message as well. How does this apply to Scripture and to preaching? Does the form of the Scripture help to shape its intent? How does the form of our sermon affect the way the message is received?

If we really believe that preachers preach so that people can hear from God, our choice is already made. We have to preach the Bible. We know that the Word of God is alive and breathing. After all, 2 Timothy 3:16 was not written in the past tense, as if God were dead, having done all his breathing in the past. Scripture is not a lifeless document that we mine for treasure like an archaeologist digging in the dust. Scripture is a living document, full of power and promise.

Frankly, the appeal of archaeology has always eluded me. A person digs in the dirt and holds some relic up for all to see. "Look at this," he says. "It is important. It is valuable. It is old." Yet I can't get past the fact that it looks like a piece of broken pottery.

Too often this is how people react to our preaching of the Bible. We dig around in the text and string together three or four abstract principles that sound important yet only make the people yawn. There is no life in this kind of preaching, no vitality. It looks like broken pottery to them. Believe me, if our preaching is only a digging in the dust, there will be no encounter with the God who lives and breathes through his Word. Don't archaeologists tend to make poor preachers?

I remember a sermon one of my students preached from the Psalms. He did a wonderful job of exegesis. His hermeneutic was flawless. His propositions were reasoned. His professor was disappointed.

"Why didn't we do it?" I asked him later when we were alone.

"Do what?" he asked, his nervousness mounting.

"Why didn't we worship?" I asked. "You spent all our time explaining what worship is, why worship is important, and what worship looks like, but in a half hour of talking *about* worship, you were successful at preventing any of us from actually *doing* worship."

The sermon is not something we listen to; it is something we do. It is an event. Preaching happens in the present tense as we connect with the God who is present and who intends to act. The Bible is alive, and we meet God in it. Don't ever let your preaching become some dry chasing after principles so as to place them under glass. When Isaiah found himself in the presence of God, smoke billowed and the doorposts shook. Let the Word loose and see what God will do as he meets the people and changes everything.

Resource Recommendation | HANDS-ON HOMILETICS

Terry Carter, Scott Duvall, and Daniel Hays have offered a simple and practical presentation of a traditional homiletic in their helpful book, *Preaching God's Word: A Hands-On Approach to Preparing, Developing, and Delivering the Sermon* (Zondervan, 2005).

Many preachers are tired; they are worn out from the pressure of trying to be interesting and trying to be God for the people. In the past, people might have been willing to grant the preacher that privilege, but no more. People know us better than that. Too many of us have failed, and few people are willing to give us the benefit of the doubt. It is hard to stand in the pulpit and claim to speak for God—especially when our stomach sticks out over our belt and our breath smells funny and our breakfast is stuck between our teeth. It is difficult to speak for God when we are so obviously flawed. Just trying will wear a person out.

We can find courage in the knowledge that preaching doesn't depend on the preacher's cleverness. Our task is simply to help people hear from God. Once the preacher understands that God has already promised to make himself known in his Word, the pressure lifts. Surprisingly, we then find ourselves motivated to a deeper and more faithful engagement with the text.

The Bible is the tool that God has promised he will bless. The Bible is living and active (Heb. 4:12). Sharper than a sword and more penetrating than a hard-rock drill, it will stab and slice the stiffest soul. It will not return empty but will always accomplish the purpose for which it was sent (Isa. 55:11). God has promised that somehow, some way, when the Bible is preached, he will have his way, in his time, whether or not we recognize it.

The Bible works. Preached faithfully, the Bible will require the listener's attention. It will persuade the postmodernist and reach the reluctant. It needs only to be preached.

The Bible Will Persuade

Preachers want to be persuasive. Proclamation is all about persuasion. When we say that preachers "pro-claim" truth, we mean that they intend to be convincing. Preachers use the Bible because nothing persuades like the Word of God.

On my own, I can be convincing. Like a politician or an advertiser, I know how to turn a phrase to change a mind. Yet my best efforts are inept compared with the power of God, who promises to make himself known through his Word. The authority of the Bible is inherently persuasive.

The key to this authority is the doctrine of revelation. That God has chosen to make himself known is the best thing I know. If God had left his Word a secret, we would not have any hope. Yet God, by his grace, has chosen not to remain hidden from us but to make himself known to us, and he continues to do so today. Hebrews 1:1 – 2 says that "in the past God spoke to our forefathers through the prophets at many times and in various ways, but in these last days he has spoken to us by his Son." Apparently, God hasn't done with speaking.

How does God reveal himself? He speaks to us through the Bible of course, the revealed Word of God. He also spoke to us through the incarnation of his Son, Jesus Christ. Jesus literally brought God down to earth. Yet God's desire to make himself known to us was first shown in the way he created us. When God formed us, he gave us the ability to recognize his voice. It is part of our wiring, so that when the Holy Spirit speaks, we recognize his voice for what it is. When a preacher opens up the Bible, we hear the voice of God because we are created in the image of God. We may have allowed our spiritual wires to corrode through neglect or misuse, and we may not have listened for God's voice for some time, but we are capable of recognizing his voice, and the preacher knows it. The preacher knows that a sermon can strike a spark strong enough to start the system going once again. People are capable of hearing from God, and they hear him through their preachers when the preachers use the Bible.

This is a remarkable affirmation. Christians dating back to the first few generations after Christ held a very high view of preaching. According to the *Didache*, the one who preached the Word of God was worthy of special honor almost as if the preacher made the Lord himself present through his preaching.[7] This document says, "My child, you shall be mindful day and night of the one who speaks to you the word of God. You shall honor him as the Lord, for at the source of proclamation of the lordship [of the Lord], the Lord is there."[8]

This instruction is jarring to those of us accustomed to taking a more critical stance toward the preachers we hear. It could make it a little harder to roast the preacher over dinner if we saw him or her as the Lord himself. As preachers, we may find the idea of the real presence of Christ in our preaching to be a burden we might not want to bear. It seems a lot to live up to.

Yet the burden might be lighter than we think. Certainly, the idea that the Lord could carry the weight of the sermon ought to be welcome to preachers used to carrying the burden alone. Preachers should not have to shoulder such a weight. It is really too much for us, which is why we preach the Bible in the first place. We have neither the wisdom nor the power to pull it off ourselves. The good news is that the power is in the Word of God. As long as we preach the Bible, we know that the Lord is present in our words. It really takes a load off.

Insight and Ideas | THE REAL PRESENCE OF CHRIST IN PREACHING

Most evangelical theology shies away from the idea of the real presence of Christ in the elements of worship, yet if we believe that Christ is present in his Word, he will be present in our preaching if we offer up his Word. How does this thinking affect your motivation to preach?

Preachers have a big advantage over others seeking to persuade. Plenty of people try to persuade us. Advertisers and politicians come readily to mind. Yet a politician could only dream of the kind of power wielded by the preacher. Some elections in the United States and Canada have raised a question about the degree to which God might endorse a certain candidate. But the preacher has more than just God's endorsement; the preacher offers the Word of God itself.

Preachers should not be quick to abandon their one great advantage. We are sometimes tempted to allow our intelligence or personality to be the persuasive factor. Many politicians have been similarly tempted, but the best ones know better. Rudy Giuliani, for one, learned that persuasion is all about the ideas.

If anyone could be justified in running on his charisma, it would be Rudy Giuliani, the former mayor of New York. His personal competence, forthrightness, and vision, seen in the aftermath of the 9/11 tragedy, inspired voter confidence. Yet Giuliani believed it was the idea that mattered, not the personality of the communicator.[9] Persuasion, he said, is not as much about communication technique as it is about the idea itself. In fact, Giuliani avoided most of the accepted standards of communication. Shunning teleprompters and the gimmicks of the professional politician, Giuliani strove to communicate the unadorned idea, trusting his sense of conviction and the power of the ideas to persuade the voters.

Discussion Question 6 | PREACHERS, POLITICIANS, AND PERSUASION

What can a preacher learn from the politician about persuasion? How is preaching like or unlike advertising or sales?

I recently listened to a recording of "I Have a Dream" at the Martin Luther King Center in Atlanta. The speech (or perhaps it is a sermon) still gives me chills. Of course, King was more a preacher than a politician. When he quoted Amos 5:24, about how justice would roll down like a river and righteousness like a never-ending stream, I got the sense that people believed him. People were not only persuaded but inspired.

Shouldn't all our sermons be like that? Sure, Rudy Giuliani had 9/11 and King had the March on Washington. We don't have such moments week by week in church, but we have ideas just as big or bigger, and we have the knowledge that we are hearing the Word of God. The moment might not always feel significant, but the message is as big as it can get.

I recently heard a pastor refer to his sermon as "the speak." I suppose that is what the preacher did. He spoke. It is what preachers do in the most literal sense. Still, the label bothered me. It seemed such an anemic way of talking about preaching. It seemed to betray a weak view of what could happen in the preaching task.

"Speaking" is safe in contemporary culture. Self-expression is something that everybody values. Nobody minds that we speak, as long as we don't seek to persuade anyone of anything. Preachers in recent decades have adopted this safe, defensive posture, hoping to be heard but afraid to offend. We speak our minds, but we're careful not to push too hard. We are cautious with persuasion. We do not want to upset the seekers for fear they might not come back.

This is understandable, but it is not preaching—not really. Biblical preaching is more confident, more prophetic. Biblical preaching is not about our speaking but about God's speaking, and that is a greater thing altogether.

God can be demanding. He is not content to offer his voice as one more opinion in the marketplace of ideas. He not only wants to be heard but also expects to be obeyed. Charles Bartow says that we speak not simply so people can make something out of what we have to say; rather, we speak so people will know that "with what we say, God is about to make something of them."[10] When a preacher gets in line with that kind of expectation, the whole event is elevated. People might actually be persuaded; they could actually change.

Younger people understand. According to research cited by Robert Webber, younger evangelicals are looking for preaching that will challenge them to a deep encounter with God. They want a significant engagement with Scripture because they understand the Bible as the means by which God speaks. They want intimacy with God and a sense of his transcendence and otherness.[11] They want more than just "a speak."

We understand this desire for encounter when it comes to worship. Most worship leaders know that worship is about encountering God. But too often we see preaching as disconnected from the worship time. In most churches I have attended, the transition is quite pronounced. The worship team finishes the final song and leaves the platform. A pulpit is brought out and put in place. The children noisily leave the sanctuary. The pastor cracks a few jokes as he activates his lapel mike and organizes his notes. The congregation changes posture and finds pencils to fill in the outlines provided for them in the program. Everything communicates that we are now going to listen to a sermon. We were worshiping, just moments ago. We are not worshiping anymore. Now we are teaching. The worship time was about encounter. The preaching time is going to be about explanations. We were worshiping. Now we are only speaking, and more is the pity.

? **Discussion Question 7** | THE ROLE OF PREACHING IN WORSHIP

What is the role of preaching in worship? Is it essential or extraneous? Does preaching aim for more (or less) than what we normally expect from worship?

The preacher who wants to persuade people will preach the Bible. The Second Helvetic Confession said that "the preaching of the Word of God is the Word of God."[12] To the degree that our preaching faithfully offers the Bible, that affirmation is true.

What could be more motivating? What could be more persuasive than the voice of God?

Choosing to Preach the Bible

He is an imposing figure, his famous eyes burning holes in the television cameras, his big black Bible brandished before him—it seems he never puts it down. "The Bible says ..." he thunders over and over again. It is as if Billy Graham doesn't have anything to say for himself, and in a sense, he doesn't. Graham has chosen to preach the Bible, and as a result, people on every continent now have heard the Word of God, have responded to it, and will live forever as a part of God's great kingdom. When we choose to preach the Bible, we are in good company.

The impact of his preaching could not have been predicted at the beginning of Graham's career. His first sermon, as described in his autobiography, was certainly not all that inspiring.[13] It was the spring of 1937, and the young Graham was a student at Florida Bible Institute. The dean of the institute, Dr. Minder, had asked Graham to accompany him to a summer conference in northern Florida. While there, they met with a lay preacher, Cecil Underwood, who asked Dean Minder if he would like to preach for him the following evening at a small Baptist church. "No," he answered, "Billy is going to preach."

Graham was stunned. To that point, he admitted, his repertoire consisted of four borrowed sermons, which he had practiced but had never preached. "We'll pray for you," said Mr. Underwood, "and God will help you."

Reluctantly, Graham agreed, but he was so frightened that he "spent the night studying and praying instead of sleeping." The next day was spent reciting his sermons out loud. By evening, he felt "confident that any one of my sermons should be good for at least twenty or thirty minutes," the standard by which any first-time preacher measures his or her readiness.

Graham entered the small meeting room and sat nervously while the tobacco-chewing song leader conducted the service. The congregation was made up of about forty ranchers and cowboys with their women. The song leader would occasionally go to the door to spit. When the time came for Graham to preach, he was a mess of nerves and perspiration.

"I launched into sermon number one," he wrote. "It seemed to be over almost as soon as I got started, so I added number two. And number three. And eventually number four. Then I sat down. Eight minutes—that was all the time it took to preach all four of my sermons!"

That has to be encouraging to some of you beginning preachers. From this humble stuff, God shaped the preacher he would use to lead more people to faith than anyone else has in human history. Who knows what God might do with you.

I saw Billy Graham on CNN talking to Larry King on New Year's Eve 1999. You probably remember Y2K. It was a fragile moment in human history. The close of the millennium had people worried that a curious glitch in technology might cripple the computers of the world.

Larry King could have chosen to talk to anyone on that night, but remarkably, he chose a preacher. I was impressed that at this potentially critical moment in the history of humanity, with a massive television audience beyond anything Graham could have paid for through his supporters' contributions, he kept his message simple. He simply preached the gospel, just as he found it in the Bible. It was not complicated, and it may not even have been deep. But if we were all to meet our doom that night, it was what we needed to hear.

 **Practical Exercise 2** | THE REAL PRESENCE OF CHRIST IN PREACHING

Interview three to five people who have been listening to preaching for a number of years. Ask them to describe the way that preaching has helped them grow in Christ. See if you can determine two or three overall principles that can help you in your preaching today.

I recently attended a dialogue headed by the archbishop of Canterbury, held at St. Paul's Cathedral in London. The subject was the governance of the world, and the various speakers offered their opinions on the United Nations and the nation-state versus the market-state and their relative levels of optimism or pessimism about the future of the people of our planet. It was a heady experience talking about such weighty matters in such a beautiful and historic venue, but at the end of the dialogue, my wife and I remained unimpressed with the rather tentative conclusions that were offered. With apologies to the archbishop, I'm afraid Dr. Graham would have handled the situation quite differently.

On May 11, 1982, during one of the more tenuous moments in the cold war up to that time, Billy Graham was given the opportunity to address the Soviet power structure at the Kremlin. Given the opportunity, most would have spoken about the nuclear buildup and the wisdom of pursuing peace. Instead, Graham gave them the Bible, which should not have been a surprise. Graham always preaches the Bible. The only way that humanity will find peace on earth, he said, is when they make peace with God through his Son, who came as the Prince of Peace. The Kremlin leaders could have easily dismissed him if he spoke about détente and other matters of policy for which he had no expertise. But they could not dismiss the Word of God.[14]

As I watched the Graham interview with Larry King, some seventeen years later, I couldn't help noticing how ancient Graham looked. The man is getting old. I was reminded of Paul's encouragement to Timothy in 2 Timothy 4:7. "I have fought the good fight," he said. "I have finished the race." The implication was that Timothy would take up the charge and continue the ministry of preaching the Word. Timothy was faithful, and others followed. Mordecai Ham was faithful, and Billy Graham heard the message from his lips. Now it is your turn and mine. Having affirmed that we will preach, the question is, will we preach the Bible?

If you want to persuade people, you ought to answer yes.

Chapter 3 | THIRD OPTION

how will you discern your message from the Bible?

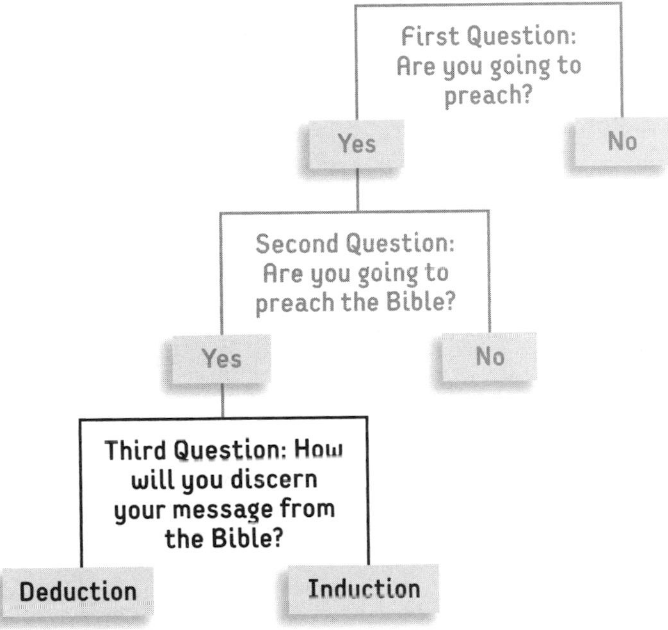

I recently bought a new digital video camera, an exciting early birthday present that will allow me to take my family-filmmaking hobby to new levels. I stayed up till 1:30 a.m. that first night, learning how to use it. These things do take some figuring out, you know.

There are two ways to learn how to use a new piece of technology. You can study the manual, or you can just take the item in hand and start messing around. Given that I tend to learn by doing, I chose the latter. I took one look at the manual, thumbed through it quickly, and set it aside. It is a lot more fun to play with the camera, discovering its joys by pushing buttons and seeing what happens. By the time I went to bed, I felt fairly confident about my ability to use the camera effectively.

I suspect, however, that some of you are not like me. You would be worried that you might do some damage if you just started ignorantly pushing buttons. Some of you like to learn systematically. You don't want to miss anything, and so for you, the manual is an essential tool.

We are not all wired the same. While we preachers tend to want listeners to conform to our learning style, we will do much better if we learn to shape our sermons to fit the learning style of our people.

David Kolb's theory of experiential learning can be helpful in this task. People learn in two primary ways. We input information, and we process information. Our third question, "How will you discern your message from the Bible?" deals with how we process information and how we go about discerning our message. Kolb says this process can take one of two forms: observation or experimentation. The world, he says, is full of two kinds of people: the "watchers," who prefer "reflective observation," and the "doers," who prefer "active experimentation."[1] If you are likely to read the manual, you might be a watcher. If, on the other hand, you prefer to learn by messing around, you might be a doer.

DAVID KOLB'S EXPERIENTIAL LEARNING MODEL

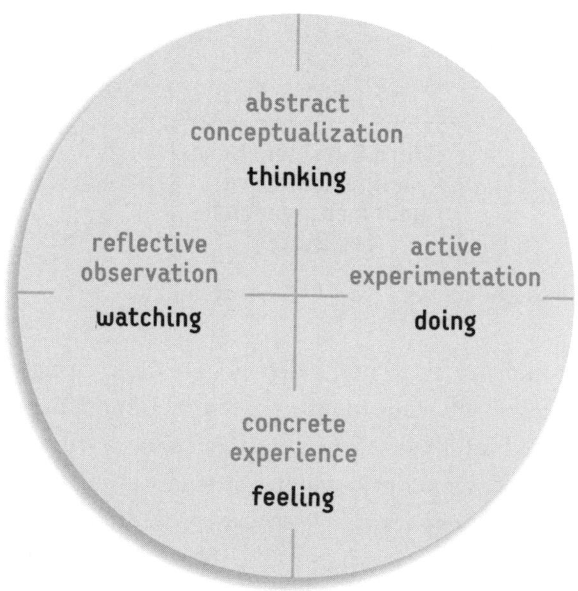

As I said, I lean more toward doing than watching, though I must admit I did eventually find the camera manual useful. Playing around does have its limitations as a learning style. Eventually some technical guidance becomes imperative; then the manual becomes very useful.

This chapter addresses the preacher's need to process the text of Scripture in order to present it to the people. Preachers, like their listeners, tend toward either reflection or action, and these tendencies are seen in how they approach the text of Scripture. Many people have observed that the Bible is a manual for living life in the will of God. Some of us approach manuals very systematically, beginning with page one and proceeding to the end. Others prefer to dip in and out as the need arises, beginning with life experience and applying the manual (the Bible) as it touches on the challenges that arise along the way. Both are legitimate ways of learning to walk in obedience to God. On this question, there is no wrong choice.

Assuming you have chosen to preach, and assuming, further, that you have determined you will preach the Bible, your third choice is how you are going to discern your message from the Bible. You have two primary options. Both choices are legitimate approaches to biblical preaching but differ in their starting points.

Option A, *deduction*, begins with the Bible and moves toward the listener. This is the approach favored by the reflective observer (Kolb's "watcher"). Option B, *induction*, begins with the listener and moves toward the Bible. This is the preferred approach of the active experimenter (Kolb's "doer"). Option A might be thought of as an *objective* approach to preaching in that it begins with the authoritative Word and immediately seeks submission to that Word. Option B might be thought of as a *subjective* approach in that it begins with the listener's need and moves toward a biblical response.

THIRD OPTION: *how will you discern your message from the Bible?*

DAVID KOLB'S EXPERIENTIAL LEARNING MODEL

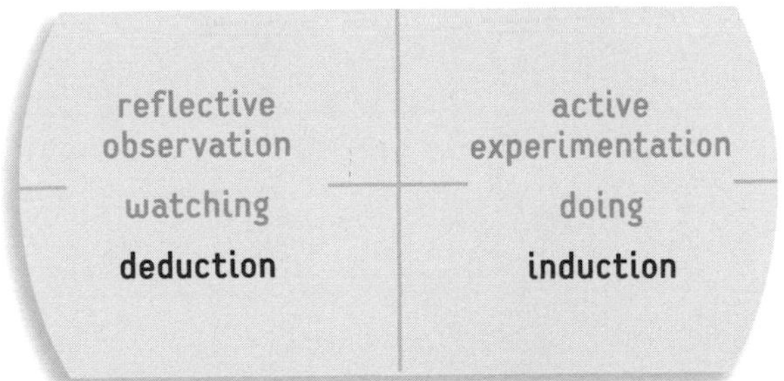

At this stage, often described as the exegetical stage, sermon preparation begins. The preacher must discover the message that God intends for the people at this particular point in time. Whether the preacher approaches the task deductively (Option 3A) or inductively (Option 3B) is the choice to be made at the moment.

Option 3A

begin with the text

Deductive Study

Third Question: How will you discern your message from the Bible?

Deduction | Induction

The professor who first taught me preaching was a humble man. The more he worked with the Scriptures, the more he was convinced of his own unworthiness. Professor Hills loved to preach because he loved the Word so deeply, but he struggled with the sense that he was somehow getting in the way. Standing at the back of the church to shake hands was especially excruciating for him. He told us how he wished he could have had a trapdoor installed behind the pulpit so that as soon as he was finished preaching, he could push a button, drop down below, and escape out the back door rather than endure the post-sermon ritual he called "the glorification of the worm."

When pressed, my professor would admit the pastoral value of greeting people after preaching. After all, they were the people he was trying to reach, and he had great love for them. But I'm not sure he was ever able to come to terms with the idea that God would use humans to communicate his truth. Deeply aware of human frailty, my professor struggled with the sense that we can't help but contaminate the message by our personal involvement in the task.

These concerns notwithstanding, the man didn't shy from preaching, and he did it well because of his rich appreciation for God's grace. That a man like him would be chosen by God to communicate his truth was a perpetual wonder to my professor. That wonder was a gift he passed on to all those who sat under his teaching.

I would characterize my professor's approach to preaching as passive, though not without passion. His passion was to be transparent in the pulpit so that the words people heard were not his but the words of God. His deep desire was to get out of the way of the Word, and this passion fueled his choice to preach and prepare *deductively*.

Begin with the Text

How will you discern your message from the Bible? You could decide to begin with the Bible. Like my professor, you may decide that your role is to be quiet before the Scripture so that God can speak.

My professor made his choice for theological reasons. I suspect, however, that it also matched his learning style. I would perceive him as a reflective observer according to David Kolb's experiential learning grid. He was a watcher more than a doer, as are most professors, which might explain why most preachers emerging from seminary lean toward a reflective style. We often adopt the characteristics of those who teach us.

A passive, reflective approach to the Bible is appropriate. Being silent before the Scripture embodies the attitude of Samuel, who prayed, "Speak, LORD, for your servant is listening" (1 Sam. 3:9). The deductive approach to Bible study does not bring an agenda to the Scripture but asks only what the text is saying. It is a submissive approach that begins with the Bible before introducing the insistent demands of life under the sun. A hard-nosed discipline is required to quiet the self, but we will make the necessary sacrifice when we understand that we are subject to our Creator and are responsible for obeying him.

Submission is never easy; we so naturally find ourselves wanting to rebel. It might have been easier on us if God had been willing to stay silent. Peter Adam notes that "one reason people prefer the company of dumb animals to that of humans is that dumb animals make fewer demands, ask no questions, and make no promises."[2] If God were silent, we would be free to make our own choices and to live our lives with self-sufficient sovereignty—a little like the family cat, who lives life on his own terms, coming to us only when he feels the need for our company. Keeping God silent makes sense to a person who feels confident enough to fill the role of god for himself or herself. Deductive preachers know that this is more confidence than any of us have reason to aspire to.

The deductive preacher approaches the text with an observant eye, seeking to assimilate the truth as it has been given, not as the preacher might wish it to be. He or she tries to come to the Bible with a mind emptied of all assumptions and preconceptions except those shaped by the text of Scripture itself. Perhaps it would be helpful, in this case, to replace Kolb's term "watcher" with "listener." "Watcher" is an appropriate term with respect to learning style, but "listener" more accurately describes the task of the preacher approaching the Word of God.

Labeling the preacher as "listener" immediately creates an affinity between the preacher and the congregation. The preacher and the listeners are one. The preacher might have the advantage of a head start, but he or she is a listener just the same. The task of the preacher and the members of the congregation are exactly the same. Both come to the Word of God with a desire to listen to what God is saying. The preacher is unique only in that he or she has the privilege of leading in the process.

Practical Exercise 3 | LEVELS OF AUTHORITY

Ideas discerned from the text have different levels of authority. That is to say, some propositions derive less directly from the Bible than others.

1. *Direct biblical authority* describes ideas that exactly correspond to the teaching of the text. The sermon preaches what the Bible teaches.
2. *Indirect biblical authority* describes ideas that are only inferred from the text.
3. *Casual biblical authority* describes ideas that are only vaguely suggested by the text.
4. *Corrupted biblical authority* describes ideas that twist the meaning of the text into something it never intended.

Choose three sermons, including one you have preached, and determine the key ideas being proclaimed. What level of biblical authority do these ideas have?

Remember that an idea does not need to have direct biblical authority to be legitimate. Nevertheless, the closer a sermon adheres to the intended meaning of the text, the more authority the sermon will convey.

H.C. Brown, *A Quest for Reformation in Preaching* (Nashville: Broadman, 1968), 36-37.

We need preachers to lead us because most of us are hearing impaired—if not physically, then spiritually for sure. I know that I am—both ways, in fact. Several surgeries over the course of my life have left the hearing in my left ear seriously reduced, which I will admit has had its advantages. Not hearing can sometimes be convenient, like when my wife calls me to some dreaded household task. More often, however, I find myself struggling and straining to discern whatever is going on. I've become very intent on hearing. You wouldn't want to sit beside me in a theater because I will constantly be asking, "What did he say? What was that? I couldn't hear." I want to know what is being said to me and I will strain to hear.

Of course, some messages are of greater value than others. I've learned to be oblivious to television commercials, junk mail, and elevator music. I try to tune myself in carefully, however, to personal messages that are of value to me. I've become adept, for instance, at sifting through my cluttered inbox to locate the important email from out of the deluge of spam. Every one of us contends with thousands of persuasive voices every day, most of which are spam: bumper stickers, infomercials, even insistent friends.[3] Yet within this cacophony is a still, small voice that must be heard. God is speaking, and it is the preacher's task to help the listener hear that voice.

Insight and Ideas | THE POSTMODERN TOWER

Postmodern thought is at least as old as the Tower of Babel (Genesis 11). While the critique of objective truth is thought to be a recent phenomenon, it was an ancient experience of humans and their God.

The primary factor contributing to postmodern uncertainty is the diversity of human culture and language. We come from different places, and we speak different languages. Given such a scenario, how could one truth fit all?

Whatever we think of the postmodern milieu, we have God to thank for it. When God scattered us and caused us to speak different languages, he planted the seeds that plague postmoderns today. Of course, it was an act of judgment, but it became a problem just the same.

Despite the real difficulty of transcending our innate subjectivity and personal experience to speak meaningfully about objective reality, God still calls on us to preach. It is important, however, to realize that when we preach, it is God who is doing all of the speaking. Preaching is not a bottom-up project. We understand God because God makes himself understood. Preaching is top-down communication.

In this we have hope. Our task as preachers is not to be so compelling that people must listen to what we have to say. Our job is to connect people to the God who is already speaking and who will work to help them hear the truth. Preaching is what God does. It is his project.

In a scene from the *The Hunt for Red October*, a Navy submarine radio operator is listening intently to detect the sound of approaching enemy subs. His challenge is to distinguish the important noises from the array of ordinary noises. It takes a trained and experienced ear to discern whether a sound is a whale swimming or a submarine propeller turning, yet the difference could mean life or death for a boatload of sailors. It is not a glamorous position. Most of the operator's time is spent quietly in a small room in the bottom of the boat, doing nothing more than listening, but when the right sound is heard, the whole crew takes notice.

This is the task of the preacher. The preacher sits alone in the study, spending long hours examining texts and listening closely. God is speaking, and the preacher needs to hear him right. Eventually, the preacher discerns the message and stands up boldly to sound the alarm. The question is whether anyone will be willing to respond. Not everyone wants to hear the truth. The truth makes demands on us, and sometimes we don't like what it has to say.

Jack Nicholson's character in *A Few Good Men* is correct. We can't handle the truth. It is not that we doubt the existence of truth so much as we are afraid of our responsibility to it. Once we know the truth, we have to accommodate it, and like making room for unexpected houseguests, accommodation is seldom comfortable.

Deductive preachers tell the truth. It is one of the reasons people have so much trouble handling them. Beyond any postmodern philosophical conviction about uncertainty principles and the supremacy of doubt, at the core, the human problem with truth is a problem of obedience. We don't want to have to adjust ourselves to the responses truth demands.

The philosophical arguments for an elastic truth are compelling. As subjective beings, fallen and finite, confined to space and time, the idea that we could define truth in any kind of objective sense seems nonsense. How would we ever know that the truth was anything greater than our own construction? Can we ever escape our bias? Probably not. We are "subjects," and our limited perspective is part of the deal.

But who or what are we subject to? To the truth, of course, which is to say, to God himself. Truth is less a concept than it is God's proper name. The God who created us defines truth in his character, his will, and his Word, and this Truth cannot be "handled." Deductive preachers do not put their spin on truth or otherwise manipulate its message; they simply preach it. God himself is speaking. Our task is to listen and obey.

Begin with the Bible so that God's voice sounds clear. Once God has spoken, the listeners will have to reckon with what they have heard.

How to Study Deductively

Taking the Bible seriously is a challenging assignment. God has put his Word in print, and printed matter always requires interpretation. The preacher approaches the task from a faith perspective, but that does not obviate the need to do the hard work of hermeneutics. Listening to God through his Word is an exacting science requiring discipline and precision.

I have heard David Jackman of the Proclamation Trust say that the preacher has two primary tasks, first to "get it right" and then to "get it out." Deductive Bible study is about "getting it right." Paul instructed Timothy to "correctly handle" (2 Tim. 2:15). Timothy was counseled to present himself to God as an approved workman, one who preaches in such a way that he has no cause for shame. This kind of homiletic craftsmanship comes with a quality guarantee. When the preacher handles the Scriptures with integrity, the listener can know that he or she has truly heard from God.

Exegesis is critical for deductive preachers, who labor to make sure that the message of the text is the message that gets heard. The preacher's task is to get out of the way of the text so that God's voice is heard, not the preacher's. This is not understood in a mystical sense, as if the voice of God were to register magically through the sound system. The deductive preacher is a scientist, a kind of homiletical mathematician. For preachers, deduction is about the laws of grammatico-historical hermeneutics and the need to apply those rules with precision.

Some might argue against the deductive insistence on precision because of the inherent fuzziness of interpretation. The intent of the author can be elusive when even the identity of the author is uncertain. Meaning can be a mystery given the time span between the writing of the text and today, yet the deductive student remains unfazed by these concerns. Like an astronomer seeking the outer limits of the observable universe, the student might find the answer lies simply in using a stronger telescope. If a matter is unclear, we don't abandon the question. We work harder. The answer might emerge through continued application of the rules of interpretation. We maintain our faith commitment, but we must not let our faith keep us from doing the hard work of study the bibilical text requires.

Insight and Ideas | THE SCIENTIFIC METHOD

1. Begin with a hypothesis.
2. Subject the hypothesis to a critical examination.
3. Apply the hypothesis and test the results.
4. Describe the findings and conclusions.

The scientist is a good model for the preacher who seeks to determine truth from Scripture. Scientists believe in an ordered universe. The physical operation of the planet is governed by certain principles. To deny these "rules" is to mock the God who set the world in motion and the scientist who works to understand its ways. The scientific method is a determined process of experiment and observation. Theories must be tested until the scientist arrives at conviction within a reasonable doubt. A scientific hypothesis can never be finally proven; it can only be disproven. The vastness of the universe defies our ability to know anything with finality. Through commonsense application of the rules of research, however, we can determine truth to a degree that allows us to function meaningfully. God himself is transcendent and beyond knowing in any purely objective sense. Nevertheless, he makes himself known to us sufficiently, though not exhaustively. He expects us to use the minds he has given us to discern truth in a principled fashion.

The good scientist begins with an open mind and a willingness to submit to the data, wherever it might lead. The scientist does not try to influence the data according to a preconceived notion but follows the information to whatever conclusion is reasonable given the facts. The data is not immune from critical examination but is subjected to a thorough questioning. If the data is truthful, it can withstand scrutiny. Having applied the data and tested the results, the researcher may make some general statements regarding outcomes. Those observations are carefully limited so as not to be twisted into unintended shapes. The observations, if valid, will then be tested by others and verified by means of other similar tests and examinations.

The scientific process describes a proper approach to biblical interpretation. The biblical interpreter takes the Scripture text and examines it carefully, knowing that it can withstand scrutiny. Having observed the data, the interpreter describes the text's intended meaning. Such interpretations are subject to further examination by others. The best responses are confirmed over time as the church across history agrees on the validity of certain convictions.

Resource Recommendation | RESOURCES ON HERMENEUTICS

This book does not intend to give a full treatment of the interpretive process. For a more detailed discussion of the work of exegesis, see Gordon D. Fee, *New Testament Exegesis* (Westminster/John Knox, 1993). The third section of the book is a "Short Guide for Sermon Exegesis," a detailed step-by-step process that preachers will find useful as they seek to understand their texts.

Grant Osborne's *The Hermeneutical Spiral* (InterVarsity Press, 1991) is a comprehensive look at the interpretation of the entire Bible.

Of course, the interpretive process is often messy. Deduction seldom follows step-by-step to an inevitable conclusion. Often it is more convoluted than linear, leading researchers down blind alleys, forcing them to retrace their steps, and causing a lot more head scratching than they anticipated when starting out. The truth is out there, though at times it seems elusive.

The quest, however, is critical. Without science, intolerable numbers would still die from chicken pox and tuberculosis. Science brought us television, timepieces, and cavity-fighting toothpaste, none of which would have been possible had scientists not believed that the truth could be discovered with effort.

I recently toured the Royal Observatory at Greenwich, England, famous as the location of the prime meridian. It is a remarkable location. I was able to take a picture of my children straddling the meridian, each standing with one foot in the Eastern Hemisphere and the other foot in the Western Hemisphere. As delightful as that might be, I would have to add that the prime meridian itself is not physically impressive. In fact, you would not realize it was there at all if it were not for a bold line cut across the pavement. The demarcation is, in fact, of human invention. Prior to the International Meridian Conference of 1884, each local region kept its own time, a system that, if continued, would have rendered impossible our current arrangements for trade and commerce. While the meridian is humanly derived, its relation to the stars is not, and that heavenly correspondence allows us to find our place on the map and in the world.

The prime meridian came about through the work of John Flamsteed, the first Astronomer Royal, who made it his life mission to produce a proper navigational chart of the heavens, mapping the location of thousands of stars. Eventually, based on Flamsteed's work, scientists were able to help people find their position on the planet, allowing them to answer that fundamental question of philosophy and physics: Where am I?

The power of the prime meridian is that it is a fixed position through which our knowledge of time and place can be understood. This is a metaphor for the effect of the Bible in human life. The Scripture is our meridian. It is the fixed position, given by God himself, through which we can understand who we are, where we are, and where we must go from here. As preachers, it calls us to a precise and careful engagement according to the long-established principles and rules of interpretation.

The challenge of interpretation is twofold: first, to understand what the text meant in its original situation, and second, to understand what it means in its present-day application. Preachers are primarily interested in the meaning for today, yet one cannot understand the contemporary significance without a clear sense of the intended meaning. If contemporary meaning is divorced from original intent, the application becomes speculative and essentially worthless.

This, according to Walter Kaiser, is what is wrong with much contemporary preaching: "The listener is often not sure whether the word of hope being proclaimed is precisely that same Biblical word which should be connected with the modern situation or issue being addressed in the sermon since the Biblical text often is no more than a slogan or refrain in the message."[4] The solution, he says, is to make sure that the sermon, derived from honest exegesis, keeps close to the text.

Insight and Ideas | READING YESTERDAY TO HEAR TODAY

We pay attention to context so that we can understand what God is saying to us today. My concern is not so much that I know what God is saying through Paul to the *Philippians* but that I hear what God is saying to *us* by means of what he said through Paul to the Philippians. I'm trying to hear from God today, but I will not be able to hear what he is *saying* until I have heard what he has *said*.

Following Kaiser, I would offer the following questions (steps) as a guide to the deductive task for preachers. I don't intend this as a full description of the hermeneutic process. Frankly, I'm assuming that most of you will have taken other courses and read other books on the subject of biblical hermeneutics. The following suggestions build on that good work, offering a condensed and simplified way of conceiving the process. As we approach a Scripture text, we must consider five questions, beginning with the matter of context.

1. Where Does It Live?

The first task of the deductive preacher is to determine the text's location in time and place. This is what Kaiser calls a *contextual analysis* of the passage. Deductive Bible study follows the first rule of real estate: the most important thing is location. Propositions do not exist in a vacuum but must be interpreted from within the context in which they were given. We must take care to ensure that each thought is understood within the flow of discussion and not atomized or fragmented.

If I asked you to define the word *love*, for instance, you might describe the great emotion you have for your wife or husband, how you feel dishrag limp whenever you walk into her or his presence. Or you might describe a more profound and determined decision made to favor your spouse with grace, commitment, and passion, regardless of his or her apparent natural state of foolishness. I imagine you continuing your discussion with some intensity despite the look of puzzlement on my face. I was talking about tennis, you see, not relationships. Etymological curiosities aside, the word *love*, in the game of tennis, is a score. It literally means "nothing." The only way you might have known that I was talking about tennis and not relationships is by taking notice of the context. Perhaps our discussion took place at a tennis match or as we were watching Venus Williams on TV. Maybe I was holding a tennis racquet in my hand. You can see how context is critical to understanding meaning.

Kaiser says that the Bible is particularly prone to these kinds of misinterpretations because of our conviction that "the message of the text in its verbalized form is the very word which God Himself wanted to be communicated." As a result, contemporary interpreters can tend to invest "every word and phrase with almost an independent meaning(s) of its own apart from its context."[5] Kaiser see this "quasi-magical" use of the words of Scripture, even when used in ways that support a generally biblical idea, as a misuse of the Bible and as disrespectful to God's intended meaning for the passage in question. The deductive preacher must instead read the passage as if he or she were one of the original recipients of the letter. We need to place ourselves as much as possible in the circumstances of the original situation to gain a proper understanding of what the writer is trying to say. Only then can we begin to consider what the words might mean today.

Insight and Ideas | SENTENCE DIAGRAMMING

Diagramming a text can be a helpful way of seeing how it works. Put the biggest idea from the text in a circle in the middle of the page. Arrange the subordinate ideas in smaller boxes arrayed around the circle. Connect the ideas with lines. Even subordinate ideas may be interconnected. The challenge is to create an overall picture of the text. Allow your study of the grammar of the passage to guide your diagram.

For an alternate approach to diagramming, see Walter Kaiser's *Toward an Exegetical Theology* (Baker, 1981) or Grant Osborne's *The Hermeneutical Spiral* (InterVarsity, 1991, 27ff.).

So the first step in deductive Bible study is to consider the text in the light of its original situation. Who was the author? To whom was he writing? What issues were in play and why did they matter? How does this text relate to all of the other texts that connect these ideas to the broader themes in Scripture as a whole? In other words, we start with context.

2. How Does It Work?

When I was in the ninth grade, I took a class called Power Mechanics. The sole project of the course was to take apart a lawn-mower engine. By seeing the engine in all of its parts, I was able to appreciate the principles of mechanical power.

In the same way, the deductive preacher's second task is to dismantle the text to understand how it works. This second level of scrutiny is what Kaiser calls *syntactical analysis*. Here we are trying to understand the literal meaning of the passage by studying the arrangement of its words and the structure of its sentences. Because this includes both a careful grammatical analysis, as well as a historical study of the usages common to the period of the author, we call this process grammatico-historical interpretation. The process can be complicated, particularly because the texts were written in ancient languages not known to preachers today unless they have had several semesters of seminary training in biblical languages. For this reason, learning biblical Greek and Hebrew is worth the effort. Failing that, an interlinear text or a Bible software program can be valuable.

Resource Recommendation | RESOURCES FOR LANGUAGE STUDY

Several excellent Bible software programs are available, such as *BibleWorks*, *The Scholar's Library*, *Gramcord*, and *Accordance*. Zondervan publishes a "Scholar's Version" of its CD-ROM Bible Study Library that is packed with resources you won't find anywhere else. Programs like these can save preachers a lot of time and deepen our appreciation for the texts that we will preach.

Syntactical analysis requires that we pay attention to the little words in the text, such as *and*, *but*, and *certainly*. These words help to clarify the relationship of one clause to another. For example, the presence of the word *therefore* always means that that section is connected to the previous section. The writer is telling us that as a consequence of what has just been said, we now must consider what follows. These words are used purposefully and provide excellent clues to meaning.

Pronouns also require the interpreter's attention. The *who, whose, whom, which,* and *that* of the text help us know to whom or what the clause is referring. Misreading a pronoun is a bit like a letter being delivered to the wrong door: great confusion can result.

Punctuation is another feature that must be considered. A best-selling book on punctuation begins with the often-told joke about the panda bear who enters a restaurant and "eats shoots and leaves."[6] Of course, a comma after the word *eats* would clarify whether or not a firearm was in use. These smallest of textual markings can dramatically alter a text's meaning, which is why Jesus reminded us of the authority of even the smallest letters and the least strokes of a pen (Matt. 5:18).

Many preachers have found it helpful to produce a diagram of the results of their syntactical analysis. A graphic picture of the grammatical structure of a passage can be a great aid in ensuring that the main thing in the text becomes the main thing in the sermon.

Insight and Ideas | SYNTACTICAL MARKERS

When you are seeking to understand the relationship of ideas in a text, it can be helpful to circle all of the syntactical markers (*and, but, if, therefore,* etc.). Mark each name, pronoun, and personal pronoun. Try to perceive the meaning of the text by means of its grammatical structure.

3. What Does It Say?

The deductive preacher's third task is to determine the accurate meaning of each word in the text, what Kaiser calls *verbal analysis.* As noted earlier, a word like *love* can have multiple meanings—sixteen of them, according to my dictionary. Affixing a specific meaning to a given paragraph requires the reader to understand the intent of each word in its context. Is the author using a figure of speech or an idiom? Are regional or cultural issues at work? For instance, in a conversation with my English friend, Nigel Wright, he referred to a woman he knew as "a real cracker." I took it from the context that this was a good thing. I told him that in parts of North America, the word *cracker* has an entirely different connotation. He assured me that he was talking about her beauty and not disparaging her as a poor white racist.

Understanding a word's meaning involves seeing the word in a series of concentric circles. In the innermost circle, the preacher looks at the author's use of the word in the immediate passage. The next circle is the author's use of the word in the fuller discussion of that particular book of the Bible. A third circle is the author's use of the word throughout his writings in the

Bible—all of Paul's letters, for example. A fourth circle is the overall use of the word in the New Testament or the Old Testament. A fifth circle might be the common use of the word as we understand it today, as we might find it defined in the latest edition of *Webster's*. The interpreter should put the most focus on the innermost circles of meaning. As meaning radiates outward, the validity of interpretation exponentially decreases, so that by the time the reader turns to dictionary.com, very little interpretative impact remains.

In other words, figure out what the author actually meant when he wrote the text. After studying the meaning of the words in the text, it might be helpful to try to write your own translation or paraphrase.

4. What Does It Mean?

Up to this point, the interpretive process has been fairly mechanical. Now the deductive preacher takes things to another level. Kaiser calls this fourth task of deductive study *theological analysis*. To stop with grammatical and historical analysis, Kaiser says, is "like carrying the football to within twenty-five yards of the end zone and then asking God's people to carry the ball the rest of the way—perhaps with a wave of the hand and a passing allusion to the wonderful ministry of the Holy Spirit in each believer's life."[7] Instead, the reader must take up the Reformation principle that "Scripture interprets Scripture." As we find a particular theme in a text of Scripture, we will want to read more broadly in the Bible to understand the overall meaning of the relevant theological concept. This is where biblical and systematic theology meet.

Theological analysis is often described in terms of "timeless truth," yet truth is never truly timeless, at least not from our perspective "under the sun." God always makes himself known in time. While it is helpful to discern the theological principles that apply from age to age, these principles must be read through the lens of the overarching biblical message of redemption. Specifically, the reader must know his or her location in salvation history relative to the text itself.

Insight and Ideas | THEOLOGICAL LOCATION

Preachers and listeners reside in a different theological location than their texts. In the diagram on the next page, for instance, the events described in the text happened sometime in Old Testament history, while the listeners occupy their position sometime after the cross and prior to the second coming. The listener must therefore look back through the cross when reading the text. This is another way of saying that our reading of the Bible must always be Christian.

For example, Greame Goldsworthy reminds us that we all read the Bible from our postresurrection position. Some texts reside in roughly the same period (e.g., the Epistles). Others only anticipate the coming of Jesus Christ (e.g., the Psalms and the Prophets). Goldsworthy insists that our preaching must always represent the person and work of Jesus Christ if it is to be truly Christian. That is to say that even when we preach from the Old Testament, we must see the themes of covenant promise in terms of their fulfillment in Jesus. "The God who acts in the Old Testament," Goldsworthy says, "is the God who became flesh in the New Testament in order to achieve the definitive saving work in the world."[8] Talking about Jesus in our sermons is more than talking about Jesus' ethical teaching. The moral imperatives of Jesus have to be read in terms of his life, death, resurrection, ascension, and promised second coming. "So often distortions of Christianity come about not by introducing totally foreign elements but by getting certain elements that are manifestly biblical out of perspective."[9] Christian preaching is always gospel preaching.

In other words, we need to make sure that our message is not overly simplistic or moralistic. The sermons we preach must be rooted in a deep appreciation for God's character and his purposes as they are realized in the world. Understanding what a text means requires us to understand the passage from the perspective of the God who inspired it.

? **Discussion Question 8** | CHRIST-IAN PREACHING

Must every sermon focus on Jesus Christ? Is it appropriate to preach without mentioning the gospel if the text itself does not allude to it? If so, what would make the sermon explicitly Christian?

5. How Does It Apply?

The fifth task of the deductive preacher is to consider application. Application is exegesis moving toward exposition. This is what Kaiser calls *homiletical analysis*. It involves framing the central ideas and propositions of the text into statements and outlines that can be preached and practiced. The purposes of exegesis are never fully realized until they are applied to the needs and concerns of contemporary life, which requires the preacher to exegete the audience itself.[10] The interpreter's work is not complete until she or he has considered how the listener will hear the ideas that are offered. How are the principles relevant, and how will they be heard? How, for instance, will an inner-city audience appreciate the agricultural motif of many of the parables? Planting and growing are not irrelevant concepts for this audience, but some form of transposition might be required.

In transposing a piece of music, the melodies and the relation of the notes are not altered, but they are played in a different key, perhaps to accommodate a different instrument or range of voice. Similarly, biblical principles must not be altered, but they can be transposed so that they can be appreciated and sung in fresh and varied settings. The preacher is the link between these different contexts.

In the end, the preacher needs to understand exactly what he or she is asking of the listener. How would the world be altered if we actually went out and obeyed the message we have heard? If we can't provide a vivid picture of an altered future under the influence of the message, we might not be ready to preach.

Insight and Ideas | THE DEDUCTIVE PROCESS

Use these key questions to treat a text deductively.

1. Where does it live? (contextual analysis)
2. How does it work? (syntactical analysis)
3. What does it say? (verbal analysis)
4. What does it mean? (theological analysis)
5. How does it apply? (homiletical analysis)

Deductive study is not unique in its insistence on interpretive precision. Inductive forms also require accurate meanings. With deduction, however, the interpretative process is where the preacher begins. The deductive preacher starts with the Bible, making interpretation the first order of business. Having heard from God, there is nothing left but to submit.

Choosing Deductive Preaching

The beauty of deductive study is in its submissive nature. Deduction is a posture as much as it is a method. It is a bowed head and bended knee. Deductive preachers understand their sinfulness and know what they must do.

Years ago, I heard Bryan Chapell preach at a meeting of the Evangelical Homiletics Society. When Chapell had finished his excellent sermon, Keith

Willhite took the platform to pronounce the benediction. "The problem with listening to Bryan preach," he quipped, "is that my fallen condition becomes all too powerfully focused."

Willhite was referring to Chapell's emphasis on the "fallen-condition focus," described in his book *Christ-Centered Preaching.* Chapell believes that the Bible was given to us because there was (and is) something wrong with us. There is always something wrong that needs repairing because we are fallen creatures, prone to wander and lacking in willingness to submit to God's authority. For Chapell, this is the key principle that ties the intended meaning of the text to its contemporary purpose for readers today. No text in Scripture was written solely for the purposes of people in the past; all of Scripture is intended to bring hope and healing to fallen people. Every text, then, has a fallen-condition focus. "The FCF," Chapell says, "is the mutual human condition that contemporary believers share with those to or for whom the text was written that requires the grace of the passage."[11] Why is this text in the Bible? Why was it important for God to include this particular text in Scripture and for us to hear from it today?

Insight and Ideas | THE "BIG IDEA"

Haddon Robinson challenges preachers to identify the "big idea" of a text by means of its *subject* (what the text is talking about) and its *complement* (what it is saying about what it is talking about).[12] The subject of Lamentations 3:22–23 is the compassionate faithfulness of God. The complement is that God's compassion never fails. This then is the "big idea" of the text: "God's compassion never fails."

Scriptures come to us in a variety of shapes and sizes. Some of them readily yield to the deductive methods here described—the Epistles, for example. Others, like the Psalms, might require a more reflective approach.

Deductive preaching is about applying these texts to the lives of listeners in the world today. The worship texts in the Psalms are not there merely to be observed as if we were a crowd of eyes-glazed-over tourists visiting a medieval cathedral. The tourist appreciates the beauty of the cathedral in a detached historic sense, not at all like the response we want from our listeners. Preachers want their listeners to read the Psalms and drop to their knees, mouths hanging open, overwhelmed by a fresh appreciation of God and his glory. Preachers want listeners to worship alongside the original recipients of the text. That is why we preach the Psalms. The historic text exists not simply to describe the detached past. Biblical history describes the activity of

God in the past to affect the reader's present. We preach the *then* to make a difference in the *now*.

Still, it is hard to avoid reading the Bible like a tourist. I remember standing before the thrones at Buckingham Palace, trying to imagine the kings and queens who had sat there. I even had the advantage of a guidebook that showed photographs of the queen sitting in the very chair that stood in front of me, but the whole thing still seemed distant and hypothetical. It was hard to put myself in that moment of the past, when my own moment was so insistent.

It is the same when I read the Psalms. I know the text wants me to worship like David. I am to feel all of the passion that he put to paper, but it is as hard for me to enter his moment as it is for me to imagine the presence of the queen. My own stuff overwhelms me; my problems, distractions, and sins keep getting in the way—especially my sins.

This is why Chapell's point is so helpful. He understands the barrier that sin presents. "By identifying our listeners' mutual condition with the biblical writer, subject, and/or audience we determine why the text was written, not just for biblical times, but also for our time."[13]

This is another way of framing the deductive concern for God's sovereignty. Every text and every sermon is intended to bring the listener into submission to the will of God. Nothing is hypothetical. Human rebellion is always at issue. Acknowledging the barrier that the listener's fallen condition presents becomes the very strategy by which the preacher overcomes the hurdle. The big idea of the sermon is how the text confronts the listener's mutiny.

There is always a problem when we insist on preaching the Bible. The question is whether the problem is something external that happens to us or something inherent in our person. Deductive Bible students like Bryan Chapell know that the problem is the sin that infests our hearts and wills. The problem is us.

The privilege of deductive preaching is that we get to put the correct name on things. Deductive preachers provide God's names for things, helping listeners learn God's vocabulary and speak God's language. Listeners who hear from God and who know what they have heard will be ready to reckon with the God who speaks today.

Option 3B

begin with the listener

Inductive Study

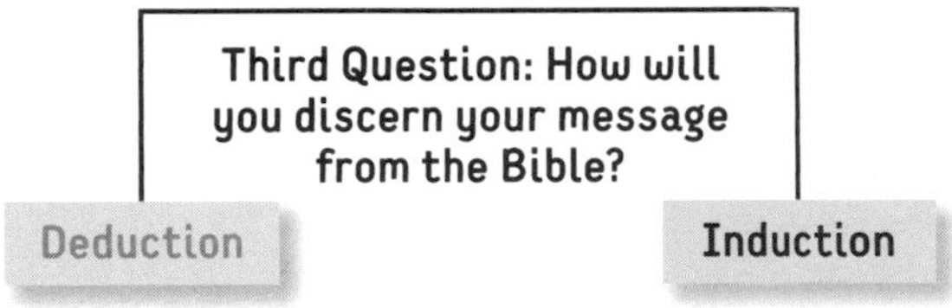

There is such a thing as too much information. Sometimes I don't want you to tell me the technical specifications and theoretical philosophy. I just want you to fix my problem. When I bring my car to the shop, I don't need a lecture on the development of the internal combustion engine; I just want the mechanic to make mine work!

When my furnace broke down last year, I called the repairman. I wasn't thrilled about having to spend the money, but sometimes that is what you have to do. The repairman came and fixed the furnace, for which I was grateful, and asked me a seemingly harmless question about my thermostat. He wondered if I had considered a programmable digital thermostat, which, he assured me, would not only keep my house warm but also save me money. I should have just said yes or no; either way, it wouldn't have mattered. The transaction would have been completed, and we both could have gone about our lives. Instead, I gave him a quizzical look that may have indicated I didn't know what he was talking about. Of course, I didn't know what he was talking about, and I was content in that happy state of ignorance. The repairman, however, in his mission to educate the populace about the dynamics of thermoelectric heating, proceeded to engage me in a twenty-minute lecture, most of which I could not comprehend. By the time he left my house, I was two hundred dollars poorer and significantly more annoyed. All I had wanted was that he would heat my house.

Listeners sometimes feel like that about preachers. Life is hard, and sometimes it doesn't seem to work. Other people seem to be prospering and succeeding, but something about my life, my set of relationships, my level of confidence, my peace of mind seems to be malfunctioning, and I would just like someone to help me get it fixed. I understand that at the heart of my problem is my messed-up relationship with God, and I know that I am to blame. I sin too much—I can't seem to help it, even though it is killing me in more ways than I want to admit. So I bring myself to church, feeling a lot like I do when I bring my car to the shop. I know it is going to cost me something, hopefully not too much, but I am willing to pay if it will help me to get my life back on the road. Just tell me what I need to do. I don't need a thirty-minute treatise on abstract theology or Bible trivia. I don't need the preacher to recite for me his master's-level research paper on a Bible text that might at some point touch my need if he could ever get around to showing me its relevance. I just want him to help me with my need.

Begin with the Listener

The attitude described above might not sit well with our deductive friends, who come to the sermon with a much different frame of mind. They might want to tell me to stop whining, sit down, and listen. Listening, both literally and in the figurative submissive sense, is what is required, and if that requires me to learn a little patience, fine and good.

The deductive approach works for those reflective observers who are content to watch and wait. But on the other side of the learning style equation is a different group of people who prefer active experimentation over reflection and observation. These are David Kolb's "doers," and for many of them, deductive preaching is just too theoretical and far too slow. Doers don't like to bog down on theory in their quest for a solution. For them, the preacher might choose an inductive, rather than deductive, approach to the sermon. The preacher who wants to reach the doers will begin with the listener and then move toward the text.

Inductive preaching takes a more subjective approach to the sermon. This is not to suggest that truth in its objective, abstract form is not important. But truth presented from the perspective of the listener can be just as valuable and just as true. Truth presented objectively can seem a little abstract to the listener caught up in the questions and complications of a hurried and harried life, while truth presented in terms of the listener's need and perspective will be welcomed and received. No doubt the preacher will need to reshape the listener's perspective, aligning it correctly with the truth, but then that is the preacher's task. Approaching the sermon from the listener's point of view will show people that they are important to God and to the preacher, who comes to bring them aid. Objective truth matters, but people matter too. People need to matter to preachers at least as much as their propositions do.

Insight and Ideas | INDUCTIVE EXPERIENCE

Ralph Lewis writes, "We gamble our lives on inductive experience every time we trust the brakes in our car to prevent us from plowing into the rear end of a stopped semi or proceed through a green light without checking to make sure the cross traffic will stop. From the mountains of life's minutiae we constantly seek patterns, principles, generalizations, truths that will enable us to confidently decide present action, predict the future and build an improved life. Thus induction constitutes the very basis for our daily living. It serves as the primary means of arriving at knowledge required for human survival."

Ralph L. Lewis with Gregg Lewis, *Inductive Preaching: Helping People Listen* (Westchester, IL: Crossway, 1983), 43.

Jesus modeled this masterfully in his encounter with the rich young man, recorded in Matthew 19. The young man recognizes his spiritual need and recognizes Jesus as one who can meet his need—so far so good. He addresses Jesus respectfully, "Good Teacher, what good thing must I do to inherit eternal life?" (v. 16).

A certain amount of self-interest is evident in the man's question. Eternal life is a good thing, and people have long sensed a desire for it. Some have crossed oceans in search of the fountain of youth, while others have recognized the potential for a spiritual solution. This young man was of the latter type, and that is what brought him to Jesus.

I must confess that if I were the preacher this man had come to, I might have handled the situation differently, which is a soft way of saying that I might have blown it altogether. I would have been tempted to focus on his selfishness. I might have told the young man that eternal life, while a wonderful gift of God, is not the primary objective we are meant to seek. I might have explained to him his need to repent of his sin and submit to his Creator. My arguments would have been sound, though they might not have been convincing. Jesus, however, took a different tack. Jesus worked inductively, beginning with what the young man gave him and moving the man from there.

The rich young man was used to buying solutions to his problems. He had money, and he was prepared to pay. He only wanted to know how much eternal life would cost. Rather than correcting his theology, however, Jesus told him just how big a check he would have to write: "Sell everything you have and give it to the poor. Then come follow me." In truth, the "come, follow me" would have been the hard part, but the young man never got to know that because Jesus quoted him a price that he would never pay.

Of course, if the young man had stayed around a little while, Jesus could have helped him understand how eternal life is not something that can be bought because none of us are capable of paying such a price. Jesus paid that price for us, and we only have to come to him for grace. Of course, that would have sounded like a lecture, and the man might not have stayed put long enough to hear it. The rich young man was a doer, a man of action, and so Jesus started with the need the man presented. Jesus told him what he had to do.

In this case, it didn't work. The man turned down the offer and walked away from the deal. Can you hear the deductive preachers, standing in the corner, muttering their exasperation with Jesus? Why didn't you explain it to him? Why didn't you tell him to submit? And of course, they are correct. The man could, in fact, have sold everything he had and given it to the poor, and his soul could still have been just as sick as ever. You can't buy forgiveness. You can't "do" yourself into eternal life. Jesus knew that, but he also knew that sometimes you start with the doing and move from there. Sometimes you begin with what the listeners give you, speaking to their felt need and moving them to the place where they can bend their knees.

The most amazing part of this story is that Jesus lets the man go. This is one of those embarrassing parts of the New Testament that we really shouldn't talk about in a textbook on preaching. What in the world was Jesus thinking? Why didn't Jesus call him back? Surely Jesus could have given him a better argument. Jesus could have been clearer. He could have been more persuasive. It certainly wasn't much of a sermon.

I cannot claim to understand everything that was going on in Jesus' mind that day, but I can appreciate the fact that he treated the man with dignity. Preachers often forget that listeners have dignity. They have been created in the image of God, which, among many things, means that they have the right to make their own choices, even bad ones. That God treats us with enough respect that he would let us reject him is one of those encouraging yet humbling mysteries. God could force himself on us. He could overwhelm us with the logic of his truth. He could force us to submit. Instead, he treats us gently and with grace. He lets us have our dignity, even if we curse him in response.

Preachers need to read this passage with care. I don't believe that Jesus' example shows us we can preach flippantly, as if the listener doesn't really matter. The fact that Jesus let the listener go shows how much Jesus valued him.

In homiletic terms, we are suggesting that the listener has "authority" in the process of preaching. We affirm the authority of the Word of God, and we uphold God's own sovereign authority over everything we do and say; humans are accountable before the sovereign will of the God who created them. But the listener has authority too. In practical terms, the listener can choose to quit listening. He or she can choose to ignore, to deny, or to defy the things the preacher says. The listener can daydream, fall asleep, or get up and leave, shaking his fist as he goes. This is the listener's right, given by God, and as preachers we must respect it. We must respect them, as human beings created in God's image and endowed with the privilege of choice. Inductive preaching is respectful preaching.[14]

Insight and Ideas | YOUR LEARNING STYLE

Every individual is different. In prayer, ask God to help you understand how you have been created. What is your learning style? Are you a watcher or a doer? Are you impatient with induction, or does deduction leave you cold?

Do you think you could stretch yourself to adopt an approach to learning that is different from your preferred style? Are you willing to consider using a different form of sermon, one that could bless those whom God has wired differently from you?

From the preacher's perspective, this is a strategic choice, not to give up on calls to submission but to make the tactical decision to begin with the listener. Listeners have a lot on their minds when they drag themselves to church. Rather than asking them to abandon the insistence of their issues and needs, the inductive preacher takes those concerns as the starting place of the sermon, leading the listeners to the point where submission is understood not only as the imperative response of a human before God but also as the necessary key to solving the problems that they have. Rather than beginning with the Bible and moving toward the listener's need, inductive preachers begin with the listener's need and move toward the Bible.

 **Practical Exercise 4 | THE FORMS OF SCRIPTURE**

Scripture texts come in many forms. Some are more deductive in approach, while others present ideas inductively. Find five deductive texts and five inductive texts. How are they similar and how are they different? How might you preach them?

Danish theologian Søren Kierkegaard put the problem in a philosophical and theological framework. Preachers are working in a difficult domain. We are fighting for the hearts and souls of people steeped in self and sin. Not only does spirituality seem dated to people jaded by what they think they know about Christian faith, but they bring hearts encrusted by years spent in patterns of rebellion. Such people cannot be won, Kierkegaard says, by simply clarifying the facts of theology.

In an age of science, we tend to downplay the seemingly soft aspects of subjective knowledge. Such thinking is thought to be illusory, unreal, or unworthy, but Kierkegaard insists that a person's experience of himself is more real than the hard facts and abstractions of science. "The domain of the subjective life, within whose boundaries all the decisive ethical and religious battles are won or lost and in whose counsels the destiny of each individual is decided is not less real for the fact that it cannot be observed by an outsider."[15]

Raymond Anderson, in an essay on Kierkegaard's approach to communication, says, "According to Kierkegaard, subjectivity cannot be communicated by lecturing, arguing, or persuading, for it is neither an idea to be explained, a proposition to be proved, a feeling to be aroused, or a pattern of conduct to be incited. Thus, if the edifying speaker begins to lecture, to argue, or to persuade, he is likely to obtain a result other than the one intended."[16] This is a particular problem for clergymen, Kierkegaard noted, when they turn to lecturing instead of preaching. What they say is usually accurate and truthful, but when preachers only encourage their listeners to reflect on the Bible and its related themes, they are taking far too remote of a position. That remoteness might be proper in a lecture, but it is a problem in a sermon.[17]

What, then, does Kierkegaard counsel? How does one encourage proper subjectivity in public preaching? "Edifying address," he believed, should be addressed personally to the listener. It should talk about concrete realities instead of theoretical abstractions. Such preaching should use the imagination and encourage the kind of process that respects the independence of the listener.[18]

Inductive preaching honors this concern for the listener's subjective interest. It does not disrespect the Bible in its efforts to show respect to the listener. It brings the listener to the Bible despite his or her possible disinclination. Induction unfolds. It leads the listener on a journey from where they are to the place that they must be. It is not inappropriate to show how the Bible speaks to the cries of the human soul. We can bring healing to the listener through our preaching of God's Word.

Discussion Question 9 | IS INDUCTION SELFISH?

Is induction inherently selfish? Inductive study takes the student's life as the starting point. Is this appropriate, or should we require a more submissive approach to the Bible and to preaching?

How to Study Inductively

My friend Dave Welch is a physician. The man has a passion for understanding and resolving medical problems. I visited his house one day and found his living room strewn with piles of medical journals and textbooks that he had been studying. His patients had problems, and Dave had to know how to resolve them even if it kept him studying well into the night.

He and I are not so different, though while he is working on the body, I am working on the soul. The preacher is a physician, a curer of souls, to use the ancient language. Listeners come like patients to the doctor, presenting problems that need to be fixed. The preacher applies Scripture like a salve (an excellent theological term), offering healing through God's Word. Listeners want me to solve their immediate problems, but I want far more than that. I want to heal their very souls before the God who gave them life.

How does a doctor fix a problem? Not unlike a mechanic fixes an engine or a plumber fixes a leaky pipe. It all begins with diagnosis. The doctor must see the problem clearly, understanding it for what it really is. In some ways, this is the greatest skill the doctor possesses. Once the problem is understood, prescribing a cure, if one exists, is relatively simple. Diseases often disguise themselves, appearing as one thing while existing as another. A misapplied prescription can sometimes exacerbate the problem.

The listener comes to the preacher with a certain "presenting problem" — a broken marriage, a broken prayer life, a broken heart. Most often, however, the presenting problem is only a symptom of something deeper and something more significantly spiritual. The wise preacher will recognize the problem for what it is and will be able to prescribe an appropriate remedy.

The listener knows only that he hurts, and he wants to feel better fast. He will not be overly interested in the deeper issues or the technical background to his pain, as important as that information might be. He just wants to be done with the crushing pain. You, as a preacher, will have to bring him along, relieving his surface pain while leading him toward a deeper and ultimately more satisfying way of life.

In some ways, deductive preaching is like preventative medicine, while inductive preaching is like emergency-room care. The office doctor can talk abstractly about healthier ways of living and how the patient can have a better way of life, but in the ER, there are no abstractions. The physician must deal with the problem and deal with it now. Only when patients begin to feel healthy can they think more deeply about that better way of life. By then, they may even be ready to do something about it.

Not every problem is acute, of course. Some of what the listener brings is chronic pain. Many people have lived with pain for so long that they are hardly aware of their pathology. Either way, inductive preaching is good for what ails.

I have heard it said that the church is a hospital, a place where sick people come when they want to get better. It is a fitting metaphor. The best hospitals have research labs, consulting offices, and emergency rooms, and while the practice differs in each room, no one would say that one or the other is illegitimate. There is a place, then, for inductive preaching.[19] It is good and proper for the preacher to begin with the listener in the emergency room, dealing with the problems and looking to build something better, for the spiritual health of the listener and for the glory of God.

How, then, does a preacher study the Bible inductively? In simple terms, induction comes to Scripture with a question to be answered or a problem to be solved. The Bereans in Acts 17:11 came to the Bible "with great eagerness and examined the Scriptures every day to see if what Paul said was true." Their inductive agenda was to see if the gospel Paul preached truly fulfilled the promise of the Old Testament. Inductive preachers help listeners sort out these kinds of questions and problems, not unlike a doctor who presents a biblical diagnosis, prescription, and prognosis for a better future under the promise and authority of God's Word.

Practical Exercise 5 | THE LISTENER'S NEED

Do an exegetical study of your congregation.

What kind of questions and problems do your listeners have? What are the acute needs? What are the chronic problems? What will you have to help them overcome so that they can faithfully hear from God?

Who are these people and where do they come from? How many different learning styles are represented? What is their level of literacy? What are some of the recent major events that have affected the congregation as a whole? What are the long-term historical influences that have shaped the theology and practice of the church?

Write a two- or three-page brief that describes the people to whom you preach.

The following four suggestions are offered as steps to an inductive sermon.

1. Start Where the Listener Is

Inductive preachers approach their study from the perspective of the listener. Like the doctor, the preacher looks for whatever problem that the listener presents. In most preaching situations, the listener does not offer a great deal of verbal feedback, so the preacher will need to anticipate the listener's *problem* or question. This requires the preacher to be in touch with his or her own humanity. Preachers are not much different from their listeners when it gets right down to it. If something is bothering the listener, it probably bothers, or has bothered, the preacher too, if the preacher can be honest enough to listen closely to his or her own heart. Sometimes events in the life of the community require the preacher's response. Living in community with the people makes obvious the questions and issues that plague the listener's mind. Preachers who know their people well will recognize the themes that need to be addressed.

Let us say that the preacher, having spent time with the people over meals, through counseling, and in worship, begins to sense a bitter spirit. Many of them are struggling to find the willingness to forgive those who have hurt them, an abusive father or a mean-spirited husband perhaps. Not everyone feels the bitterness directly, but its existence in some is leading to a degree of tension in all. The unity of the body is threatened because some people are carrying an unforgiving spirit, while others are finding it difficult to tolerate the pervading negativity. Few but the preacher recognize how this root of bitterness is poisoning the atmosphere. All that the people know is that it doesn't feel good to be part of the community. Of course, bitterness will not be the only problem the church is facing at a given point, but if it is one of the things impeding the health of individuals and of the congregation, the preacher will want to bring God's wisdom through his Word.

Resource Recommendation | PREACHING THAT SPEAKS TO WOMEN

Induction requires that we begin with the listener's perspective, that we put ourselves in the place of our listeners, which can be difficult with respect to gender. Traditionally, women have been very gracious in the way they have listened to the men who have preached to them. That patience could wear thin, however, if men persist in ignoring the specific needs and learning styles of women. Alice Matthews's book *Preaching That Speaks to Women* (Baker, 2003) is a good place to start for those who are seeking to understand how to speak more meaningfully to women.

2. Clarify the Situation

Providing a *diagnosis* for the problem requires effort on the part of the preacher. While the doctor scours journals and databases for insight into a problem, the preacher turns to the Scriptures. The doctor's solutions are found in the physical properties of the body, while the preacher's solutions are found in the spiritual properties of the soul. These solutions are theological, not medical, and are found through study of the Scriptures.

Inductive preachers need to take the listener's presenting problem and reshape it in the form of a research question—something that can be resolved through further investigation or experience. Often the listener is asking the wrong question or looking in the wrong direction. What feels like indigestion might actually be a problem with the heart. Inductive preachers need to begin by getting a clear picture of what is wrong before they can offer a solution. In some cases, the question will need to be restated in terms of God's perspective on the matter. The preacher's task is to clarify the situation, helping the listener see the issue for what it really is.

Insight and Ideas | THE LISTENER'S VOICE

Preachers looking for powerful communication will learn to speak with the listener's voice. Framing issues and questions in the listener's voice is an effective means of drawing people in to the sermon and helping them to care.

"This is hard, isn't it?"

"Are you thinking what I am thinking?"

"Isn't this great?"

The listener responds to the sermon as the preacher offers it. Good preachers will anticipate the listener's response to various elements (positive or negative) and give voice to these reactions in the space of the sermon. This helps listeners feel included and draws them in to deeper engagement.

Wayne Gretzky was the greatest hockey player in history, not because he was the strongest skater or had the hardest shot. He wasn't physically large, nor was he the most skilled. The thing that set Gretzky apart was his ability to anticipate. He always knew where the puck was going to be before anyone else did, and he seemed to have an innate sense of what the other players were going to do before they did it.

Anticipation is not only a great athletic skill but a great homiletic ability as well. Preachers who have the courage and the skill to anticipate what listeners are thinking and to give voice to these things in the sermon will preach to great effect.

In inductive study, exegesis and theology come together. The preacher will identify the broad theological categories to which the problem belongs and then will turn to the specific texts in Scripture that provide wisdom relevant to the situation. Theology provides the categories, while exegesis provides the data. Through exegesis, the necessary information is brought forward. Through theological reflection, the information is unified and made coherent.[20]

In our example, the preacher prayerfully discerns that bitterness must be rooted out to create a healthier atmosphere in which the people and the church can grow. Of course, the preacher is theologian enough to understand that bitterness itself is not the problem. Bitterness is only the symptom. This poisonous feeling is the result of something deeper: an inability to forgive. The preacher turns to the Bible in search of wisdom, prayerfully seeking texts that will inform them of a better way. One such text is Matthew 18, which is initially quite frightening to consider. Verses 34–35 suggest that if we can't forgive those who hurt us, we can't expect God to forgive us. Forgiveness, Jesus says, must be perpetual. If your wife deserts you, forgive her. If your father abuses you, forgive him, and if he does it again, forgive him again. This is hard medicine, not easily swallowed.

"How many times should I forgive?" Peter asks. "Up to seven times?" To Peter's thinking, seven times seems extravagant. Any of us who have been deeply hurt would agree. We could possibly produce the grace necessary to forgive a backstabbing friend once, and perhaps with superhuman effort—prayer and fasting and the like—we could do it more than once. But to forgive seven times would be something only an apostle like Peter could be capable of.

"Not seven times," Jesus says, "but seventy-seven times." The implication is clear. The Christian forgives every time. There is no limit, and for many of us, it would seem, there is no hope. Who is capable of such a thing?

Practical Exercise 6 | PROBLEMS WITH YOUR PREACHING

Take three sermons you have recently preached and rethink them from the perspective of your listeners. What kinds of questions would they ask about these sermons if they had the chance? Where might they argue with what God is saying? How deeply do you feel these same concerns? How difficult is it for listeners (yourself included) to submit to what God is saying in these sermons from his Word?

3. Offer a Solution

Exegetical and theological reflection leads to a *prescription*, a solution the listener can apply. The preacher will offer the listener a means of resolving the problem. Here is where the preacher's task becomes more difficult than the doctor's. The doctor can give the patient a bottle of pills or, in more serious cases, turn to more aggressive surgical solutions. In both cases, the prescription is physical and clearly defined: "Take two aspirin and call me in the morning," or more seriously, "You're going to have to come in for surgery." Preachers normally call this stage the *application* of the sermon. Inductive preachers understand that the sermon will be appreciated only to the degree that its application is found helpful by the listener. The problem is that the preacher's prescription is not always as definitive as the doctor's.

Larry Crabb describes the patient who came to him with a pressing problem. "I want to feel better quick," he said.

"I paused for a moment," Crabb said, "then replied, 'I suggest you get a case of your favorite alcoholic beverage, find some cooperative women, and go to the Bahamas for a month.' "

"Are you a Christian?" the man asked. "Your advice doesn't sound very biblical."

"It's the best I can do given your request," Crabb answered. "If you really want to feel good right away and get rid of any unpleasant emotion, then I don't recommend following Christ. Drunkenness, immoral pleasures, and vacations will work far better. Not for long, of course, but in the short run they'll give you what you want."[21]

The preacher's prescription won't always be immediately recognized as potent by the patient, but a biblical-theological solution is what the listener needs. The preacher leads the listener to a place of obedience and submission to the God who loves him or her and wants to bring healing, if not physically, then spiritually and eternally.

The prescription for bitterness, for example, is not easy. It will require careful application and more than just a simplistic order to forgive. The listener already knows that he should forgive his brother, but he hurts too much to do what he knows is right. Principles and propositions are helpful in the abstract, but they don't do a lot of good when the patient is in pain. The answer will come only as the listener begins to understand the degree to which he has personally been forgiven by God. Only when he begins to feel forgiven and to feel something of the wonder of that forgiveness will he be able to offer forgiveness to others.

The preacher's prescription, then, is to help the listener feel forgiven—to know the extent to which he or she has been forgiven by the God who has been gracious and to appreciate what a marvelous thing that is. Having truly tasted grace, the listener will loosen his hold on the bitterness that has been crippling him. Healing will begin.

Insight and Ideas | THE INDUCTIVE PROCESS

Use these keys as you prepare yourself to preach inductively.

1. Start where the listener is (presenting problem).
2. Clarify the situation (diagnosis).
3. Offer a solution (prescription).
4. Anticipate the future (prognosis).

4. Anticipate the Future

The *prognosis* describes the future state of the patient. The doctor can offer patients the probability that if the problem has been correctly diagnosed, the cure should work—as long as a cure exists. In the preacher's case, the cure always exists, at least for the most fundamental problem: human estrangement from the creator God. The doctor faces the prospect that the patient will eventually die no matter how effective the doctor is. The preacher knows that the homiletic cure is ultimately eternal; it offers the prospect of everlasting life.

Bitterness is a serious problem. An unforgiving spirit reveals an unbelieving heart, and unbelief will lead us away from God and from his heaven. But we can find the capacity for forgiveness in the grace God first gave us. In so doing, we find not only that we begin to feel better but that we *are* better. We relate better to one another, and we relate meaningfully with God.

In our scenario, the listeners came to the sermon sporting a problem with bitterness, but the preacher was able to fix the problem, not by applying a band-aid to the wound, but by leading them to God's healing of the underlying cause. They are thus reconciled to God.

The inductive approach, then, can be seen as the opposite of the deductive approach. In a sense, deductive study begins with the prognosis (reconciliation with God), or the final expected result, and moves back toward the listener's situation. Induction, on the other hand, begins with a problem and moves toward ultimate reconciliation and submission. In both cases, God and man are restored to their right proportions and relationships.

Induction takes a problem-solving approach to the sermon. The inductive preacher begins with the listener, making use of whatever need the listeners bring and moving them toward God's will for their lives. In the end, they find themselves in a position far more advanced than what they might have expected. They came looking to feel better or to understand better, and they leave having actually become better in a sense deeper than they could have asked for or imagined.

Choosing Inductive Study

Fred Craddock was the first to champion an inductive approach to preaching. As he saw things back in the early 1960s, deductive preachers were not always completely honest about their process. The truth is that deductive preachers tend toward inductive study in their preparation. To have a message to preach, they first have to study the text for themselves so that they might discover what God is saying. This puts them at an advantage over the listener, Craddock felt. While the preacher gets to enjoy the thrill of discovery in his or her study prior to preaching, listeners are spoon-fed the message. All the fun has been removed.[22]

Let's say, for example, that a friend of yours gives you a jigsaw puzzle for your birthday. You love puzzles. You can get lost for hours in a puzzle. But rather than giving you the present nicely wrapped in paper and bows, your friend gives you the present unwrapped.

"Here is your gift," he says. "I hope you like it. It's a puzzle."

Oh, you think to yourself, that's great, I love puzzles. I would have enjoyed unwrapping the present and discovering that for myself, but never mind.

"I hope you don't mind," your friend continues, "but I already finished it for you. I thought I would save you the effort of putting it together."

You watch in disbelief as your friend hands you the completed puzzle glued to plywood and nicely framed. "Would you like me to hang it on your wall?" he asks.

Okay, it is a nice picture, and if you had finished the puzzle yourself, you might have considered putting it on your wall, but there is no way in the world you are going to hang a puzzle that somebody else completed.

"In most sermons," Craddock says, "if there is any induction, it is in the minister's study, where he arrives at a conclusion, and that conclusion is his beginning point on Sunday morning. Why not on Sunday morning retrace the inductive trip he took earlier and see if the hearers come to that same conclusion?"[23]

Discussion Question 10 | THE JOY OF DISCOVERY

Why are preachers hesitant to let listeners in on the joy of discovery? Why do we tend to want to keep this to ourselves? Are we afraid that our listeners will distort the result if we let them participate? Is this concern justified? Will they not do what they want with the sermon whether or not we give them permission?

In Craddock's view, the preacher is robbing the listener of the joy of discovery. "It hardly seems cricket for the minister to have a week's head start (assuming he studied all week), which puts him psychologically, intellectually, and emotionally so far out front that usually even his introduction is already pregnant with conclusions."[24] In deductive sermon structure, "there is no democracy here, no dialogue, no listening by the speaker, no contributing by the hearer. If the congregation is on the team, it is as javelin catcher."[25]

The preacher who throws javelins may offer a penetrating point, but how many listeners will survive to tell about it? Craddock's solution is for the preacher to recreate imaginatively in the sermon his or her thought process so that the listeners can arrive at the same conclusions for themselves.

The suggestion is appealing. The benefit is more than just a matter of maintaining listener interest, however. Listener apprehension is also strengthened through induction. Craddock continues, "A second reason for stressing inductive movement in preaching is that if it is done well, one often need not make the applications of the conclusion to the lives of the hearers. If *they* have made the trip, it is *their* conclusion, and the implication for their own situations is not only clear but personally inescapable."[26]

One might want to argue with Craddock on this point. The sermon does not belong to the listener. It is not up to the listener to create the conclusion. God owns the sermon. It is his message, and a preacher ought to feel fully within his or her rights to proclaim it. Still, Craddock is correct in stating that an inductive approach to the sermon allows the listener to feel respected as a participant in the process.

Whether or not we follow Craddock's model closely, it is easy to see the benefit of choosing an inductive approach to preaching. Induction matches the shape of our lives. Induction honors the fact that listeners have no choice but to perceive life and truth and God himself from their earthbound perspective. Induction, then, is about the movement of thought from the subjective listener to the objective God, rather than the other way around. But in both cases, God speaks, leaving the listener with no choice but to reckon with what God has said.

Chapter 4 | FOURTH OPTION

how will you communicate the message?

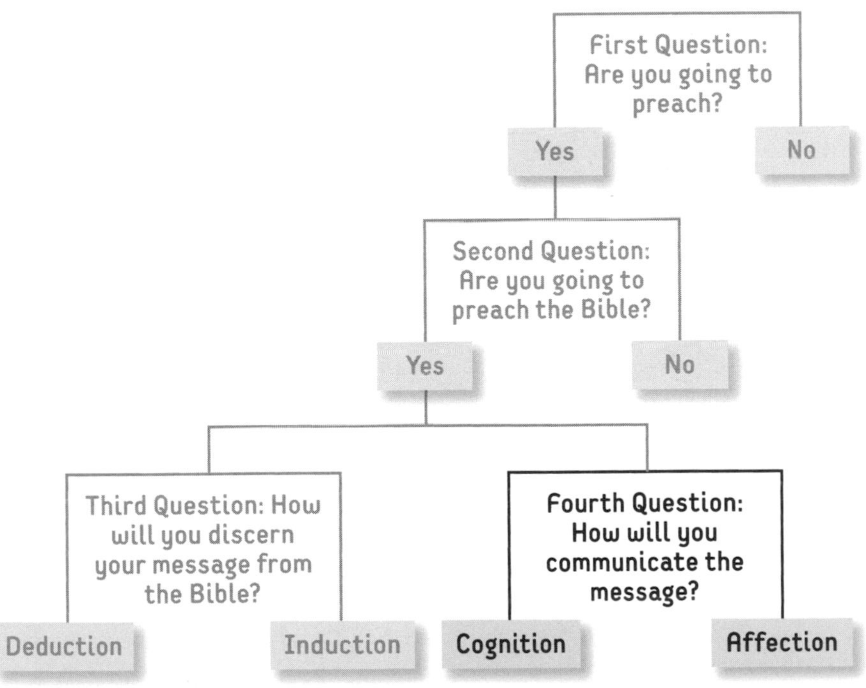

First Question: Are you going to preach?
Yes
No
Second Question: Are you going to preach the Bible?
Yes
No
Third Question: How will you discern your message from the Bible?
Deduction
Induction
Fourth Question: How will you communicate the message?
Cognition
Affection

A year or two ago, I took my family to the museum to see a traveling exhibition of the work of Leonardo da Vinci. The exhibit featured carefully constructed reproductions of the great artist's inventions. There seemed to be little that he had not applied his mind to—everything from human kinetics to the properties of flight. Also displayed were copies of his notebooks, which are full of philosophical insight, technological innovation, and artistic inspiration. The highlight of the exhibit was an "exact" copy of the *Mona Lisa*, a copy so good that it is often used to replace the original piece on display in the Louvre.

In this day of specialization, it was wonderful to interact with a man who was able to cross disciplines so effortlessly. I loved how he was able to integrate the fruits of science and technology with the grace and glory of art. He was the original "Renaissance man." I think he could have made a pretty good preacher.

Preaching is a science. It is a technical discipline that requires meticulous study and careful construction of the sermon. Homiletical textbooks describe the "functional elements" of preaching and the technical "steps to the sermon." Seminaries emphasize the study of biblical languages to ensure that preachers are "rightly dividing the word of truth." This is appropriate, given that preaching is the presentation of God's truth as mediated by his Word. As the saying goes, God is in the details, and preachers need to get it and him right.

In the movie *A Beautiful Mind*, Nobel Prize–winning mathematician John Nash is portrayed as being on a compulsive search for what he called the "governing dynamics." He is shown describing the most common occurrences by means of the language of mathematics. The movement of a flock of pigeons or the interplay of young people in love could all be communicated and to some extent explained by means of algorithmic equations. All of life has an underlying logic. Like the unseen circuitry inside a computer, every function has its reason. Preaching seeks to expose those reasons, displaying the truth that is too often hidden from our sight. Preaching requires precision.

At the same time, preaching is an art. It is not limited to rational, linear forms. A beautiful sermon can inspire and motivate. If the face of Helen of Troy launched a thousand ships, we must admit the power of beauty to move people to action. Many great preachers have learned to treat the sermon like a canvas, offering the right blends of form and color to impress meaning on the listener and move him or her to the intended response.

It has become common to think of art as a medium without a message. It would be difficult, for instance, to determine the meaning behind a piece by Picasso or by Jackson Pollock. Still, as Marshall McLuhan reminds us, there is a message even in the medium. As the great cathedral builders of Europe knew, making something beautiful can be worship. Preaching can appeal to this more intuitive part of the mind that God has given us. Preaching can speak to the heart.

David Kolb sees both approaches, science and art, as means by which people input information. He says we can offer people "abstract concepts," which will appeal to the "thinkers" in the crowd. Or we can offer them "concrete experience," which will appeal to the "feelers."

DAVID KOLB'S EXPERIENTIAL LEARNING MODEL

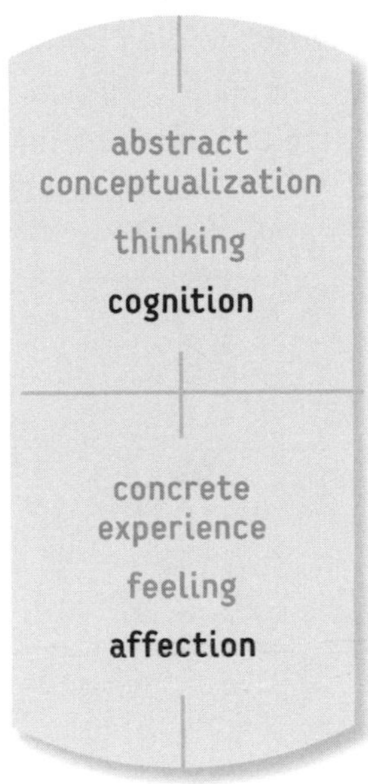

I have seen both of these approaches used in churches. On a recent Sunday, I attended Hillsong London in the morning and All Souls Church in the evening. I love both of these churches, but for quite different reasons. At Hillsong, I feel God's presence. I am inspired by the music, the preaching, and the way people relate to one another. I love the tangible sense that God is present and that he is acting among us. The affective "feeler" in me loves it. All Souls, on the other hand, is known for its commitment to expository preaching. The legacy of John Stott lives on in the church where he served as rector. When I go to All Souls, I know my mind is going to be fed. I know I will leave having profoundly met with God in his Word.

Not long ago, I shared these experiences with Ian Dickson of Belfast Bible College. "But the sermon is the medium that is capable of expressing both," he said excitedly.

Exactly.

Preaching can be art, and it can be science. It can even be both.

Having discerned the message of your sermon, through either deductive or inductive means, the next choice you have to make is how you will communicate your message. The goal is to craft your message so that it can be received by the congregation. You can choose a cognitive style, which will appeal to the thinkers, or an affective style, which will appeal to the feelers. *Cognition* involves the correct ordering of ideas in the mind. *Affection* deals with emotional intelligence and the impact preachers can make on the heart. As with the choice between deduction and induction, there is no wrong choice here. Either style can be effective in helping people hear the voice of God and respond appropriately to what they hear.

So which will you choose?

Option 4A

focus on the idea

Cognitive Style

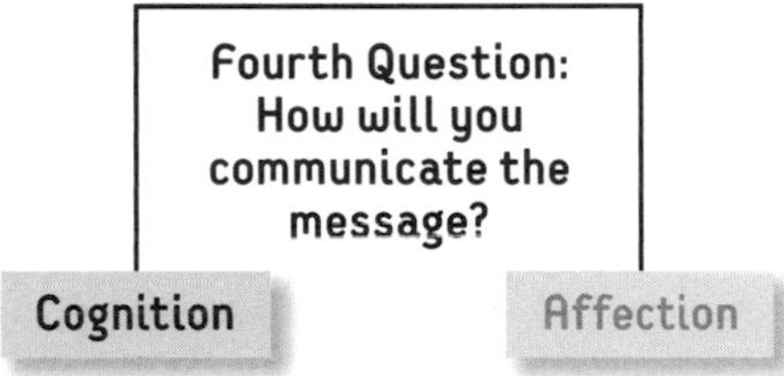
Fourth Question:
How will you
communicate the
message?
Cognition
Affection

"Just the facts, ma'am."

Do you remember the television series *Dragnet*? Whenever long-suffering police detective Jack Webb came across an overwrought housewife or an emotional victim, he would try to cut through the feelings and get at the heart of the matter: "Just the facts."

Emotions are legitimate. Sometimes the things we experience are crushing, and we just have to feel what we feel. Yet when it comes to finding healing, facts become imperative. We need someone who can help us think, someone who can remind us of the truth. The victim needs to feel what he or she is feeling, but Jack Webb will not be able to do his job unless he can set the facts in order. Understanding truth does not always immediately relieve the pain we are feeling, but it can ensure that we do not make emotional choices that lead to further trouble.

Focus on the Idea

The key to cognitive preaching is to focus on the ideas in the sermon. While imagery is useful, the primary emphasis in the cognitive sermon is on the propositions. Truth is taught by precept, and it is in the ideas of the sermon that truth is clearly realized and understood.

"Let me understand the teaching of your precepts," the psalmist wrote, "then I will meditate on your wonders" (Ps. 119:27). The psalmist understood the value of cognitive preaching. "Oh, how I love your law!" he wrote. "I meditate on it all day long.... I have more insight than all my teachers, for I meditate on your statutes. I have more understanding than the elders, for I obey your precepts. I have kept my feet from every evil path so that I might obey your word" (Ps. 119:97–101).

Notice that the psalmist's commitment to the ideas (precepts, statutes, laws) of Scripture gives rise to obedience and a more righteous way of life. There is a reciprocal relationship between the psalmist's commitment to obedience and his reading of the Word. Studying the truths of the Bible creates a hunger for righteousness, while living a righteous life creates a hunger for God's Word. "How sweet are your words to my taste," he writes, "sweeter than honey to my mouth! I gain understanding from your precepts; therefore I hate every wrong path" (Ps. 119:103–4).

Psalm 1 pictures a righteous man who meditates on the law of God night and day. The result is that the man is like a tree beside a river, deeply rooted and well nourished. In contrast to the righteous man are the wicked, who do not pay attention to the truth of God. They are like chaff, the worthless husks that blow away as the grain is tossed in the wind. The ideas of Scripture are what allow us to be rooted in truth and enable us to find the nourishment we need.

Cognitive preaching is committed to providing people with the principles of Scripture that will stand across time. Second Timothy 3:15 says that the Scriptures are able to make us wise for salvation. "All Scripture is God-breathed and is useful for teaching, rebuking, correcting and training in righteousness" (3:17). The fully equipped person (3:17) is one who has the truths of Scripture deeply embedded within him, and it is for this purpose that we preach (4:2).

The back of Campus Crusade's *Four Spiritual Laws* booklet contains a diagram that features a train with various cars. The cars represent aspects of the human experience. "Fact," for instance, is shown as the engine, while "feeling" is the caboose. The booklet makes the point that you can't drive the train by the caboose. Put the engine in front of the train, and everything that is linked behind will follow along in place. Feelings are unreliable and are easily counterfeited, while facts are self-evident. "The train will run with or without the caboose. However, it would be useless to attempt to pull the train by the caboose. In the same way, as Christians we do not depend on feelings or emotions, but we place our faith (trust) in the trustworthiness of God and the promises of His Word."[1]

Of course, a sermon can have too many facts. Part of the challenge of communicating clearly is keeping the discussion focused.

Like most children, my daughter, Katelyn, has sometimes struggled to keep her room tidy. She is older now and is very proud of the way she keeps her things, but it wasn't always that way. I remember one time she came downstairs and complained that there was "nothing to do."

"Come on, Katey," I said, "there are plenty of things to do. You've got a whole toy store up in that room just waiting to be played with. There is no end of toys, games, books, dolls ..."

But she was insistent. "No, Daddy, there is nothing to do!"

So I took her upstairs, and after one look at her room, I knew exactly what she meant. It's not that there was nothing to do. The problem was that there was too much to do and that it was everywhere, strewn across the floor and piled without purpose. The room was a cluttered mess!

I walked into her bedroom, being careful not to break anything by stepping on it, and picked up one of her long-forgotten toys. "How about this," I said. "Oh," she said, her face brightening, "I forgot about that." She took it in her hand, and she was fine for the next hour or so.

Practical Exercise 7 | PROPOSITIONS THAT SHAPE OUR PREACHING

Our preaching is shaped by principle. List five propositions that have helped shape your convictions about preaching. For example:

- God speaks when his Word is preached.
- Truth must be applied to the listener's life.

Sermons are often like this. They are cluttered. Everything in the sermon is good; there is just too much of it. The listener can't get hold of the ideas because there are too many of them. Everything jumbles together and turns into goop. If we took a single element and looked at it carefully, we would see its value, but in the undisciplined mix of the sermon, that element is almost inaccessible.

In preaching, the old adage is true: less is more. The clearest, most compelling sermons have the simplest structures. They don't attempt too much. They are deep by being profoundly simple, not by being complex and cluttered.

Flannery O'Connor (or was it Ernest Hemingway?) once said that the editing process is a lot like killing your babies. You gave birth to your work, and it is extremely painful to put some of it to death. But there is always next week. The things that are set aside for this sermon might be just what you need for another sermon later on.

Haddon Robinson has suggested that every sermon ought to have one "big idea." "A sermon should be a bullet and not buckshot," he said. "Ideally each sermon is the explanation, interpretation, or application of a single dominant idea supported by other ideas."[2]

Resource Recommendation | COGNITIVE SCIENCE AND THE MIND

The nature of the mind is much in dispute among cognitive scientists. Some, like Daniel Dennett, describe the mind as a complex, organic machine, not unlike a computer or calculator. Others take a more theological approach, arguing for a consciousness capable of communion with God. Preachers can learn from research into the cognitive process but must retain a sense of body and *soul*.

For further study, see Gregory Peterson, *Minding God: Theology and the Cognitive Sciences* (Fortress, 2003).

Saying that the sermon ought to have one main idea is easier in theory than in practice. It takes a great deal of discipline for the preacher to be able to focus all of his or her energies on a specific proposition. When you spend the better part of a week falling in love with a text in Scripture, it can be difficult to bring the whole thing under the discipline of a single concept. Bible texts are rich and detailed, and the more we study them, the more wonders we discover. Yet if we try to communicate all of those ideas in a single sermon, we will create more confusion than clarity. Many times a text will feature a big idea, a bigger idea, and a biggest idea. Which of these ideas we choose to preach on is less important than choosing one of these ideas and preaching a message that has unity and focus. It doesn't take me long to tell when a student really understands what he is trying to say and when he has not been able to finally put his finger on it. Preaching rings true when the preacher is compelled by a single big idea.

If we can convince our listeners of one truly big idea week by week, we will see lives change in ways beyond our imagining. The truth will embed itself like a seed deep in the congregational ground. Eventually, it will break out into blossom and bear fruit.

How to Use Cognition

Cognitive preachers strive to instruct the listener. If we are going to understand God, we have to know exactly who he is. If we are going to obey God, we need to understand what he expects. The cognitive preacher works (either deductively or inductively) to ensure that the listener has been given the necessary information and that he or she understands it correctly.

Imagine the listener's mind as a kind of filing cabinet. The cognitive sermon works to put all the information in the correct folders and in the proper drawers. Or think of the mind as a complicated piece of computer code written by God. A virus has infected the code, fatally altering key blocks of information and causing the data to be disarrayed. The listener cannot function properly according to the designer's intent if the code is in error. The preacher, then, works to fix the code, rooting out the virus and replacing it with the right information, making sure that all the correct code lines are in the right places so that the synapses fire correctly and the mind works as designed.

Discussion Question 11 | PREACHING AND TEACHING

Is there any difference between preaching and teaching? Deductive study sounds very much like the work of a teacher. Does preaching demand something beyond deduction? Or could good teaching embrace that "something beyond" as well?

In this, the preacher is not unlike a teacher who seeks to educate the listener. While a good teacher is concerned with teaching students how to think, the teacher also makes a major effort to explain to students what to think. In other words, the teacher provides the student with the information necessary for a well-ordered mind. If one is to be successful in a given area of life, let's say aeronautics, the student must learn a vast body of information before his or her creative-thinking skills can ever begin to be applied. The history, theory, and basic information relevant to the discipline of flight must be mastered. Helping students achieve this is what a teacher does.

It is also what a preacher does. Given that God has revealed his nature and his will through his Word, the preacher needs to educate the listener in these things. The Bible is a large book, not only in its number of pages but in its scope and intellectual depth. The listener initially comes to the sermon uninformed and theologically unsophisticated. The cognitive preacher accepts the challenge of not only providing the listener with the necessary concepts but also explaining how the information should be processed.

For two years, I sat under the preaching of Harold Bullock, pastor of Hope Community Church in Fort Worth, Texas. I'm not sure I have ever known a preacher more respected by the audience than Harold. The people of Hope Church love his preaching because they profit so much from its wisdom. These people take their sermons seriously. Pencils scribble rapidly whenever Harold preaches because the people know that the information he is offering them is critical to their success in living life with God. Harold's intellect, his innate sense of wisdom, and his deep sense of the Scriptures combine to provide a teaching experience that touches people powerfully. He is, in a sense, reprogramming them, correctly ordering the ideas and propositions of Scripture so that the people are able to think rightly and live appropriately. As a result, Harold's teaching has raised up a vast network of leaders and church planters who have gone out to follow his example in educating people in the truths of God's Word.

The goal, of course, is to see lives change. I suppose it is natural to see cognitive instruction as a rather tame exercise of the intellect, as if information carries no consequence, but teaching preachers like Harold would reject that kind of thinking. Ideas have consequences and are offered not only to add to the listener's store of knowledge but also to change the listener's physical and spiritual responses to God.

Take the question of preaching and teaching. Many have tried to distinguish between preaching and teaching as if teachers share information, while preachers change lives, but that distinction might not actually be helpful. When someone says, "George is a better teacher than he is a preacher," we think we understand. When pressed to articulate the difference, however, things become more complicated. It may be George is a little dry in his presentation or perhaps he is lacking in passion. That might leave him deficient in the preaching category, but does it automatically mean the man can teach?

One of the reasons preachers are unappreciated in contemporary culture is that they keep trying to change people's lives. Teachers are better accepted because they are thought to be benign. The teacher shares information but isn't concerned about persuading anyone, or so it is thought. Put it like that to a real teacher, however, and see how he or she responds.

Any teacher worth her whiteboard wants to change lives. Great teaching is not solely about information transfer, as if the lecture were a biotechnical cognitive download. There is that, of course, but teachers want so much more for their students. Teachers want to be dangerous. They actually want to change lives — just like preachers.

Preachers and teachers have more in common than what is often thought. The teacher wants to change lives, and the cognitive preacher understands that lives will change once people have a correct understanding of truth.

Discussion Question 12 | IMAGES AND IDEAS

Are ideas more important than images, or are the two roughly equal in their expressive power? Is there something dangerous about an image without an idea? What about an idea without a corresponding image?

Cognitive preaching is not a form of sermon so much as it is a means of communication common to multiple homiletic forms. A cognitive sermon can, for instance, unfold inductively, or it can declare itself deductively. The cognitive nature of the sermon will be seen in its attention to the mind in order to gain the listener's assent. Preachers who choose cognition as their primary means of communication should give attention to the following recommendations.

1. Use an Outline

In preaching, the primary means of explaining truth is the outline. Whether using a pedagogical tool like the lecture or a more interactive tool like discussion or experiment, the effective teacher first makes a logical and clear outline of the material to be taught. Similarly, preachers have long understood the value of a sermon outline that puts the presentation in an ordered and rational framework.

The first textbook on preaching to gain a significant following was *On the Preparation and Delivery of Sermons*, written by John Albert Broadus in 1870. Broadus, building on the work of Aristotle and the classic rhetoricians, ensured that cognition would be the primary focus of the sermon for decades to come. For Broadus, the shape of the outline was critical.

Insight and Ideas | JOHN BROADUS ON THE OUTLINE

Sermon outlines must have

- unity
- order
- proportion
- progress

Broadus's first concern was that sermons have *unity*. Many sermons, Broadus said, are actually two or three little sermons in succession. "Whether the unity be that of a doctrinal proposition, of an historical person, or of a practical design, in some way there must be unity."[3] Robinson, in his emphasis on the one big idea, is simply following the heritage championed by Broadus and those who have followed. Everything in the sermon needs to pull together. A sermon might offer several good ideas, but if they are in competition with one another, fracturing the focus of the listener, they will do more harm than good.

Second, Broadus counseled a concern for *order*. This is to say that the preacher must consider how the various parts of the sermon relate to one another and to the whole. "Good order requires first of all that the various ideas comprising the unit of consideration be carefully distinguished from one another; secondly, that they follow one another in sequence, making for continuity; and, thirdly, that the order of thought shall move toward a climax."[4] Getting the pieces of a sermon in the proper order means that the preacher understands how the elements relate logically. Certain elements need to be established prior to other elements if the sermon is to make sense.

Third, Broadus wished that the sermon present its various ideas in *proportion*. Not every aspect of the sermon needs to be given identical emphasis or time in the sermon but must rather be seen in terms of the proportional weight of the idea relative to the overall intent. Having established primary ideas, the subsequent ideas can be treated more lightly. To give a supportive element as much focus as the big idea of the sermon is to create confusion for the listener.[5]

Fourth, Broadus asked for a sense of *progress* in the sermon. In other words, the sermon must move, and that movement must be forward. "Some sermons," Broadus said, "have been called 'Ferris wheel' sermons. They move 'round and round,' but they do not move forward to a climax."[6] The climax of the sermon is indicated by its objective. If the preacher has a clear sense of what he or she is seeking to accomplish, the sermon can then be built so it moves toward the objective. Everything that gets in the way of that purpose can be jettisoned.

It is helpful, Broadus suggested, that the key ideas of the sermon be clearly divided and identified, not only to make the train of thought plain to the listeners but also to assist the preacher in encouraging logical correctness. The number of divisions is not set, but fewer is usually better. Each division must be clearly distinguished, memorably described, and critical to the achievement of the objective. Broadus preferred two divisions for his own sermons, though he acknowledged that three-point sermons seem to be a lot more common.[7]

2. Use the Language of Literacy

Literacy, as a kind of language, is the form best suited for the careful presentation of ideas. Colloquial language might be too informal when the goal is to gain an understanding of the truth. Precision matters when truth is at stake.

According to Aristotle, the substance of the ideas are critical to persuasion, not the arousing of prejudice, pity, anger, or other similar emotions, which have nothing to do with the facts.[8] Such appeals to the personality of the listener can manipulate a message.[9] To that end, the cognitive preacher will not invoke flowery eloquence but will communicate in plain language. To say that the sermon is literate is to say that care has been given to the words of the sermon so that they communicate a precise and accurate message.

Cognitive preachers tend to be manuscript preachers since a manuscript gives the preacher the best chance of getting the words right in the pulpit. The ideas are important, and they need to be stated clearly and punctuated with confidence. Points misstated or unclear can cripple the whole project. A good set of notes can ensure that the preacher will not make critical mistakes or forget key information.

Resource Recommendation | POSTMAN'S AMUSEMENT

Neil Postman, in his book *Amusing Ourselves to Death* (Penguin, 1985), makes the case for linear cognition better than anyone else. While not everyone agrees with his conclusions, he is helpful in showing how Western culture has moved away from literacy and logic toward more entertaining ways of managing public discourse.

The shape of the manuscript can vary. Some preachers prefer to write their sermons in full, giving every word in print just as it is to be preached. Others prepare a partial manuscript, committing only the outline and key phrases to paper.

A full manuscript offers the preacher the greatest amount of confidence. If the preacher has every word laid out, there is less to be nervous about. The preacher can concentrate on the message rather than on how it is worded, confident that if the Holy Spirit can guide a preacher's choice of words while in the pulpit, he can certainly do the same in the preacher's study. Manuscript preachers wake up comfortably on Sunday mornings, knowing that the sermon is well in hand and that there will not be a major blunder.

Of course, the downside is that it can be difficult to present a manuscripted sermon and retain the vitality and presence that would normally be welcomed in a sermon. People don't want a preacher to read to them. Full-manuscript preachers must make sure they are so well prepared that their sermons are not merely read but are confidently and artfully offered to people in the moment. A sermon should feel not like it came out of a can but that it lives and breathes and speaks life to people.

Notes can be prepared in many ways. Ideally, the manuscript sermon will not be laid out in the typical paragraph fashion you find in a book ...

but rather by using shorter sentences

laid out to show the relation of the ideas

in a manner that is more readily viewed at a glance.

A larger type font can be helpful.

So can bold print!

Or color highlighting.

Most preachers have found a way of laying out their notes that suits their personal style. Ask to see the notes of preachers you respect to see how they are done. You will likely find everything from the preacher's scrawlings on a three-by-five-inch card or Post-It note to several pages of typewritten script. Sometimes preachers will record the detailed arguments but leave the stories and illustrations for extemporaneous delivery. Other preachers prefer to craft their statements in unfinished phrases, which leads to preaching that

sounds more natural
encourages more eye contact
allows the preacher a little room to be creative

Words matter to a cognitive preacher. Whichever form of notation the preacher chooses, it must aid him or her in communicating the big idea with clarity and precision.

3. Offer a Competent Presence

The demeanor of the cognitive preacher will be professional, if not quite formal. You will want to communicate that the message matters, not only with your words but also by your presence. Careless dress can send the wrong message, suggesting a lack of seriousness. If your dress is casual, perhaps your message is as well. One would not expect a politician to present a major speech in anything but a suit and tie. A businessperson dresses to communicate competence and seriousness when addressing the shareholders.

Of course, such things are always culturally determined. I recently toured the National Portrait Gallery in London and was struck by the variety of clothing styles worn by English monarchs over the centuries. Henry VIII dressed very differently from George V, whose attire was again different from that of Charles I. The only principle that applied across the ages was that they all dressed their best, whether that meant frilly collars or button-down shirts. What exactly we will wear depends entirely on the venue and the expectations of the people. You will dress differently for speaking at a camp meeting than you will for speaking at a banquet, but we should always look like we care about the event and about what we have come to say.

I sometimes carry a tie in my pocket when traveling to speak. The tie can easily be put on or taken off depending on the expectations of the crowd. What I don't want to do is to make it impossible for my listeners to hear what I am saying because of something as minor as a tie. I understand that some of us don't feel comfortable in a tie or in a T-shirt, or whatever the convention might be at a given event. Isn't it more important that we be true to who we are? No. It is not. The sermon is not about you and your comfort. If you care about your listeners, you will do anything in your power to help them hear from God. If the people want you in a tie, then don't be a fool. Wear the tie. Besides, if you really feel your personality is defined by what you wear, you have spent too much time in shopping malls.

Discussion Question 13 | APPROPRIATE DRESS

It seems there is no longer a standard for dress in the pulpit or in church. As churches begin to meet in warehouses and shopping malls, the expectations of the past have dwindled. Older believers remember when dressing well indicated one's desire to bring their best to God in worship. Younger believers tend to think that being comfortable in God's presence is more important. Is there any bottom line when it comes to how one dresses when preaching? How do factors like age and socioeconomics affect the question?

As with dress, the cognitive preacher's manner will portray competence and a seriousness of purpose. The preacher's gestures will be firm but not intrusive. Remember, the words themselves are what matters. Pointed gestures should only support the ideas being spoken without overwhelming the message itself. The preacher's voice will be strong and clear. Not only will a mumbled message imply that the preacher doesn't think the words matter, but the words will not be clearly heard. Conviction is expressed with a direct and powerful voice.

4. Use Aids That Serve Understanding

Cognitive preachers will use those material aids that will assist the clear communication of the ideas of the message. Visual aids and object lessons will be used only if they are critical to enhancing the listener's understanding of the point. If the object lesson is too flashy, it can become more memorable than the point itself. Of course, the same can be true of sermon illustrations. Visual aids are a more physical form of bringing light and color to the ideas of a sermon. Anything beyond that should be avoided.

The foremost material aid for the cognitive preacher is the pulpit itself. For many people, the pulpit is a symbol of the communication of God's Word. Centrally located, the pulpit is a visual picture of the importance of the preaching of the Bible in the congregation. For the cognitive preacher, however, the pulpit offers added value as a place to lay one's notes.

Some pulpits are just too small. I recently watched a preacher try to work with a flimsy music stand in an outdoor setting. Not only was it too small to hold her several pages, but a breeze came up and sent many of them flying. Unfortunately, the distraction made a shambles of her sermon, though it did provide a little humor.

? **Discussion Question 14** | THE USE OF THE PULPIT

Must a cognitive preacher use a pulpit? If the preacher knows the material well enough to preach extemporaneously, can the pulpit be left behind? Or is the pulpit a symbol we cannot afford to lose?

For more background, see my article "The Place of the Pulpit," www.preaching.org/pulpit.html.

If a pulpit is to be used, it should be large enough to lay two full-size pages of notes alongside one another and also have room to rest one's Bible when not in use. The pulpit should be just high enough so the preacher can see the notes without bending to look down, but not so high as to obscure the congregation's view of the preacher. The pulpit should be attractive without being ostentatious, so that the focus is on the message and not on the furniture.

Many cognitive preachers are turning to projection technologies to add impact to their sermons. PowerPoint software allows the preacher to lay out the ideas and outline of the sermon so that the listener does not miss them. Sometimes the ideas go by too quickly for a listener to grasp them. Projecting the main ideas on the screen gives the preacher confidence that these points not only will be heard but also will be remembered. Retention improves when a listener not only hears what is said but reads it as well.

Using projection technology effectively is not as easy as it might appear. Like a child with a new toy, preachers initially want to make use of all the bells, beeps, and transitions the technology offers. Wise preachers understand that more is not necessarily better. Simple images and constructions are almost always stronger. As a rule of thumb, twenty-five words on a single slide might be a maximum, and twelve to fifteen slides in a presentation might be an outside limit. Of course, none of it will matter if the slides cannot be seen. Try sitting in the back row with a normal Sunday morning light array to see how easily the screen can be seen. Font sizes of less than twenty-eight points might be difficult for some people to read. Generally, white fonts against dark backgrounds read well. Colors ought to contrast without clashing. Remember that the best slides will not have much impact if the projector bulb is too weak. If the image is dull, it will frustrate people more than enhance the message. If you're going to spend money on this kind of technology, make sure you spend enough money to make the investment worthwhile. Eighteen hundred lumens might be a minimum standard for a small church building.

Resource Recommendation | POWERPOINTERS

The development of PowerPoint slides is as much an art as it is a science. For help with developing excellent slides, check out www.presentationpointers.com.

A favorite strategy of cognitive preachers is to include printed notes in the sermon bulletin. These notes, offering the sermon's text, big idea, outline, and key ideas, can be printed either in full or with blank spaces that the listener is able to fill in. Asking the listener to fill in blanks or add his or her own comments is a way of encouraging careful listening. The listener can take the notes home and study them further when the issues discussed are particularly urgent.

These practical aspects related to communication style all serve to enhance a sermon that focuses on the idea offered by the text. Subsequent chapters will look more specifically at the form these sermons take.

Choosing Cognitive Style

Preachers choose the cognitive style as their means of presentation to help their listeners think correctly. The conviction is that when we think rightly, we will act rightly. We will obey God once we believe God. Preachers who want to change behavior will be intentional about changing listeners' beliefs.

John Piper is a quintessential cognitive preacher. His book *The Supremacy of God in Preaching* reminds preachers that their task is to represent God and his glory by means of the sermon.[10] Piper achieves that task by carefully enunciating the principles that support correct thinking about God and his will.

In one of his sermons, Piper tells the story of a woman in a small group Bible study he was leading who found it impossible to forgive her mother. No matter what the group said, the woman made it clear that there was no way and no circumstances under which she could forgive her mother for the way that she had been treated as a child. Piper says that no matter how hard the group pleaded with her about the biblical commands to forgive and about how God had forgiven her, the woman was adamant.

Resource Recommendation | DESIRING GOD

John Piper's website, www.desiringgod.org, offers insight into Piper's approach to preaching and theology, along with access to his sermon manuscripts.

Piper begged the woman to consider Matthew 6:15 and its claim that if we do not forgive the sins of others, God will not forgive our sins. "Don't you realize," he said, "that if you are unwilling to forgive your mother, God won't be willing to forgive your sins and you won't go to heaven?" But it was all to no avail. His words had no impact on her. "She was not the kind of person who was governed by principle," Piper said, "or by the Word. She was emotion driven ... and that emotion was impervious to biblical words."[11]

Emotion, for Piper, was the problem. The believer in Christ is to be formed on the basis of principle. The problem with emotion is that it can interfere with the Christian's ability to believe rightly on a principled basis by faith. While Piper values emotion when it is rightly directed, his manner of preaching is built on the premise that believers grow when they understand the truth.

As an example, the sermon from which this story was taken consists of four points. The points serve as the complement to the sermon's subject. The title, "Battling the Unbelief of Bitterness," is described by means of the four propositions. In fact, the title could be reconstructed as a question: "How does the believer battle the unbelief of bitterness?" The four points, then, provide his answers to the question: (1) believe that what the Good Physician prescribes for you is good, (2) cherish being forgiven by God, (3) trust that God's justice will prevail, and (4) trust God's purpose to turn the cause of your anger to your good. These points do not require sequential treatment. The fourth point, for instance, is not dependent on the third. It would be important, however, to give all four points. For Piper, the four propositions work in concert to give a full-orbed appreciation for God's intention. Anything less would be an incomplete statement of the truth of God's Word on the subject.

Piper wants to help the listener think correctly. The key to being a forgiving person, according to Piper, is to believe what God has said. In another example given in the same sermon, Piper says it is like the doctor saying, "Put away coffee." "You just have to believe him," Piper says. "If you believe him, you will do it."

No cognitive preacher could have said it better.

Option 4B

focus on the image

Affective Style

Fourth Question: How will you communicate the message?

Cognition | **Affection**

My son, Kirk, made a relevant comment while doing his homework. "I've decided," he said, "that there are two things that are way overanalyzed."

"What are they?" his mother asked.

"Art and poetry," he declared. "Somebody paints a picture because they think it looks nice or writes a poem because they think it sounds nice, then everybody else has to turn it into some great intellectual thing."

I think I understand. I enjoy viewing art. My experience of poetry tends to be limited to its expression in music, but I like it just the same. I appreciate that poetry and art offer the opportunity for deep intellectual appraisal, but like my son, sometimes I would rather be spared all of that. Sometimes I like a piece for reasons I could not even explain. Is that such a bad thing? Analysis would choke the simple delight I find when I experience something beautiful or notice something grand.

I recently heard two music critics debating the merits of a new U2 album. One critic was enthusiastic about the evocative images and the potency of the musical sound. The other critic wanted something more. For him, the band needed to offer a more intellectually coherent message. He wanted to know how U2 would change the world.

The first critic, however, was having none of that. For him, the specifics were insignificant. It was the sweep of images and the overall impact that stoked his passion. The band, he said, had created a soundtrack for the times, filling in the spaces with a way of feeling in the world. For this critic, the album worked on an affective level. The cognitive impact of the music was less important.

This debate points out the two ways people comprehend the world. Whether or not we appreciate the music of U2, we ought to be able to grant the affective possibilities for comprehending truth. While we might want a more definitive message from those who purport to influence the culture, we must admit that people are moved through affective means.

Preaching also works on an affective level. Preachers can help listeners feel things. A good sermon can lead a listener to get angry, to be hopeful, to feel wonder, or to any number of other responses to God. Effective preachers know the power of human emotion to affect the will and to motive change in the listener's response. While preachers want to give the listener reasons for faith, informing the person's view of God, sometimes the listener just wants to know that he or she is not alone. When the listener comes to know that he or she is loved by God, analysis can seem superfluous.

Focus on the Image

While cognitive preaching focuses on the ideas of the sermon, affective preaching focuses on the images. The preacher touches the heart of the listener through the pictures and descriptions of the sermon, creating a desire for change that works at a different level than logic does. We might not be able to give all the reasons for our desire to change, but we know what we must do. This kind of preaching is wired for the "feelers" more than for the "thinkers" of David Kolb's learning paradigm. While some might question the validity of emotional forms of apprehension, seeing them as inferior or elementary, psychologists and educational theorists would see cognition and affection simply as being different.[12] I prefer to view the matter as an example of God's creative genius. God has created us with the capacity both to think and to feel. That some people might be bent more toward one than the other should not be a problem for preachers who understand how to communicate in either or both styles.

My wife and I both enjoy the movies, but we have very different experiences when we visit the theater. I tend to focus on the ideas. Karen locks on to the images. When the movie begins and the opening sequence rolls, I will note the title and all the actors who are listed. Karen doesn't even notice that there are words on the screen. I literally have to draw her attention to the words or she will barely even know they are there. Of course, image details that elude me completely will not escape her gaze. We're different, which is one of the things that make our marriage such a pleasure.

Karen, of course, is not the only affective thinker who experiences the world through images and intuition. The world is full of people who perceive the world with their right brain, though not many of them make it to the pulpit.[13] The highly cognitive nature of seminary life tends to attract left-brain thinkers, who naturally gravitate toward cognitive forms of the sermon. This can make it difficult for affective thinkers, who actually might not be able to hear a cognitive sermon, at least not in any helpful sense. Preachers who insist on high levels of cognition in their preaching inadvertently impose a kind of intellectual prerequisite for their sermons. That entrance standard may be higher than many listeners are able to reach.

I have often felt this way myself. I love learning about Jesus. I have a large capacity for intellectual apprehension when it comes to the great themes of theology. Still, there are limits, not only to my capacity for intellectual intake but also to my ability to understand. The more I learn about God, the more I learn I cannot know. God is bigger than I am, and that is just the way he ought to be. A god fitted to the capacity of my intellect would not be much of a god. God eludes me, even as he enfolds me in his eternal plan.

Practical Exercise 8 | INTERNET SEARCH

Search the Internet for a sermon that utilizes affective style and one that uses cognitive style as its dominant approach. Try to find excellent examples from both categories. List at least five major differences between the two sermons. Which sermon would you prefer to listen to?

Strangely, this awareness only feeds my faith. Peter wrote, "Though you have not seen him [Jesus], you love him; and even though you do not see him now, you believe in him and are filled with an inexpressible and glorious joy" (1 Peter 1:8). This is called faith, the substance of things hoped for and the evidence of things not seen (Heb. 11:1). None of the ancient heroes of faith could give much of an intellectual argument for building their arks or leaving their homes. Their motivation was of a different quality, no less powerful for its seeming lack of logic. Of course, obedience to God is never irrational. It only appears so to those who have not known the love and fear of God. The heart has its reasons.

Jonathan Edwards understood the power of what he called the "religious affections." Edwards understood the difference between the mind and the will. The mind, he believed, offers humans the capacity to perceive and to speculate. The will, he said, is "that by which the soul does not merely perceive and view things, but is some way inclined with respect to the things it views or considers."[14] Some things draw us and some things repel us. The point is that "the soul does not behold things as an indifferent unaffected spectator, but either as liking or disliking, pleased or displeased, approving or rejecting."[15] We feel things, and these feelings motivate us to action.

Edwards believed that this affective pull of the soul is a legitimate and important aspect of the spiritual life because it is through affective impulse that the will is compelled to act. Understanding leads to the best intentions, but affection leads to action. "The religion which God requires and will accept," he said, "does not consist in weak, dull and lifeless wouldings, raising us but a little above a state of indifference."[16] If we are serious about our faith, Edwards said, and our heart is not "strongly exercised," we are nothing. These matters of faith are so crucial that there is not much use if the effect on our hearts is not "lively and powerful."[17]

Practical Exercise 9 | THE RELIGIOUS AFFECTIONS

Jonathan Edwards listed the following "religious affections": love, hope, desire, joy, sorrow, gratitude, compassion, zeal. Name four more religious affections and describe how they could be utilized in your preaching.

What are these religious affections? Hope, love, joy, desire, sorrow, gratitude, compassion, zeal—these are things that affect a listener's heart. Edwards called them the "springs of action," and any experienced preacher knows how powerful they can be. Listeners are motivated when they gain hope, feel loved, sense joy, or become grateful. Any understanding of faith that does not produce this kind of holy affection in the heart will not lead to the kind of active response that God requires.[18] Preaching must lead to response, and it will not do so unless we touch the heart.

Preachers too often concede this territory to the worship musicians. We accept that worship can touch the emotions, but somehow preaching is supposed to be different—perhaps even above the exercise of mere feeling. Yet this sense does not account for the way God works as we see him in the Bible.

Have you ever wondered why God demanded the tabernacle to be beautiful? Why all the incense if a correct approach to God was only through the mind? In Exodus 31, God chose a craftsman named Bezalel to make the tabernacle beautiful. God had gifted this man, filling him "with the Spirit of God, with skill, ability and knowledge in all kinds of crafts—to make artistic designs for work in gold, silver and bronze, to cut and set stones, to work in wood, and to engage in all kinds of craftsmanship" (Ex. 31:3–5). Bezalel, Oholiab, and all the other craftsmen did their work to near perfection. "The Israelites had done all the work just as the LORD had commanded Moses. Moses inspected the work and saw that they had done it just as the LORD had commanded. So Moses blessed them" (Ex. 39:42–43).

Discussion Question 15 | CROWD SIZE

How does the size of the crowd affect your presentation? Is there an optimum size for certain kinds of presentations? How should we alter our preaching as the crowd of listeners grows in size?

God wanted a beautiful building, which is a little surprising to some of us. I was raised in a conservative denomination, heavily influenced by the Puritans. Our buildings were never beautiful; they were utilitarian but never physically attractive. These days I visit the old cathedrals of Europe, and I marvel at their majesty. I know, of course, the dangers of worshiping structures and how a building can be more a testimony to the builder's ego than a gift of worship to creator God. Still, a part of me longs for a sense of beauty in the places where I worship.

The sermons I grew up listening to were not beautiful. Just like the buildings they were offered in, the sermons I heard were more functional than they were inspirational. They offered ideas and precious few images. They worked on my head but offered very little for my heart. The sermons were meaningful but they were not beautiful, and I think we were the poorer for it.

God exceeds my attempts to understand him. While he honors and encourages my exercise of intellect, my finite mind has its limits. There are aspects of God's character and will for which there are no words. At such times, we come closer to understanding him with an image or with words that describe a picture. There comes a point when all I can do is stand with my mouth hanging open, lost in wonder, love, and praise. At times like this, only these images of awe, the language of the affections, will suffice.

In my first year of college, we used to sing a special hymn in chapel. I believe it was one of the professor's favorites, and it soon became one of mine as well, for it spoke to what I had come to understand with my mind but could only express through my heart: "I stand amazed in the presence of

Jesus the Nazarene and wonder how he could love me, a sinner condemned, unclean. How marvelous. How wonderful is the Savior's love for me."[19] These beautiful words express the feelings of the heart even as they affect the actions of my will.

Resource Recommendation | EMOTIONAL INTELLIGENCE

In his groundbreaking book, *Emotional Intelligence* (Bantam, 1995), Daniel Goleman describes a different way of knowing. Sometimes, he says, "smart is dumb." Sometimes "cognition isn't enough."

As an illustration, Goleman cites the difference between two *Star Trek* characters, Spock and Data. Spock, from the first series, embodied the idea that emotions have no place in the pursuit of intelligence. In the second series, *The Next Generation*, Data emerges in Spock's place. Data is different in that he yearns for the "higher values of the human heart—faith, hope, devotion, love—[which] are missing entirely from the coldly cognitive view."

Daniel Goleman, *Emotional Intelligence* (New York: Bantam, 1995), 40–41.

How to Use Affection

Affective preachers help listeners experience God through his Word. The experience is not the goal of the sermon but the means by which the goal is attained. That goal is a deepened appreciation for God's truth and a more faithful obedience to its demands.

Nothing like this can happen unless the preacher is fully engaged in the preaching moment. The preacher cannot appear detached if the goal is to touch the listener's affections. The affective preacher does not so much describe the truth as embody it. The preacher participates in the sermon not only as one who tells the truth but as one who portrays it.

This portrayal must be authentic. The preacher cannot merely act the sermon out. Actors know how to evoke affective response from listeners, but the actor deals in artifice. The preacher deals in truth. Method actors, for example, are taught to identify with the character to the extent that they are no longer really acting. The method actor *becomes* the character, embodying the identity of the character to such a degree that actor and character are virtually indistinguishable. This approach comes closer to that of faithful preaching but still falls short. Preachers cannot afford to act. Affective preachers must live their sermons. Their message must overtake them, engulfing them physically and intellectually so that absolutely nothing is artificial. The affective preacher personifies the message.

In my book *Preaching with Conviction*, I encouraged preachers to commit a significant portion of their preparation time to something called "assimilation." What I was suggesting is that preachers might be intentional about finding ways to embody the message in actual life before they ever get around to preaching it. This is the most neglected aspect of preaching, yet I don't know anything that has improved my own preaching and my passion for the sermon as much as this deliberate effort to work the sermon through in my own life under Christ.

Resource Recommendation | ASSIMILATION

Chapter 5 of my book *Preaching with Conviction* (Kregel, 2001), describes the process of assimilation.

"It's one thing to have a message from God. It's another to have a sermon constructed that will allow you to communicate that message. But it's yet another thing altogether to be so captivated by the message that you're truly prepared to preach with depth and passion."

Kenton C. Anderson, *Preaching with Conviction* (Grand Rapids, MI: Kregel, 2001), 110.

Recently, only a few minutes before I was expected to preach, I realized that an issue in my marriage was getting in the way of what I was planning to say in the sermon. I knew that I couldn't say what I wanted to say with integrity when my wife was sitting in the crowd in front of me. I realized I needed to act on the message if I was going to be able to preach it, so with three minutes to go before the start of the service, I got up from my place in the front row, went to Karen, told her I was sorry, and made things right before the worship ever began. It took some courage for me to make that move, but I can tell you that acting intentionally to embrace my message personally made a radical difference in my ability to deliver an affective sermon. It was also the right thing to do for my marriage.

Preaching is more than just the words we say. It is who we are, and it is what we do. In the last few decades, we have experienced a remarkable improvement in our ability to worship holistically. In our worship, we have learned how to integrate heart, mind, soul, and strength in ways that inspire a fully human response to God. It is time we learned to do the same with our preaching.

Some months ago I attended a performance of the Cirque du Soleil. The experience was emotionally overwhelming. On one level, I was impressed by the acrobatics and sheer physical prowess of the performers, but that in itself would not have been enough to work the effect I was experiencing. It was the beauty of the performance that stunned me. Far beyond the faultless technical prowess displayed by the performers, the aesthetic splendor of the show made me feel and think in ways I had not planned. It was not enough that they left me gasping at the acts of strength and coordination; they also moved me with the flow of color and music and the fluidity of their movements. Everything was structured to make me feel something. Of course, I wasn't sure what exactly I was supposed to feel—wonder perhaps, or a vague sense of joy; it was all very inexact—and though I left the giant tent feeling moved, to what I wasn't certain.

I left thinking about my role as a preacher. I would love it if my sermons could leave the listener so profoundly affected. The difference is that when someone is moved by my preaching, I know where he or she is moving to. Preaching has a deliberate trajectory. It aims at action, so when listeners are affected, they know what they are supposed to do about it. Preaching helps people encounter God. Whenever people encountered God in Scripture, they were shaken by the experience, physically and emotionally (e.g., Isaiah 6). Our preaching could have a similar effect.

Preachers can be more affective in their style by paying attention to a number of specific elements. The key is for the preacher to take ownership of the motivation of the listeners, deliberately using means designed to shape the listener's response.

1. Arrange the Images

Affective preaching creates an experience for listeners through the use of images. Preaching is, and always has been, poetic. That is to say that preachers paint pictures with words to evoke a specific response. According to David Buttrick, the preacher needs to take responsibility for how the sermon forms in the listener's consciousness.[20] Preachers can shape this forming, Buttrick believes, by ordering the way thoughts move through the listener's mind, by choosing images that connect, by watching their point of view, and by creating a sense of immediacy in the presentation of these word pictures.

Sermons *move.* They are not static set pieces; they flow across the consciousness of the listener. Preachers who desire to create an experience for listeners will try to shape this movement, seeing the sermon not as a static set of linear ideas but as a series of movements. In this sense, the sermon is like a concerto played by an orchestra; the listener experiences the music as a series of linked pieces, or movements, that combine to create an overall impression. Buttrick suggests that the sermon's movements can be intentionally designed to lead the listener to the desired state of motivation. The preacher takes the ideas of the sermon and imagines them in terms of lived experience. Abstract ideas can remain hypothetical, but concepts framed in terms of real-life story, example, analogy, and metaphor are not so easily avoided. Real-time problems, struggles, and opposition must be faced squarely.[21] The experience is not always comfortable.

Resource Recommendation | AFFECTIVE MOVEMENT

David Buttrick's landmark *Homiletic* (Fortress, 1987) suggests that preachers need to think about how sermons "form in consciousness." Though I don't endorse all aspects of Buttrick's theology, his approach to affective formation is helpful. Buttrick asks us to pay attention to these features:

- the "movements" of the sermon
- the "image grid"
- point of view
- the mode of immediacy

David Buttrick, *Homiletic: Moves and Structures* (Philadelphia: Fortress, 1987), 24.

Most preachers give little thought to how the *images* connect in their sermons. Images and stories are offered only for their illustrative value and not for their affective power. Images are connected to the sermon by their ability to enliven the idea, but these images are not required to cohere in any other way. They could be anything, a story about football, a nursery rhyme, an object lesson, with no apparent similarities between them. For Buttrick, however, images ought to bear some kind of evident relation to one another. The *image grid* is his term for the sermon's web of stories and metaphors and the way that they interact. Rather than gathering a series of "impact illustrations," Buttrick prefers to weave a series of images, examples, and illustrations that have a common theme or connection to give the sermon unity.[22] The model here might be the poet who crafts images to create an affective result.

In a sermon taken from Psalm 8, I chose to focus on images of majesty and royalty to build on the idea of majesty in the text: "O LORD, our Lord, how majestic is your name in all the earth!" (v. 1). The best place to find an image is always in the text itself. In that sermon, I offered Huckleberry Finn talking about kings, Tolkien's *The Lord of the Rings*, and a story about a recent trip I took to Buckingham Palace. Each of these elements had a unique purpose in the sermon, but they all related to the theme of royalty and fed the sense of majesty I was building through the sermon. Together, they helped to keep the listener focused in one direction and on one experience.

Insight and Ideas | COULD A VOICE COACH HELP YOU?

The best preaching will not be of much use if we cannot be heard. Not all of us are blessed with powerful, resonant voices. We can all improve on what we have, however. I am naturally soft-spoken, but I have learned a lot through the vocal training I received while singing in college choirs. You might consider hiring a voice teacher for a few lessons to help you learn how to project and resonate your voice. We don't all need to sound like James Earl Jones, but we do all need to be heard.

Point of view heightens the listener's ability to participate in the sermon. The preacher can show the sermon from several different perspectives. How would a young mother experience this story? What about a young businessman, a malcontent teenager, or a retired senior citizen? Buttrick suggests the preacher select a particular point of view for each section of the sermon and hold that viewpoint through the entire movement.[23] Offering the sermon from a particular perspective keeps the sermon from deteriorating into abstractions. Whether or not the listener shares the exact perspective chosen by the preacher for that movement, the fact that the preacher has taken a point of view locates the move in the life and experience of real people, making the sermon more accessible to everyone. We can listen better when the preacher is talking about real life, even if it is somebody else's life.

As much as possible, affective preachers will offer their images in the mode of *immediacy*.[24] If the sermon is to come alive for the listener, it needs to be offered in the present tense, as if it is actually happening in the present. Stories told in the mode of immediacy live and breathe. The preacher imagines the smell of ancient Jerusalem, the dust and grime, the coolness of the water used to wash the disciples' feet. Immediacy is a sensual mode of preaching. Events are not over and done, but they unfold, inviting the listener to participate in an experience of the Bible. Like a movie or novel that draws the listener in, the preacher approaches the sermon not like the stereotypical history professor but like an embedded journalist describing events as they happen.

2. Adopt an Oral Style

Orality, more than literacy, creates a sense of presence for the listener by offering language that can be experienced more than analyzed.

"Oral" is the language of almost half the North American population. According to statistics gathered by the U.S. National Center for Education Statistics and Statistics Canada, 42 to 48 percent of the general population in North America is either completely illiterate or functionally illiterate.[25] This is not to say that these people are not intelligent, just that they process thought in different ways. As Grant Lovejoy put it, "The question is not simply whether people can read, but how well they learn through literacy-influenced forms of communication."[26]

These statistics are shocking until we consider how much most people read. It is not so much that they cannot read as that they choose not to, which ought to be obvious when one stops to notice the offerings at any airport newsstand. When our primary reading material is about as literate as a children's picture book, one begins to see the problem.

Resource Recommendation | ADULT LITERACY IN NORTH AMERICA

Check these websites for information on adult literacy:

http://nces.ed.gov/naal/

www.abc-canada.org/literacy_facts/

There is a fundamental difference between oral language and written language. A person who is reading has the opportunity to take time to reflect. One can scroll back and reread sections that were at first unclear. Readers of written language are able to process detailed outlines and complex language. Multipoint sermons can be readily understood when put into print.

Oral presentation is different. It happens on the fly, and it happens quickly. People who listen to oral presentations track a flow of fleeting ideas without the possibility of pausing for reflection or stopping to pose a question. This is not a problem because oral listeners are adept at handling information rapidly, as long as the information is offered in the oral language. The problem comes when we try to offer literate constructions orally. It doesn't work very well, particularly for the masses of people who never read serious newspapers and are incapable of handling complex argumentation, at least in oral form. Preachers have to take this issue seriously. It could be that we have created an unnecessary barrier to the gospel with our complex, precise, multipoint, linear presentations.

Resource Recommendation | THE ORAL UNIVERSE

"We—readers of books such as this—are so literate that it is very difficult to conceive of an oral universe of communication or thought except as a variant of a literate universe."

If that thought challenges you, have a look at Walter Ong's book *Orality and Literacy* (Routledge, 1982).

Walter Ong describes a student of his in an inner-city classroom who refused to take notes while listening to the lecture. Perhaps the student was unable to take notes. He simply sat in his chair, rocking slightly, eyes mostly closed as he took the presentation in. To use Ong's words, the student was getting "with it," imbibing the material almost organically. In the end, Ong discovered that the student had mastered the lecture as effectively as many who had taken notes in the traditional fashion.[27] The point is that oral process is not inferior or superior to literate process, though it may be more affective.

How does the preacher prepare a sermon for oral delivery? In the initial stages of preparation, little needs to change. The preacher still needs to study the text and construct a sermon that will help people hear from God. The stage of putting words to the sermon is when adjustments can be made. Contrary to common wisdom, sermons do not need to be written. In fact, the act of writing a sermon may be the very thing that cripples its orality.

According to Clyde Fant, John Broadus preached a series of sermons at Calvary Church in New York that was very well received. Having been urged to publish the sermons, Broadus took to editing the stenographer's transcription of the sermons. He was so horrified by what he read that he called off the whole project, not because anything was wrong with the sermons themselves but simply because he couldn't bear to read them. What is well spoken is not the same as what is well written. As Fant put it, "What suits the ear does not suit the eye."[28] So, Fant argues, if spoken speeches look bad when written, could the corollary also be true? Do "written speeches sound bad when heard"? Invariably, Fant says, they do.[29]

To overcome this problem, preachers are usually told to "write like they speak." Fant questions whether such a thing is even possible. "Learning to speak and learning to write are difficult enough in themselves without learning to hybridize the two. And why do it anyway? Why not prepare for the oral medium in the first place?"[30]

Resource Recommendation | ORAL LANGUAGE

In *The Sermon Doctor*, Harry Farra offers several suggestions intended to help preachers adopt a more oral tone in their preaching. These include using the following:

- more personal pronouns
- more variety in kinds and lengths of sentences
- more repetition of words and phrases
- more single syllable words
- more contractions
- more interjections
- more quotation and dialogue

Harry Farra, *The Sermon Doctor: Prescriptions for Successful Preaching* (San Jose: Author's Choice, 2000), 125.

The problem is with the manuscript. A manuscript gives the preacher only three options: (1) One can read it, though few want to listen to someone reading to them from the pulpit. (2) One can memorize it, but that is a road to disaster. The preacher who memorizes the sermon spends most of the time trying to remember those well-crafted sentences so elusive during the live event instead of focusing on the ideas, the people, and the presence of God. (3) One can become familiar with the manuscript in the study but then do without it as much as possible in the pulpit, a proposal that is much easier in concept than in reality.

Fant's option is to eliminate the written product altogether in favor of something he calls "the oral manuscript."[31] He suggests that the preacher complete the basic exegetical study and the structure of the sermon, then take the various "thought blocks" suggested by the sermon structure and preach them aloud, free-associating until the thoughts begin to settle into a pattern useful for preaching. Fant counsels that, after growing comfortable with the flow of thought, the preacher write a "sermon brief" consisting of a few "directional statements" that suggest the oral trajectory of the sermon. The key to this process is that the product derives from the exercise of speaking and not from writing. It has not been punctuated or edited. It could not be submitted for publication, but it could be preached.

My own practice for many years has been similar. I work hard on sermon exegesis and construction. I do not believe in "winging it." Having developed a sermon structure that seems profitable, I love to work the words out loud. I have worn out a small section of forest trail near my office while preaching to the trees. I have "oralized" other sermons while cutting my lawn or going for a run. I will admit that manuscript preaching feels more comfortable on Sunday mornings, but I will also own that being a little on edge those mornings has made for sharper preaching.

Perhaps the greatest hindrance to a sense of affective presence in preaching is the preacher's set of notes. Preachers dependent on a sheaf of papers will have difficulty communicating on a personal level. The good news is that the paper is not necessary. Extemporaneous preaching has a long and respected history.[32] One does not have to trust in a set of notes to be authoritative. Perhaps it is again a question of how well the sermon has been assimilated into the fabric of the preacher's being.

Orality makes sense for preachers who want to use affection. The oral sermon is alive and fresh, happening in the moment as God speaks through his Word.

3. Establish a Physical Presence

Affective preachers will do whatever they can to be present with the people. Experience is enhanced when listeners sense that the preacher is in the moment with them so that they are participating together in the sermon event.

Much of what gets communicated in preaching is conveyed physically through body language. Generally, you will not want to think too much about what you are doing with your body. If you are passionately engaged, it will show in the way you carry yourself.

Gestures make a difference, but they ought not to be manipulated. Reining in a particularly annoying gesture can be difficult because these things tend to be unconscious and involuntary aspects of our personality, which is just the way we want them. The more we are engaged with our material, the more natural and powerful our mannerisms will be.

Still, there are some things we will want to watch for. Generally, keeping your hands in your pockets for lengthy periods should be avoided. You will want to keep them out where people can see them so that you can make good use of them. Be careful of overusing "stock" hand gestures or facial expressions. These can grow tiresome to the adults and entertaining to the younger members of the congregation. I remember, as a teenager in church, counting the number of times our preacher made use of certain favored gestures. Pounding pulpits, by the way, should probably be done sparingly these days. Ideally, the preacher wants to present a warm and welcoming persona in the pulpit.

Insight and Ideas | WATCHING VIDEO

It might be helpful to view videotapes of your preaching from time to time to judge your physical presence. Of course, nothing is more painful. Videotape tends to accentuate all our annoying mannerisms and physical idiosyncrasies. The goal is not to eliminate them entirely. Part of who we are as people is presented through our bodies. Using our hands, our faces, and our bodies is a great way of communicating presence.

It is a good idea to keep the Bible visible. This is a powerful, though subliminal, aspect of affective presence in preaching. The number of "biblical preachers" who never show their Bibles amazes me. Some preachers keep their Bibles hidden behind the pulpit. Others have so many Scripture verses embedded in their notes or in PowerPoint presentations that the Bible itself does not need to be read. My understanding is that the power is in the Word itself and not in the physical pages. In my own study, I use a digital Bible more than anything else, but not when I am preaching. This is a symbolic issue. I like what it says to the congregation when they see the Bible in my hand and when they see me reading from it. I use a small black Bible that I keep in my hand throughout the sermon, and I never put it down. I like the idea that people can see with their eyes that this sermon comes from God's Word.

Another aspect of physical presence is the preacher's manner of dress. Unlike the more formal and professional dress adopted by cognitive preachers, affective preachers tend toward casual dress as a means of helping the listener feel comfortable and unintimidated. The precedent for casual dress has long been established in the business world. Corporations like Microsoft have found that allowing their employees to dress casually communicates that the company cares and is not about "controlling" their people. Most important, a casual dress policy communicates that the company does not favor (for promotion) those who have the good fortune to have been born affluent. This latter point should be of interest to preachers who want to communicate the accessibility of the gospel to all, regardless of social class or financial standing. Casual dress is a simple and nonverbal way of communicating equality before the Word of God and its accessibility to all who come to listen.

Still, preachers handle the Word of God in the house of God. Sloppiness in dress will be interpreted as disrespectful, and for good reason. Even in the business world, *casual* is not a synonym for *careless*. In fact, "business casual" has become a category of dress complete with its own set of rules, many of which could be helpful to preachers.

Of course, such rules defy codification. Nothing is more culturally conditioned than clothing. What is appropriate in Southern California (i.e., Rick Warren's famous Hawaiian shirts) might not fit the bill in Atlantic Canada or in central London. Generally, descriptions of "appropriateness" in dress will give rise to fits of laughter when examined a few short years later. Styles change. The key is to know the culture and expectations of the church or setting and to dress accordingly, not so far above the people as to create distance but alongside the people to create an atmosphere of presence.

4. Use Material Aids Intentionally

Attention must be given to the *material aids* an affective preacher uses, taking care to calculate and calibrate the effect of the use of pulpits, projectors, and other such aids to the sermon.

Pulpits have not always been a part of Christian experience. Jesus certainly did not use one. Over time, the central position of a fixed podium in the church came to symbolize a theological prominence for the preaching of the Word of God, as though the presence and position of the furniture represents the authority of Scripture in a visible and tangible way. Some liturgical churches offer a "lectern" for readings and announcements so that the pulpit can be kept solely for the high purpose of preaching. It is therefore not without pause that the preacher abandons "the sacred desk."

One of the lessons of the Reformation, however, was that the Bible belonged to the people, and the preaching of the Word was not bound to officially sanctioned and authority-laden locales. Reformation preaching happened in fields, in houses, and in streets without any pulpit whatsoever. While the pulpit may well serve as a symbol of authority, it is worth remembering that the pulpit, and the ecclesiastical authority it may represent, must not place boundaries around the preaching of the Word.[33]

The act of leaving the pulpit, however, is also symbolic. The preacher who walks out from behind the pulpit offers a nonverbal affirmation of interest in and presence with the people. By coming out from behind the pulpit, the preacher is saying, "I like you. I want to be close to you as we talk about these things. You can trust me."

This movement, however, is not without risk. Fred Craddock said, "The pulpit reminds me that I am one of a long line of people whom the church has called to preach and teach. It's a humbling thing to approach the pulpit. With no pulpit, I come on stage, and I am the center."[34] Craddock's point is well taken. The sermon is not about the preacher. Still, there is something to be said for the extemporaneous immediacy of pulpitless preaching. A sermon can be just as faithfully researched and carefully constructed without requiring a literate pulpit style that might be less effective in this television-dominated age. It's hard to imagine Jay Leno doing his nightly monologue from behind a pulpit.

PowerPoint and LCD *projectors* have brought technology to preaching in a way not seen since the introduction of the microphone. A microphone is designed to bring the speaker closer to the listener by making his or her voice easier to hear. At the same time, it gets between the speaker and the listener with its booming artificiality. Projection technology has a similar way of creating both distance and presence at the same time. Microphones and projectors mediate the preacher's presence. Ironically, the technology separates the preacher from the people despite its being intended to make the preacher and the message more accessible. Preachers who want to emphasize a sense of presence will have to be careful about the use of such equipment.

Resource Recommendation | PHOTO RESOURCES

To find excellent photos for use in sermon PowerPoint presentations, consider subscribing to worshipphotos.com or to photos.com. Several other websites offer inexpensive, royalty-free images (sxc.hu; dreamstime.com). An even cheaper option is to make use of Google's powerful image search engine.

Adobe Photo Elements is a relatively inexpensive software program for manipulating images and overlaying photos with text.

Affective preachers use projection technology not so much to clarify outlines as to display images and visual metaphors. Such images can be purchased via the Internet or can be produced in-house. Some preachers will use their own digital photos in order to get the image right. The best slides are often created using image-production software that allows the designer to creatively merge words with images in ways that communicate an overall concept.

Projectors can also be used to project video clips or movies. The use of video allows the preacher to connect with listeners on their own terms and in the language of their culture. You might want to consider using gifted people from your congregation to do customized pieces for your sermons. Inexpensive digital video cameras and editing software allow churches to produce their own "on the street" interviews, dramatizations, and music-video style enhancements. Such approaches allow the preacher to involve others in the process of putting truth into the context of life.

At the same time, however, using video has its pitfalls. Video can easily give listeners permission to occupy their accustomed seat as spectators, something preachers must be careful to avoid. Video can eat up precious time and interrupt your carefully designed sermon flow. A video clip is a kind of supercharged sermon illustration, subject to all of the strengths and weaknesses of such illustrations and then some. It creates a world for the listener to inhabit. Many times that world is more compelling than the world of the sermon itself. Listeners can get lost in the world created by the video and lose touch with the actual intent of the sermon. Finally, preachers need to be particularly careful with clips taken from movies, which can be seen as giving license to listeners to view things that might be substantially less than the pure and lovely things of good report that Paul describes in Philippians 4:8.

Insight and Ideas | MOTION PICTURE "UMBRELLA LICENSES"

Remember that most movies carry copyright restrictions. Movies rented at the video store, for instance, cannot be shown at church-related functions without permission. Blanket copyright permission for most motion-picture companies is available, but the rules vary from country to country. Using imagery from movies can be helpful, but we must do it with integrity. For more information, go to www.mplc.com.

Still and video projections are only two of the more contemporary uses of visual enhancement in preaching. While perhaps not as trendy, a good old-fashioned *object lesson* still has power. Often seen as a staple of the "children's sermon," wise preachers will not be afraid to employ the power of a visual object to draw people closer and involve them more intimately in the sermon. Jeremiah once hid a linen belt under a rock to help his audience visualize the ruin of Judah and the spiritual decay of Jerusalem (Jeremiah 13). Preachers today ought to continue this long-established pattern.

Material aids are valuable, but they should be used with the confidence that the greatest visual effect in preaching is the image of the preacher standing and delivering the Word of God. Preachers are going to have difficulty competing with Hollywood or with the multimedia offerings found on cable. But no one exceeds the preacher in terms of standing up and speaking. It might be worth asking whether the preacher actually needs technological reinforcement. The strength of preaching is that a human being, having heard from God, helps others hear from God as well. The energy and passion of such a preacher might be visual stimulation enough.

Discussion Question 16 | IS POWERPOINT WORTH IT?

Is using PowerPoint worth the effort? Creating great slides requires skill in graphic presentation and computer technology, not to mention the homiletical and theological prowess necessary to develop a sermon in the first place. While the preacher could be expected to bring the latter, the former skills might be in short supply. On top of that, producing the piece takes a lot of time (which could be spent studying the text), and the whole production could be crippled by a power outage, a burnt bulb, or a computer glitch. Is there anything we can do to overcome these difficulties (like teaming up)? Or is using PowerPoint unnecessary, or worse?

Choosing to Preach Affectively

When we think of affective preachers, Charles Haddon Spurgeon does not spring immediately to mind. The "Prince of Preachers" did not have access to the technologies of our day, yet he was a master of using words to create an affective experience for his listeners.

The impact of Spurgeon's ministry is well known. For more than forty years, his preaching attracted capacity crowds to England's largest auditoriums. His printed sermons, numbered in the dozens of volumes, have nourished readers and preachers in every part of the world. Spurgeon would credit his impact to God's sovereignty and dependence on God's Word, but the student of preaching will want to study how Spurgeon's sermons are constructed. One underappreciated aspect of Spurgeon's preaching is his use of the five senses to create an experience for his listeners.

This appeal to the senses was a deliberate choice. In a detailed study titled "Sense Appeal in the Sermons of Charles Haddon Spurgeon," Jay Adams catalogues the great preacher's use of sensory language. According to Adams, instances of sight appeal rated far above that of the other senses. Appeal to hearing was unusually frequent. The sense of touch was next in usage, followed by smell and taste almost equally.[35]

Spurgeon's purpose was to get the listener involved in an experience. Speaking of the death of Christ, he encouraged listeners to paint the picture for themselves: "Let your thoughts draw the outline, your love fill in the detail; I shall not complain if imagination heightens the coloring."[36] Spurgeon himself was not afraid of coloring in those details. "Do you mark him in your imagination nailed to yonder cross! Do you see his hands bleeding, and his feet gushing gore? Behold him."[37]

Practical Exercise 10 | SENSE APPEAL

Examine your notes from a recent sermon for evidence of sense appeal. How often did you appeal to the listener's sense of sight, smell, hearing, taste, and touch? See if you can find at least five ways to add further appeals to the senses in this sermon.

Appealing to the listener's sense of hearing, Spurgeon said, "Can Christ's name be forgotten? No ... the winds whisper it; the tempests howl it; the seas chant it; ... the beasts low it; the thunders proclaim it; earth shouts it; heaven echoes it."[38]

For the sense of touch, he said, "Out with your finger! Dear soul, out with your finger! Do not go away till you have touched the Lord by a believing prayer of hope."[39] One can imagine thousands of listeners reaching out, their index fingers pointed. Such was the effect of Spurgeon's imaginative powers.[40]

None of this was accidental. Spurgeon understood that preachers have it in their power to help the listener experience the presence of God through the way they use their words. "God gives his ministers a brush," he said, "and shows them how to use it in painting life-like portraits, and thus the sinner hears the special call."[41]

Affection is not a way of manipulating people into a shallow faith. Faith must always rest on the person and promises of Christ. This does not mean, however, that the preacher must avoid affective means in order to keep the sermon theologically pure.

Affective preaching has a rich and venerable history. While contemporary technologies give today's preacher an advantage, excellent preachers have always found ways to motivate the heart. Choosing to preach affectively is not a way of propping up weak material or shoddy preparation, like the preacher who wrote in the margin of his notes, "Weak point, shout louder!" It is a matter of taking more responsibility, owning more than just the ideas. Affective preachers choose to shape the images that will compel listeners to reckon with the living Christ.

PART 2

structures

A good map makes a difference. I learned that on vacation as I drove my family across the North American continent and back. We spent two very miserable hours in a storm late one night in Buffalo, New York, trying to find our way across the Canadian border. It would have been a lot easier if our map had been up to date. An old map might look similar to the territory. Some place names might be the same, and a few roads might look familiar. But an old map can still get a person very, very lost.

Resource Recommendation | CATEGORIES OF PREACHING

The categories of preaching have changed dramatically over time. Note the difference between Broadus's listing more than one hundred years ago and Dave Stone's more recent listing.

John A. Broadus (*On the Preparation and Delivery of Sermons*, 1870):

the topical preacher

the expository preacher

the textual preacher

the textual-topical preacher

Dave Stone (*Refining Your Style*, Group Books, 2005):

the creative storyteller

the scholarly analytic

the cultural prophet

the unorthodox artist

the direct spokesperson

the revolutionary leader

the practical applicator

the convincing apologist

the passionate teacher

the engaging humorist

the persuasive motivator

the inspiring orator

It is time we had some new maps for preaching. The old maps were suitable in their day. The places that they mark still sound a bit familiar, but a preacher could get lost if she tried to follow one of the old maps. Maybe the most well-worn map of the preaching landscape was written by that pioneer homiletic cartographer, John Albert Broadus. Broadus's map described the textual sermon, the topical sermon, the textual-topical sermon, and the expository sermon. While these categories may have served the preacher of the late nineteenth century, they are not sufficient to describe all of the territory explored by preachers today.

We need a new map of the preaching landscape that describes more than what we know as the traditional listener. A good map will give us insight not only into the quality of our preaching but into the manner of our listening as well. It will assist the contemporary preacher by showing the possibilities of a biblical communication across cultures.

Our new map of the homiletic landscape derives from the four choices we have made. The four options become the four poles on our homiletic map. The first thing we notice is that the poles combine to define territories where listeners choose to live and where sermons take their shape. The resulting terrain features a variety of sermon forms as the poles combine to create a series of unique structures for biblical preaching.

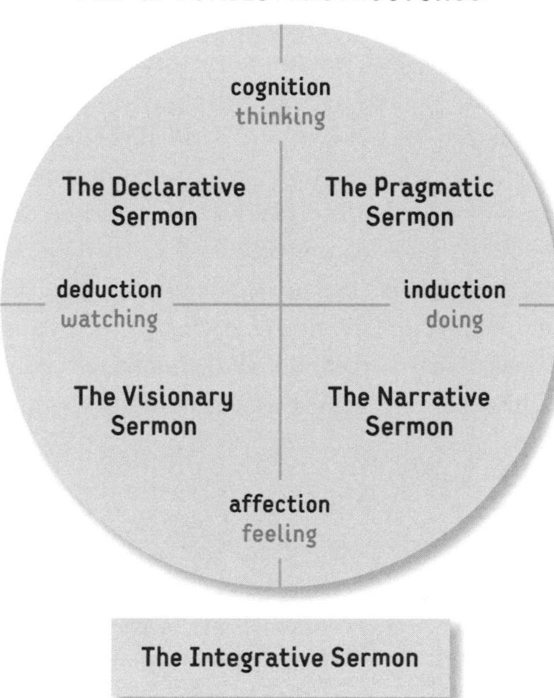

Where deduction meets cognition, we find the home of the *declarative sermon*, favored by classic biblical preachers who value traditional approaches to biblical exegesis. Preachers and listeners living here tend to be watcher-thinkers (Kolb's "assimilators"). These are the "cogdedians," people who won't want to "waste time" telling too many fluffy stories.

The junction of cognition and induction is where you will hear a *pragmatic sermon*. "Cogindian" sermons seek to solve problems for listeners, using biblical truth. People in this territory tend to be doer-thinkers (Kolb's "convergers"), the kind of people who look for biblical solutions to practical problems.

Crossing induction with affection, we find the *narrative sermon*, custom-made for all the doer-feelers (Kolb's "accomodators") who live in this territory. These "indaffians" like nothing more than a good story to guide them into truth.

If you want to hear a *visionary sermon*, you might want to move to the deductive-affective territory. "Affdedians" are watcher-feelers (Kolb's "divergers") and are motivated by a powerful vision of the future.

Finally, we find stubborn "free-traders" who refuse to be pinned down and would rather roam the globe. These homiletic wanderers offer the *integrative sermon* in the attempt to speak meaningfully to all four approaches to preaching and learning, perhaps even in the same sermon.

People tend to inhabit the territories where they are the most comfortable. Listeners who appreciate stories tend to live in inductive-affective territories. Preachers who want to speak powerfully to them might want to read the map carefully. Sometimes people live in particular territories for theological reasons. For instance, some live in the deductive hemisphere because they believe that submission, rather than solution-seeking, ought to be primary. Others have no strong reason for living in a particular territory. They just have always lived there, and they have no intention of leaving. A preacher who offers a lot of analysis to people living in the inductive hemisphere is going to come off like a foreigner. It will be as if he is speaking a different language.

Insight and Ideas | WHO SHOULD CHANGE, THE PREACHER OR THE CONGREGATION?

It is common for a preacher to want to change the listening style of the congregation. There are many good reasons for attempting this. Sometimes the community around a church changes, and if the discourse of the church doesn't change, the church will limit its ability to speak to its community. Any such attempts, however, should be undertaken slowly and wisely. Subtle changes can be introduced over time rather than radically altering the approach all at once. Talking about the need for change is always a good idea. Remember, though, it is always easier for the preacher to change to match the congregation's style than for the whole congregation to change to match the preacher's style.

Many examples of preachers and many homiletic models can be found for each of the territories. In most cases, these models are not specific to one territory but range across the lines into other lands. The borders tend to be porous, though some people will always argue for the need to police them diligently. It is probably fair to say that these models are all "mostly models." That is to say they are found mostly in one territory or another but can find a home beyond their natural borders as well.

It is not lost on me, by the way, that the model matches up fairly well with planet Earth. On the whole, the Southern Hemisphere, for instance, does tend to be more affective and emotive than the Northern. The Western Hemisphere does tend to be a little more deductive in its ways of public discourse than the Eastern. This suggests that our preaching styles will increasingly be affected by the globalization we are seeing in the world. I visited a church of two hundred people in London, for instance, that had thirty-five different nationalities represented. There has to be a lot of different learning styles represented at that church. Such situations will not long be limited to the larger urban centers.

Insight and Ideas | PERSONALITY TESTING

David Kolb's experiential learning paradigm has been shown to parallel aspects of the Myers-Briggs Type Indicator. The MBTI might be a helpful tool for analyzing your personal approach to preaching. For more information, see David Kolb, *Experiential Learning* (Prentice Hall, 1984), 78.

MAP OF HOMILETIC STRUCTURES

cognition
thinking

The Declarative Sermon **John MacArthur Jr.**	The Pragmatic Sermon **Rick Warren**
deduction watching	induction doing
The Visionary Sermon **Rob Bell**	The Narrative Sermon **Eugene Lowry**

affection
feeling

The Integrative Sermon
Kent Anderson

The structural examples given in the following chapters are not the only ways that people preach today. They are not even the only ways that people practice "pragmatic preaching" or "narrative preaching," and so on. They are, however, my attempt to describe what might be viewed as "best practice" in biblical preaching according to the various styles. In addition to each of the structures, we'll take a look at a sample sermon from a contemporary preacher who might be said to exemplify that approach: Rick Warren (pragmatic sermon), Eugene Lowry (narrative sermon), Rob Bell (visionary sermon), John MacArthur Jr. (declarative sermon), and Kent Anderson (integrative sermon).

I am also aware that some who preach in one territory might not have a lot of patience for those who preach in other territories. Some preachers believe their model is the only viable approach to faithful preaching. I respect them for their views. I know that their approach is founded in honest conviction. I have, however, attempted to make the case that biblical preaching can take a variety of forms. It is my hope that these structures will encourage us all to fulfill our task with excellence wherever God has placed us and to whomever God has called us.

Chapter 5 | MAKE AN ARGUMENT

the declarative sermon

example: John MacArthur Jr.

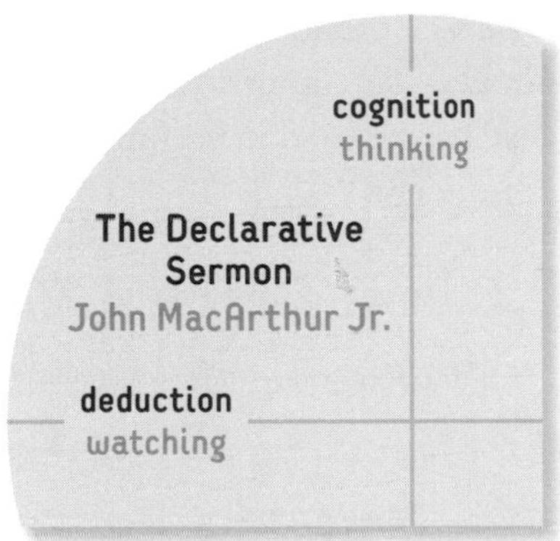

Among the primary forms of the sermon, the most common is the *declarative* sermon. Declarative preachers present arguments for the gospel. Like a lawyer, the preacher arranges the facts and puts the case before the people in as convincing a manner as possible. The sermon is deductive in orientation, which is to say that the ideas of the sermon are given more than they are discovered. It is cognitive in form, which means its appeal is logical more than it is emotional. Thus, this form of preaching appeals to those who learn through watching and thinking.

This is the kind of preaching I grew up listening to. My childhood pastor, A. J. L. Haynes, served more than forty-one years as the pastor and sole preacher at my home church. I remember him as a man of unquestioned authority. His sermons, as I recall, were detailed and determined. If the adults in the church felt free to challenge his authority, I never heard about it or saw any evidence of the dissent. Rather, I think the people found it comforting and encouraging to sit under his teaching. This was a man who could make an effective argument and who could declare the Word of God with conviction.

Declarative preaching, the dominant sermon structure of the twentieth century, should not be dismissed as suited for a time past. The power of a confident word carefully argued and firmly founded on the Scriptures will never pass its prime.

How to Make an Argument

Understanding the elements of an effective argument is important if you want to learn how to preach the cognitive-deductive sermon. How does a lawyer present an argument that will convince a judge and jury? How, then, do preachers offer the ideas of Scripture in a way that will convince those gathered to listen?

An argument is a set of statements used to convince someone of the truth or importance of a particular idea or conclusion. Arguments are built on *premises*, or statements used to support the idea being argued for. Premises are not examples or illustrations but statements of fact. The number of premises that can be used is unlimited; however, premises ought to be relevant and self-evident.

Insight and Ideas | MAKING ARGUMENTS

Poor Argument: Even if the premises are true, the conclusion is false.

Strong Argument: If the premises are true, the conclusion is very likely to be true.

Sound Argument: If the premises are true, the conclusion must be true.

A *poor* argument is one in which, even if its premises are true, the conclusion is false. This would be the case when the premises given are immaterial to the conclusion being argued for. Your conclusion ought to flow naturally from the premises. For instance, the statement "Many Christians believe abortion is morally abhorrent" is true. This, however, does not prove the argument that abortion is wrong, because moral truth is not established on the basis of the opinion of "many Christians." The premise might be emotionally compelling, but it does not provide logical warrant for the conclusion.

A *strong* argument is one in which, if the premises are true, the conclusion is very likely to be true. For example, the existence of God could be argued for on the premise that the beauty and design evident in the world could not be the result of random chance. This argument is compelling, particularly to those predisposed to the conclusion, but it is not ironclad. Though rare or unlikely, random events can produce beautiful or ordered results.

A *sound* argument is one in which, if its premises are true, its conclusion must be true. The argument is valid in that the conclusion is rationally deducible from the premises or the logical consequence of them. Take, for instance, the argument that Jesus' death proves God's love for us. If we accept that Jesus is God's Son (first premise), and if we agree that sacrifice is a meaningful way of displaying love (second premise), then the conclusion must be sound. Of course, the challenge is to make sure you are working with agreed-upon premises.

Take C. S. Lewis's famous argument that good men don't claim to be God unless they are God.[1] The premises are unarguable:

- People who claim to be God when they are not God are either crazy or deceitful.
- Crazy or deceitful people are not good men.

The conclusion is sound because the premises are sound. Now apply the same argument to Jesus' claim:

- Jesus claimed to be God.
- Jesus was not crazy.
- Jesus was not deceitful.

These premises provide a strong, though not sound, argument for the divinity of Jesus. It is unlikely that Jesus was either a lunatic or a liar, but this statement cannot be established beyond a shadow of a doubt. What can be said is that, as Lewis said, either Jesus was who he said he was (the Son of God) or he was not a good and moral teacher. That much is certain.

Insight and Ideas | IS ANYBODY PRAYING FOR YOUR PREACHING?

Who is praying for you as you preach? Have you recruited anyone to support you through the ministry of prayer? Do you keep them informed of your sermon themes and the needs of your listeners so that they can pray more meaningfully?

Spurgeon was once asked the secret of his preaching power. In answer, he took the inquirer down to the "engine room" of the church, where more than five hundred people were praying for the sermon half an hour before the service began.

Consider, further, the argument offered in the phrase "Jesus loves me, this I know, for the Bible tells me so." It is an encouraging expression of childlike faith, but as an argument, it has weaknesses. The song's conclusion is based on two premises: (1) the Bible tells me that Jesus loves me, and (2) everything the Bible tells me is true. The first is unquestionably true. The second is more problematic, at least from a purely rational perspective. Whenever a premise (or in this case, a book) offers itself as its own proof, we have a circular argument, which is never, by itself, conclusive. One might feel subjectively certain about such things, but such a feeling is a very different thing from knowledge.[2]

But could the argument still be sound? Yes, it could be, because there is no way to *dis*prove the second premise. There can be sound arguments that are not known to be sound, which is where faith comes into play.

Faith is the stuff of preaching. Biblical preachers constantly appeal to faith as an appropriate and meaningful response to the gospel. Still, declarative preachers will want to watch their arguments. It is legitimate to appeal to the listener's faith. It is illegitimate to argue for a conclusion on the basis of premises that are irrelevant or that can be shown to be false, whether the fault is deliberate or unforeseen.

The "Jesus loves me" example is particularly important for preachers. Much of what the preacher argues is based on the premise of biblical authority. This puts the sermon on an uncertain footing, at least from a logical perspective. To bolster cases that seem overly dependent on faith convictions, many preachers will be tempted to use unsound premises to support conclusions that seem weak in purely rational terms.

It may be, for example, that there is no sound argument for the resurrection. The premises used to support Jesus' miraculous return to life (the absence of a body, the witness of the disciples, the claims of Scripture, among others) might support a strong argument, but ultimately the proposition depends on faith. That is fine. Arguing for faith is appropriate. What we do not want to do is to overstate our case ("The evidence demands affirmation of the resurrection!") or to try to hoodwink our listeners through spurious arguments ("Resurrections are common") that ultimately do more to undermine faith than support it.

The answer is to ensure that the sermon is built either on premises that are unassailable or on propositions that are demonstrated in Scripture. The authority for the argument is, then, either sound in logic or founded on the Bible, or both. Faith in the authority of Scripture will not be convincing to every listener, but the preacher proceeds in the confidence that God will stand behind his Word. The cognitive appeal of the argument finds strength in its fidelity to the presentation of the Bible.

Lawyers, in their role as professional arguers, serve as a model for the cognitive-deductive sermon. In fact, classic expository preachers are familiar with the language and practice of lawyers. Sermons are fashioned into "briefs." Outlines use legal numbering systems (i.e., 1.1, 1.2, 2.1, etc.). Points are shaped into apologetic "evidences" for faith. Sermons often sound like the closing argument at the end of a *Law and Order* episode (only longer). This is not inappropriate given the preacher's desire to "make the case" for the gospel.

The *cognitive* nature of the legal argument is deliberate. Intuitive or emotional arguments are not accepted as probative. Judges charge juries to be dispassionate in their deliberation. Cases are made based on the facts and not on the concern one might feel for the victims or for the defendant. Of course, this dispassion is probably more theoretical than actual. The murder trial of O. J. Simpson is only one of many famous cases in which a conviction was thwarted more by emotion than by fact. Good lawyers know the rhetorical power of an intuitive appeal. Still, the lawyer's primary tool is the logical argument. An argument is understood to be persuasive to the degree that it is rational and relevant.

Practical Exercise 11 | PAUL'S POINTS

Study Romans 8 and attempt to order the arguments that Paul makes. What are the primary arguments? What are the supportive statements? Put them in logical order.

Classify Paul's argument. Are his conclusions poor, strong, or sound?

Legal argument is also *deductive*. The lawyer comes with a case to prove. Unlike the detective who needs to build a case from elements not yet known, the lawyer marshals all the known facts of the case and presents them with conviction. The lawyer begins with the conclusion of the matter—a crime has been committed, the defendant is guilty—then gives all of the reasons (premises) that warrant the judgment.

The cognitive-deductive preacher, similarly, comes to the congregation (the jury) with a case to make. The message is given in the Word of God. The preacher unpacks the Word, arguing for conviction based on the truth as God has made it known.

The lawyer as logician is an attractive model for preachers who want to make their arguments from Scripture. The clarity and precision of logic is appealing to those searching for means powerful enough to persuade. It must be remembered, however, that the lawyer's task is more difficult than it seems. Construction of a clear and logical argument is complicated by the fact that there is another lawyer on the other side of the aisle. The legal argument is dialogical in that it must contend with counterarguments designed specifically to discredit and destroy the opposition's case.

Legal arguments are not static but are a process of combative discussion between parties opposed to one another's interests. During this process, conclusions are drawn, reasons are offered, counterarguments are raised, and new premises are introduced. The system is not pure and inert but contentious. Effective lawyers expect the unexpected. Anticipating objections, they strive to prepare arguments that can be defended against new information and contrary arguments.

Discussion Question 17 | THE LIMITS OF ARGUMENT

Some would say that the appeal of argument is limited in these postmodern times. People today seem content with contradiction. They are adept at slipping out of the logical traps that apologetic preachers like to set for them. Given this phenomenon, is there a limit to the usefulness of argument in preaching today? What are the pros and cons of using argument?

Preachers would be prudent to take a similar approach. Preaching is a process involving real people in dialogue. Many of these people approach the sermon from a contrary perspective. It may, in fact, be wise for preachers to assume this is the case. The Word of God is countercultural and sometimes counterintuitive, because the kingdom of God is not of this world. Preachers often take on impossible cases, arguing that people should embrace such contrary concepts as marital fidelity, financial stewardship, and personal selflessness. Convincing people to give their lives to Christ will not be easy. If a lawyer for the people were arguing against the preacher's points, it might actually be helpful. It might sharpen the preaching.

With or without the lawyer on the other side of the pulpit, preachers ought to be aware that the sermon is dialogical, which is to say that people will argue back, though perhaps not orally. The real deliberation takes place in the listeners' hearts. The sharpest preachers will work to anticipate how the jury of their listeners will hear the arguments being made.

Another advantage lawyers enjoy is that the rules of process are understood by all members of the court. A judge presides over the lawyers' arguments, not necessarily to decide on the case—that is the task of the jury—but to ensure that arguments are fair and in accordance with the standards of the court. The preacher's listeners have no such protection. Of course, the Judge of all does preside over proceedings in and out of the sanctuary. Preachers tempted to manipulate listeners through slick and deceptive arguments ought to consider their accountability. Preachers can be disbarred from their task, if not through human authority, then ultimately and finally by God himself.

Unfortunately, the preacher-lawyer comparison is not necessarily flattering to the preacher. What do you call twenty lawyers at the bottom of the ocean? A good start. Judging by our jokes, lawyers are not the most esteemed members of the professional class. Come to think of it, neither are preachers.

The problem with lawyers (and the preachers who emulate them) is ironic. Lawyers, through persistent use of logic, are able to support convictions that violate common sense. This irony is not lost on lawyers who are not above using it to their advantage. Jonathan Swift described lawyers as "a society of men among us, bred up from their youth in the art of proving by words multiplied for that purpose that white is black and black is white."[3]

The problem stems from the "words multiplied." Preachers, like lawyers, can gain the reputation of being "fast talkers," stringing together impressive-sounding arguments that are entirely unconvincing to those unfamiliar with the jargon. The very words designed to communicate precision can obscure the truth from people who haven't learned the language.

To be fair, these problems are seldom intentional. Preachers (and lawyers) want to build convincing cases. This leads them to marshal as much evidence as possible in support of their claims. Piling up premises, however, can produce more confusion than clarity. Sometimes less is more. Listeners can have a hard time just keeping on the trail of the argument, given all of the subsidiary points the preacher intends to support the argument but that often end up only leading listeners astray.

The answer for declarative preachers is not to give up on the argument but rather to offer good arguments for the gospel, arguments that will encourage many to faith in Jesus.

Preaching the Declarative Sermon

The *declarative sermon* is born of the idea that the listener attends to the sermon as it is given. This kind of sermon is accepted as a word from God which all must obey. It appeals to listeners who appreciate a reasoned argument and who respect objective truth. Preaching a declarative sermon is about instructing listeners in the way they must go. The primary concern is that the sermon be clear, because the message must be understood. If the message is seen as logical and truthful, it will be inherently persuasive. Creative approaches to presentation are not strictly necessary. The Holy Spirit will work powerfully to apply the truth as it is offered.

Insight and Ideas | THE DECLARATIVE OUTLINE

Introduction

Body

- *Point 1*
  - explanation
  - illustration
  - application
- *Point 2*
  - explanation
  - illustration
  - application
- *Further Points*

Conclusion

This confidence is reassuring in a time when so many voices question our ability to know truth. But while an epistemological skepticism seems sensible in these postmodern times, the philosophy is not always realized in everyday practice. When our car needs repair, we want a mechanic who will fix it correctly, according to the rules. We do not want our technicians to operate intuitively, following their muse, when determining how to set up our carburetor. Some people are willing to trust their health to an alternative-medicine practitioner, but most of us want to know that our cardiologist has done her homework when she inserts the scalpel. No less is expected of the declarative preacher when it comes to surgery of the soul. In a world where opinions are a dollar a dozen, it is nice to know that the preacher has the facts straight. The truth is that we rely on the cognitive-deductive approach in just about every other area of life. Why not in preaching too?

The declarative sermon uses an *outline*. Such a sermon has a simple structure: an *introduction*, a sermon *body* comprising a series of multiple sermon *points*, followed by a *conclusion*. Elements of the sermon are linked by means of *transitions*. The points are the premises of the sermon and should combine to produce a sound argument. While each functional element can stand alone, the preacher seeks to follow a meaningful progression from point to point to reflect the Scripture appropriately and thus make a convincing case.

Listening to the declarative sermon can be refreshing when there is a willingness to submit. A simple message clearly put is a wonderful tonic, in the same way that a clear and simple set of instructions is welcome when you are trying to install a new piece of software on your computer. So, in the spirit of clear instruction, let me suggest the steps that lead to an effective declarative sermon. Feel free to build on these steps to suit the needs of your people and your personal preferences.

1. Pray

Your purpose is to help people hear from God. You are coming submissively to the text to hear his voice. You need to pray.

The whole sermon-building process ought to be washed in prayer, but here at the beginning of the process, the preacher will want to make a special effort to connect with God by his Spirit in prayer. A long walk with God might be in order, or perhaps a time of silence in a closet or other solitary place. If we are going to know what God would have us say, we are going to have to pray.

2. Choose Your Text

Affirming that we should preach the Bible raises a practical problem. How do we determine which text we will preach? The problem bothers preachers not so much because of a difficulty finding an appropriate text as because of the embarrassment of riches the Bible provides.

Insight and Ideas | "FORECASTING" THE MESSAGE

Preachers who want to be clear and unambiguous will make their point evident right from the start of their sermon. Such preachers "forecast" their messages, indicating to the listener exactly what they want to convince him of before they get into their arguments. This classic deductive strategy keeps things clear and helps keep the listener focused on the task at hand.

C. H. Spurgeon confessed to feeling frustrated when attempting to determine the specific text that the Holy Spirit would have him preach. "Do what I would, no response came from the sacred oracle, no light flashed from the Urim and Thummim; I prayed, I meditated, I turned from one verse to another, but the mind would not take hold."[4] My somewhat presumptuous response to Spurgeon might be to relax. Just preach the Bible. I do not wish to speak lightly of the work of the Holy Spirit in guiding us to just the right text, but the truth is, if the text is in the Bible, it warrants preaching.

Many preachers have found it valuable to preach consecutively through books of the Bible. Others prefer to identify texts that seem to be of particular help to their congregation in its present time and situation. Either approach is fine, as long as the texts are found in the Bible. Sequential preaching through biblical texts can be a meaningful way of preaching the whole counsel of God. It is hard to duck the difficult texts when you come across them in the normal flow of preaching through a book.

In my first year of senior pastoral ministry, I chose to preach through the gospel of Mark. I thought it would be good to begin with the life and ministry of Jesus Christ. Eventually I came to chapter 10, which gave me a little jolt when I realized what I would have to preach. I cannot imagine that I would have chosen to preach on divorce in my first year of ministry in that church, but there it was in the text. It could not be avoided, though I very much might have wanted to do so. I preached the passage, and the sermon went well. People needed to hear what God had to say on the subject, but because it was part of an overall strategy, no one could accuse me of specifically picking on them. It was in the text, so I preached it, and that was all there was to that. In the end, I was pleased that the text led me to this subject. The issue needed to be addressed, but I probably would not have had the courage to go there had the text not forced my hand.

Insight and Ideas | STRATEGIC PLANNING FOR PREACHING

Strategic planning is an important aspect of choosing one's text. It has become important for preachers to choose their themes well in advance to allow for effective marketing (publishing brochures and such) and to provide worship teams and production assistants with the opportunity to prepare. Biblical preachers, however, sometimes have difficulty assigning titles to sermons before the texts have been studied. A preacher who works through books of the Bible could, however, announce the texts that will be studied and describe a general theme that arises from those texts. Getting too specific too soon can cause the preacher to inadvertently skew interpretation before it even starts.

In choosing the specific passage for the sermon, the preacher must be careful to choose a complete unit of thought in the text. Sermons built from textual fragments will offer fragmentary truths. A complete unit of thought could be a single sentence (as with one of the Proverbs), or it could run several chapters (as with some Old Testament narrative texts—the Joseph narrative at the end of Genesis, for instance). The key is to start at the beginning and end at the end, no matter how long or short the resulting text might be. In the case of a longer text, you don't need to feel obligated to address every theme the text suggests. Stay focused on the big idea and let the text lead you to say only those things that must be said. That should be enough.

3. Discover the Big Idea

Sometimes called the theme, the "big idea" is the central proposition of the sermon. It is the sermon in a nutshell—the thing that God wants to say through this text, at this time, to these people. The big idea is discovered through a detailed process of deductive exegesis intended to help you understand not only what the text meant to its original audience but what it means today to those who will listen to what you say when you stand before them to speak.

This theme statement must be derived directly from the text of Scripture. There ought to be direct biblical authority for this statement. Careful exegesis is imperative so that you can say in good conscience that what the statement preaches is what the text teaches. Having understood what the text said to its original audience, the preacher looks to frame the theme statement in terms of what God is saying in the present.

 **Practical Exercise 12** | WRITING "BIG IDEA" STATEMENTS

Write a theme statement (a "big idea") for a sermon from John 3:16. Make sure it is a full declarative sentence of no more than ten or twelve words that offers both a subject and a complement.

For example:

"People love justice, but Jesus just loves" (1 Peter 2:22–25)

"Christians win by losing" (Matthew 16:25)

Choose five more passages from throughout the Bible and do the same.

The big idea of the sermon should be stated in a simple declarative sentence of no more than ten or twelve words. Avoid all conjunctions and linking words that would turn the statement into more than one idea. You don't want to preach on God's love *and* grace. Choose one or the other and preach that.

The statement needs to be a complete sentence comprising both a subject (what you are talking about) and a complement (what you are saying about what you are talking about). "The love of God," for instance, is a sentence fragment—a subject without a complement. You need to tell the listener what you are saying about what you are talking about—that the love of God is reliable or that the love of God is eternal. Without a complement, the big idea does not declare anything and cannot be proclaimed. Remember, you are not writing a subhead for a term paper; you are writing something that you will actually have to say in the sermon.

The big-idea statement should flow nicely and have a "ring" to it so that it can be easily stated and restated throughout the sermon. You will want to use this statement often so that it embeds itself in the listener's mind. It is almost impossible to repeat the big idea too often. I've heard as many as twenty repetitions in a single sermon, and it was not too much. The statement needs to be the refrain that lingers in listeners' minds as they leave the meeting. It should be so ingrained in your own thinking that should your husband or wife nudge you in the middle of the night, you could recite it to him or her without further thought.

4. Determine Your Point Structure

I have a friend who collects ancient arrowheads. Each of the many relics in my friend's collection is unique in color, size, and shape, but one feature is common to all: they each have a point.

So should our sermons. Most people are familiar with the frustration of sitting through sermons on perfectly good Sundays only to emerge with a blank look on one's face and a question on the lips: "What was the point of that?" God speaks for a reason. He has a point, and so must our sermons.

The point is a remarkably useful physical element. The point is the part of any tool that allows for focused penetration. Points allow one to focus impact with precision. Without a point, clothes could not be sewn, battles could not be won, and rockets could not fly. Without a point, sermons cannot hit their mark and penetrate the soul. Points are imperative.

Cognitive-deductive preaching requires the preparation of an *outline*, or a logical array of points that unite to declare the sermon's big idea. Of course, some texts lend themselves more naturally to outlining than do others. A sermon from Romans 5:3–5 almost outlines itself: (1) tribulation produces perseverance; (2) perseverance produces character; (3) character produces hope; and so on. Outlining a poetic text from the Psalms or a narrative text from the Gospels can be a lot more challenging, however. The preacher will need to take considerable care when forming deductive outlines from inductive passages.

The key to outlining biblical texts is to let the exegesis of the passage lead the process. Let the text call the tune. If the text has four points, the sermon will have four points. If you have a one-point text (as is likely with a narrative passage), you will have a one-point sermon. Be careful not to import a theological construct on a text that doesn't intend it. Even if what you are saying is sound, you haven't helped people hear from God if you do not honor the intention of the text in Scripture.

The resulting outline could take a variety of forms. In essence, the points of the sermon are the premises of the argument and need to be arranged most logically. Some sermons will pursue a primary point while using multiple supplementary points in support of the big idea. Other sermon structures could be syllogistic. For example:

- If point A is true,
- and point B is true,
- then point C must be true.

Alternatively, the sermon could follow a multipoint parallel construction, offering several propositions that work in concert to advance the sermon theme. For example:

- Point A is true,
- point B is also true,
- and point C is true as well.

? Discussion Question 18 | ALL FOR ALLITERATION?

Alliteration ("The purpose of the cross, the person on the cross, the power of the cross ...") is a favorite technique of declarative preachers, but is it more trouble than it is worth? In the attempt to find another *p*-word, do we risk twisting the sermon into saying something that the text does not intend to say?

There is no "correct" number of sermon points, despite the common inclination to use three of them. Often some points will seem stronger than others. You will need to decide whether all of them are necessary. No one sermon needs to say everything the text says.

Sermon points need to be written in a form that can be spoken. Ideally, they will have a little punch to them so that they stick in the listener's mind. There should be a logical flow of thought from one point to the next so that transition statements do not have to bear too heavy a load. Once completed, a recitation of the sermon points would be almost as if the entire sermon has been given in brief.

5. Explain Your Points

Declarative preaching seeks to convince listeners of truth, but they won't be convinced of anything if they don't understand the points the preacher is making. *Explanation* is an unadorned description of the most important propositions, given to aid the listener in understanding the text. Explaining is communicating. It assumes the listener will need help in appreciating what the text is saying and what it means. Explanation, then, is about *organization* and *restatement*.

Organization helps the listener by distinguishing major issues from minor ones as well as by setting things in proper order. The challenge is to discover the main aspect of the text and make sure it is the main aspect of the sermon. The preacher attempts to order the relevant ideas, sequencing them so that primary propositions are supported by lesser ideas. Irrelevant and unnecessary thoughts are omitted so as not to confuse the listener.

Practical Exercise 13 | SYNTACTICAL MARKERS

The little words in the text (*yet, for, but*) are significant in understanding the relationship and relative weight of ideas. These *syntactical markers* provide clues to the organization and meaning of the passage.

The word *therefore* in Romans 12:1, for example, is a powerful indicator of how the application ideas to follow respond to the theology described in earlier chapters.

The word *unless* in Matthew 18:3 shows that entry into the kingdom of God *depends on* our becoming like little children.

Take five passages consisting of at least five verses and circle all of the syntactical markers.

Prioritizing ideas can be important in determining the intent and application of a text. A careful reading of Mark 4:35–41, for instance, shows that the text exists to point to the divinity of Jesus Christ ("Who is this? Even the wind and the waves obey him!" v. 41) more than to encourage believers to "bear up" under the strain of "the storms of life." This is not to say that life cannot be stormy. It is to say, however, that any encouragement to bear up comes to us as a consequence of a deepened awareness of Jesus' divine nature. "If the wind is subject to him, then I can rest in his care." Arguing that the listener should persevere in times of storm without first establishing the text's primary Christology is about as helpful as telling the listener to just "hang in there." Prioritizing the main idea ("Jesus really is God!") over the less consequential idea ("I should take courage") not only gets the meaning right but deepens the force of application as well.

The sermon structure for this text must therefore be organized around the disciples' awakening to Jesus' divinity. Jesus challenges their fear not because the storm is not fearful but because their fear is a consequence of their lack of faith in his power and willingness to care for them. Confidence, then, is faith in Jesus' power over the elements. We will be persuaded to be confident because our Christology makes it logical.

Explanation also requires *restatement.* Having organized the material, the preacher will further need to put the material in words the listener can understand. It may be that the text is not all that incomprehensible; however, the listener will understand the text more fully when the preacher can find new ways of expressing truth in language the listener can recognize. Restatement includes definition, translation, and description.

Definition is a matter of helping listeners understand the meaning of the words. The preacher restates the terms, using words more familiar to the listeners—in essence, translating the text so it can be more easily described and apprehended.

People speak and hear in different ways depending on their culture and language. The Bible is separated from all of us simply because of the amount of time that has passed. Preachers try to describe ancient settings to contemporary people, many of whom weren't paying attention during their high school lecture on ancient Mesopotamia. Preachers need to be able to translate unfamiliar words, expressions, and customs into equivalents recognizable to the listener. For example, few contemporary listeners know that a *shophar* was a ram's horn used in ancient times to sound a warning or a summons. Most listeners would know what the "eye of a needle" is, but they might be poorly equipped to understand Jesus' exact reference when he suggested that a camel could penetrate it more easily than rich people could enter God's kingdom.

Once the listeners understand the premises, logic can have its effect. The argument begins with the preacher's explanations.

6. Illustrate Your Points

If explanation aids understanding, illustration deepens it. Illustration utilizes concrete images from the listeners' lives to help them understand abstract ideas in analogous living situations. Illustrations "color in" the idea, bringing a new degree of depth and vitality to the discussion. Sports-minded people might think of the explanation as the "play-by-play," while illustration is the "color commentary" of the sermon. (This example itself serves as a kind of illustration.) *Metaphor* and *story* are two primary forms of illustration, both of which function analogically, or by substitution of an image for an idea.

Insight and Ideas | ELEMENTS OF ILLUSTRATION

Metaphor

Aligning the idea with something analogical from the listener's experience and understanding.

Story

Describing the idea in terms of real-life instances, whether real or imagined, so that the listener can appreciate the idea in context.

Metaphor plants a word image in the mind of the listener that is similar to the bare idea. "This is like that," the preacher says. Often the analogue is something that is closer to the life experience of the listener. Metaphor, then, is a heightened means of restatement. Paul's list of qualifications for boasting in Philippians 3:4–6 ("of the people of Israel, of the tribe of Benjamin ...") can be described in terms of his resume, or his CV. When the preacher tells the congregation that the text shows Paul giving his credentials to the Philippian church, just like a potential pastor might send his profile to a church search committee, the preacher has placed the ancient text in the context of the contemporary listener. Metaphor is a means of offering examples that aid in understanding. Paul himself uses a metaphor in the same text when he suggests that his own righteousness is "rubbish" (Phil. 3:8) or something worse.

While *story* can serve many homiletical functions, in the declarative sermon, story serves primarily to illustrate propositions. Story is not the primary element of the sermon. It is, however, useful in supporting an understanding of the primary ideas by describing them in terms of their implications as the truths play out in real-life situations. Declarative preachers need to take care when using stories, as they are extremely powerful. A story can obliterate the point when it is too large or too compelling. Piling stories on top of one another like meat in a sandwich is also counterproductive. After a while, they have a way of canceling each other out.

Insight and Ideas | MNEMONIC PUNCH

Attempt to write point statements and transitions with some mnemonic punch.

"Just do it!"

"I have a dream ..."

Such phrases evoke worlds of meaning in just a few simple words. Create mnemonic hooks that will plant themselves in the listener's mind and keep growing over time.

An illustration is not just a "breathing space" in the sermon, as if it were only there to serve the same purpose as a television commercial, allowing the listener an opportunity to mentally go to the refrigerator. Illustrations must always move the sermon forward, serving a productive purpose in the structure of the message.

7. Apply Your Points

While illustration fleshes out the explanation in life experience, *application* pushes those implications into specific action items for each listener. Illustration says, "Let me describe what this looks like in real life." Application says, "Let me show you how this is lived in *your* life." Applications vary in terms of specificity and degree. Some applications are broad, even abstract, suggestions that give the listener room to consider his or her own means of appropriating and enacting the truth in question. Other applications are more pointed and specific in their requirements of the listener. Applications also differ in terms of their objective. Some applications seek to affect the listener's belief structure; they seek to change the way we think. Other applications intend to change our behavior.

Generally, applications ought to be as concrete as possible. Suggesting that listeners help their neighbor with their gardening might be more helpful than simply counseling the listener to "love their neighbor"—or perhaps not. A neighbor finicky about the health of his petunias might not appreciate interference. The challenge is for the listener to find a specific means of involvement that the neighbor would appreciate as loving. It is difficult to customize applications with such specificity for every listener in a crowd. You will need to be careful to preach the applications that are necessarily implied by their texts ("Love your neighbors") and then suggest more concrete implications ("You might want to consider helping your neighbor with his yard"). The suggestions will trigger additional, more appropriate steps the listener might be able to take. Make sure that application items are measurable, so that the listener can readily identify when he or she has done the thing that God expects.

We have to believe that the Holy Spirit is operating in the application of his Word. God does make clear what he wants out of the sermon. We don't want to get in the way of what he is doing, but we sure want to encourage it.

8. Develop an Introduction

The *introduction* of a declarative sermon exists to focus attention on and stimulate interest in the particular subject at hand. You might be surprised that the introduction doesn't come into play until step 8, but it is for good reason. Delaying the formation of the introduction until after the points are in place keeps us from pointing the train in the wrong direction. It is remarkably easy to send the train down the wrong track with a powerful, but not necessarily relevant, story or image. Get your message straight first; then form an introduction to fit it.

Insight and Ideas | THE FIRST NINETY SECONDS

You have no more than about ninety seconds to capture the listener's attention at the beginning of a sermon, and that might be stretching it a little. Of course, you can always regain the listener's attention, but it helps if you can grab it from the start.

Starting immediately into detailed cognitive discussion is like trying to start your car when it is thirty degrees below zero. Or it is as if the people show up at the airport to get on the plane, but you've already got it up to 25,000 feet. "Come on up," you say. "That's okay," they answer. "We'll see you when you come back down to earth."

An introduction ought to be brief so as not to compete with the substance of the sermon, as found in its points. A quotation, a surprising statistic, or perhaps a brief but interesting story from common life might be all that is necessary to get the sermon moving. While the cognitive deductive sermon tends toward ideas over images, the introduction is a place where imagery can be used to good effect in capturing the listener's attention.

A good introduction does not need to be very long at all. In fact, it probably shouldn't be. Listeners will give you only a few brief moments to establish your claim on their attention. If you are not grabbing them quickly, they will move on in their minds to something that interests them more—the football game they saw last night or the report that is due at work first thing in the morning. You don't have a lot of time to work with. When you think how quickly you and I change channels with the television remote, you will realize just how little time you have. Our listeners have a remote control in their heads, and they are not afraid to use it. One story is probably better than two or three strung together. As was said earlier, multiple stories or ideas can cancel one another out in the listener's mind since pieces of individual stories can get confused with one another. It is far better to build one element well so that it stands out and retains its power.

Many preachers rely on their personality to gain attention. This is not entirely inappropriate. If God has blessed you with personal charisma, feel free to use it. It is part of who you are, and who you are is part of what God uses in the communication of his truth. Just remember, however, that your task in declarative preaching is to connect people with God and his Word, not with you. You probably don't want to be overly noticeable in the preaching process. You don't want people to say, "What a wonderful preacher!" at the end of the sermon. You want them to say, "What a wonderful God!"

9. Create Your Conclusion

Earlier I suggested that the introduction shouldn't be written until after the points are in place. With the *conclusion*, it could be just the opposite. One could argue that you should write your conclusion first. This is because the conclusion is the point in the sermon at which the big idea is most powerfully put to the people. Everything has been moving toward these final moments. The points have been made. The stories have been told. Now is the time to close the deal. Having brought the listeners to a place of deepened understanding, the preacher expects them to do what is required.

As with introductions, sermon conclusions might make stronger use of imagery to create a sense of motivation. This is not the place for a further set of points ("The first thing we learned is ... The second thing we learned is ..."), though a brief restatement might not be out of place. You have already made your points, and the opportunity for teaching is over. Now you are trying to motivate a change. You are calling for a verdict, and a response is now required. The whole thing is moving to a point of reckoning, when the listener will decide what he or she will do.

The preacher can help the listener by suggesting specific, concrete action steps that could be taken in response. You need to be intentional and direct. If you don't speak in real-life terms, the listener might remain content to leave the sermon in an abstract and general form. What do you want the listener to do or to be? While you cannot tell the listener exactly what he or she must do ("Quit your job, go to Africa ..."), you can give a range of possibilities that will stimulate the listener toward applications that make sense in his or her own life situation.

You may want to call for some kind of formal response, as in an altar call or a show of hands. These approaches are often culturally conditioned. I have preached in some churches that would have fired the pastor if he neglected to have an altar call at the end of the sermon. Other churches would find that kind of thing distasteful. But there are many ways to call for response. People could be invited to come forward after the sermon is over to meet with others for prayer. People could be invited to write their responses to the sermon on cards that are handed out. Or the preacher could invite people to agree to "homework"—something they will do upon their return to work or home. The declarative sermon offers an idea, but that idea is intended to change a person's life.

10. Manage Your Transitions

Having constructed the sermon form, the preacher will want to give attention to the flow of the various elements. Preferably, no great gaps will need to be overcome in moving from one point to the next. If such gaps exist, it might indicate a serious flaw in the outline, which the preacher will need to address. Don't be afraid to stop and fix the problem. It might be painful, but eliminating a point that is getting in the way is a better option than standing up to preach a confusing message. On the other hand, the difficulty might be addressed through simply-phrased transition statements that will ease the movement from element to element.

Sometimes transition is eased by the way the points are labeled. If the points are well conceived and properly labeled, the transition need not be overly difficult. In one of my sermons taken from 1 Peter 2:22–25, I used the following point statements:

- Jesus didn't get justice (v. 22).
- Jesus trusted God for justice (v. 23).
- Instead of justice, Jesus loved (v. 24).

In this case, transition flows naturally without much elaboration. This is because each statement builds on the previous statement, linking key words and turns of phrase.

11. Title Your Sermon

While some preachers prefer to title their sermons earlier in the process, perhaps in order to publish them on the church webpage or in the newspaper, I have found it better to leave the sermon title as the last piece to be put in place before I begin the preparation of my notes. I am looking for a relatively creative title that is capable of capturing attention and directing thought toward the truths to be told in the sermon. There doesn't seem much purpose in a bland title except as a simple label for the message. I want something that will grab people's interest and point them in the right direction, which is difficult to find before the sermon has been written.

Insight and Ideas | SERMON TITLES

A sermon title should be interesting without giving too much away. A subtitle can be used when the preacher wants to put a more descriptive statement (perhaps the sermon's theme) alongside a more creative lead title.

For example:

> "Just Love: Love and Justice in the Life of Jesus" (1 Peter 2:22–25)
>
> "Living Comfortably: Christians Are Comfortable with Suffering" (2 Cor. 1:3–7)
>
> "Preaching with Your Feet" (Rom. 10:14–15)

12. Prepare Your Notes

Because of the cognitive nature of the presentation, a declarative sermon usually requires a manuscript (see chapter 4A). There are some exceptional preachers who are able to preach detailed exegesis extemporaneously, but most declarative preachers will find they need to take at least a skeleton outline into the pulpit. Of course, if there are notes, there will likely be a pulpit. Just be sure not to hide behind it. Don't let your notes and the pulpit become hindrances to the communication process they are supposed to serve.

For Example: John MacArthur Jr.

One of the better-known practitioners of declarative preaching is John MacArthur Jr. In his book *Rediscovering Expository Preaching*, cowritten with members of The Master's Seminary faculty, MacArthur offers a stirring apology for Exposition with a capital *E*. The task he sets forward is formidable, requiring the preacher's full store of skill and commitment. "A small amount of skill and ability," he says, "will never enable a preacher to teach doctrine, expound on the deep things of God, convince the stubborn mind, capture the affections and will, or spread light on dark realities so as to eliminate the shadows of confusion, ignorance, objections, prejudice, temptation, and deceit."[5]

MacArthur's emphasis on instruction is seen in his desire to banish ignorance and to convince the mind through a careful understanding of God's Word. He writes, "If the preacher is to detect the errors of his hearers and if he is to free men from their strongholds of ignorance, convince their consciences, stop their mouths, and fulfill his responsibility to proclaim all the counsel of God, he must be skilled in the Word. This is the preacher's only weapon — the most powerful, two-edged sword of the Word, which alone cuts to the depths of the soul and spirit."[6]

Highly suspicious of the influence of psychology in contemporary preaching and its inordinate focus on the listener, MacArthur would prefer that the focus of the sermon be God and God alone. Robert Thomas, MacArthur's colleague, describes the case for a deductive, "begin with the Bible" approach to preaching: "Biblical preaching's authenticity is significantly tarnished by contemporary communicators who are more concerned with personal relevance than with God's revelation. Scripture unmistakably requires a proclamation focused on God's will and mankind's obligation to obey."[7]

Prayer is a major focus in MacArthur's preaching. He tells of often praying till he falls asleep on Saturday night, waking to resume praying again on Sunday morning: "I drift off to sleep praying through my message and awaken Sunday to pray again. As I dress to go to church, I pray with my mind focused on the message and trying not to let anybody or anything distract me."[8]

Sermon Example | "THE MAN OF GOD"
1 Timothy 6:11 – 14

In the appendix of his book *Rediscovering Expository Preaching*, MacArthur reproduces a set of his preaching notes. These notes are extremely helpful in appreciating his approach.

The notes, given in his own hand, are striking — bold underlining, large asterisks, and fat pointed arrows that festoon the pages. One can see MacArthur's passion for the text simply in the way he writes his notes.

The points of the sermon are simple: The man of God can be recognized by

- what he flees from (v. 11a)
- what he follows after (v. 11b)
- what he fights for (v. 12), and
- whom he is faithful to (v. 13 – 14).

MacArthur's preaching tends to be heavy on explanation and light on illustration. When he does illustrate his ideas, it tends to come in the form of a biblical reference or a quotation from church history. MacArthur admits his personal disinterest in storytelling. "I am not into storytelling," he says. "I fail to see the value of multiple, long, drawn-out illustrations. I think you can make a point effectively with a simple analogy. After all, the only value a story has is to pull up the shades so somebody can see a teaching more clearly. If you can do that with a brief analogy, you can keep the flow going better."[9]

Admitting the emotional impact of a story, MacArthur prefers to stick with Scripture. "Stories have emotional impact, but they are lightweight compared with Scripture. People respond to a story with the idea, 'Now I can sit back and hear this nice story.' I call it communication in the light vein.... I want them to stay at my level of intensity.... I tell a story when it is appropriate, but this happens only rarely.[10]

While one could criticize MacArthur for his lack of respect for narrative and other creative forms of communication, watcher-thinkers appreciate his direct approach. MacArthur's example blesses those who value traditional exposition. If the goal is to explain the text and clarify God's expectations, his preaching succeeds wonderfully. Having heard from God in the presence of the Holy Spirit, preachers like MacArthur know the listener will understand his or her accountability and will respond appropriately.

Template for the Declarative Sermon

Preacher: ________________ **Date:** ______________ **Text:** ____________

Title (Subtitle): ____

Good titles are creative and compelling, offering listeners a reason to listen, without giving too much away.

Theme (Big Idea): ____

State the main proposition in a complete declarative statement of fewer than ten words with no "ands."

Introduction: ______________________________

____

Use an interesting story, an arresting quotation, or a useful statistic to gain the listener's attention.

First Point: ______________________________

Explanation: ______________________________

Illustration: ______________________________

Application: ______________________________

Points are the premises that put forward the sermon argument. They ought to follow the logic of the text.

Second Point: ______________________________

Explanation: ______________________________

Illustration: ______________________________

Application: ______________________________

Third Point: ______________________________

Explanation: ______________________________

Illustration: ______________________________

Application: ______________________________

Conclusion: ______________________________

____

The conclusion calls for a specific, measurable response from the listener in obedience to the message.

Example of the Declarative Sermon

Preacher: John MacArthur Jr. **Date:** 2003 **Text:** Luke 8:4–15

Title: The Rocky Soil

Theme (Big Idea): The superficial believer appears genuine but abandons faith when trouble comes.

Introduction: Salvation is such a wonderful gift. It is almost impossible to understand why anyone would not be interested. Why do people reject the gospel?

First Point: Response to the gospel depends on the heart.

Explanation: It's not a matter of the quality of the message or the skill of the messenger; it is a matter of the heart condition of the hearer.

Illustration: It is amazing to me when our society tries to figure out the reasons people do evil things. Why would mass murderers kill people? . . . There's always a clinical way to explain it.

Application: I've met people like this, and I can make a fair presentation of the gospel. But you know when you've run into pavement—the heart beaten hard by sin and unbelief—and whatever of the gospel you put there, Satan snatches it away, so this person may not believe and be saved.

Second Point: The rocky soil receives the gospel with joy.

Explanation: The rocky soil represents those who, when they hear, receive the word with joy. . . . They are receptive. They are interested. . . . And they receive it with joy. But these have no root.

Illustration: Paul told the Colossians about the true believer who continues in the faith, contrasted with those who believe for a while.

Application: People will respond to the gospel for the wrong reasons: because they're at the end of a broken relationship, because they've gone through a divorce and lost their wife and kids, they've lost their job, they've been told they have a terminal disease ... they believe that if they give their life to Jesus, he will fix everything that's wrong in their life. Those are reasons to make a superficial response to the gospel.

Third Point: The rocky soil doesn't understand redemption.

Explanation: Some people want to get in on the Jesus party. They like the music, maybe.... So they crash the kingdom, but they've never been robed in righteousness.

Illustration: In Matthew 22, Jesus describes a king who has a banquet for his son and invites everybody to come. But there's one guy who crashes the party without a robe.

Application: Remember what Jesus said: Take that man who doesn't have the robe, and throw him in outer darkness.

Fourth Point: The rocky soil quits when trials come.

Explanation: If you look at the field, you don't see the rock underneath. The soil looks good. The plant pops up, but under the scorching sun, because there's no root, it can't go down and get the water. It perishes.

Illustration: Wasn't everything supposed to be better? Everything got worse. I had people who used to love me and who now hate me. I had people I used to hang around with and we got along fine, but now because I claim to be a Christian, they resent everything about me and want nothing to do with me. Now I have a whole new group of enemies.

Application: They believed for a while, but they left as soon as Jesus started to talk about a price to pay.

Fifth Point: True believers remain faithful through testing.

Explanation: A true disciple stays, bears fruit, remains abiding in the vine, permanently bearing fruit.

Illustration: I've debated this for years in what's called the "lordship controversy."

Application: The true conversion takes place when what the person hungers for is to be delivered from a deep, overwhelming burden of sin into righteousness before God.

Conclusion: There are many people in this shallow condition. And some of you here are in that condition. You're superficially attached to Jesus for whatever reasons. You may feel emotional about it at this point, but you're not going to survive if you didn't come to him because you were utterly and totally overwhelmed with your sinful condition and its consequences, and the cry of your heart was for a righteousness you knew you needed to escape judgment and have a relationship with God.

Evaluating the Declarative Sermon

Preacher: ________________ **Date:** ______________ **Text:** ____________

What would you say was the one big idea that the preacher was trying to communicate?

___

___

To what degree was the big idea faithful to the biblical text?

(circle one) 1 2 3 4 5

What points or reasons did the preacher use to convince you of the big idea?

___

___

To what degree did you find these reasons convincing?

(circle one) 1 2 3 4 5

What kinds of responses did the preacher challenge you to make?

How likely are you to follow through and make these responses?

(circle one) 1 2 3 4 5

Describe the preacher's manner and appearance during the event.

To what degree did the preacher's manner enhance the sermon?

(circle one) 1 2 3 4 5

Offer any further comments you think might be of help.

Chapter 6 | SOLVE A MYSTERY

the pragmatic sermon

example: Rick Warren

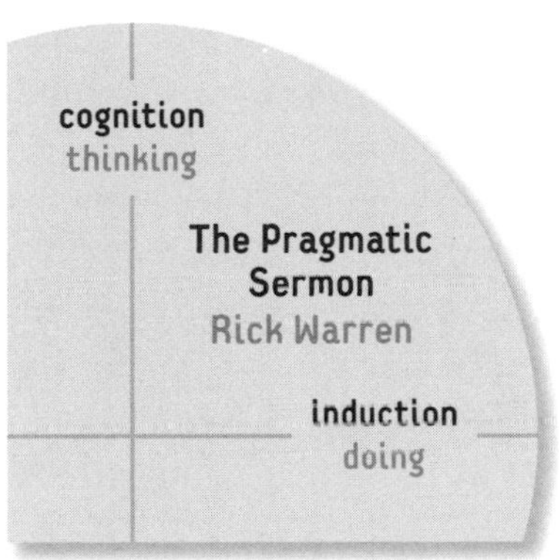

The *pragmatic* sermon is the preferred manner of preaching in the seeker-focused churches that began developing in the late twentieth century. Like a detective, the pragmatic preacher works to solve mysteries for people. With the Bible as his or her casebook, these preacher-detectives appeal to Kolb's "doers" and "thinkers," helping them think through answers for the questions they encounter while living life. Such preaching is inductive in that it starts with the need of the seeker-listener and moves toward a solution. It is cognitive in that it focuses on the ideas of the sermon and builds on the assumption that if the listener can learn how to think rightly, he or she will be able to live rightly.

This kind of preaching continues to be extremely popular, particularly among North American baby boomers. Pragmatic preaching has been the fuel of the megachurch, fitting the need-solution focus of these fast-growing churches like a glove. Pragmatic preaching is immediately relevant, as it starts where the listener lives — in a difficult marriage, a failing business, or a place of spiritual uncertainty. The market for this kind of preaching is virtually insatiable, given the complexity of life in the new millennium.

Life is bigger than we are and more complicated than we ever thought possible. People, crippled by their questions, come to preachers seeking understanding. Our expectations are not very high. We don't expect the preacher to be some smug answer-man. If he were, we probably wouldn't believe him—besides, it wouldn't be much fun. We would, however, like to think that we could get some kind of handle on how life works. We want to know what we can do to become more like Christ, more successful in our life with God. The world is mysterious. Perhaps the preacher can help us learn what we can do.

How to Solve a Mystery

One day when my wife and I were out walking, we came across a film crew shooting a mystery movie at Somerset House in Central London. The courtyard had been filled with smoke, creating the illusion of a thick foggy morning. The fog was a metaphor for our own lack of knowledge about what we were looking at. It looked like a Sherlock Holmes movie, but we couldn't be sure until we asked one of the extras. Could we recognize any of the actors? Would we recognize the story? Had we read this one before? I have heard that filming is a slow-moving and tedious process, and this was certainly the case here. Actors were looking for ways to pass the time between takes. The carriage driver had to continually exercise the horses. Nothing was happening, but still we couldn't pull ourselves away.

Insight and Ideas | POSTMODERN MYSTERY

We are growing weary of the scientists. Every time they answer one of our questions, they turn around and hand us several more we had never thought of. The more we tune our microscopes and strengthen our telescopes, the more mystery we see—quantum mechanics, subatomic uncertainty, parallel universe theories—the more educated we become, it seems, the more we realize how little we know. Perhaps ignorance really is bliss.

Postmodern philosophy in its popular manifestation is a deepened awareness of our inability to comprehend the mysteries.

There is something attractive about the unknown. We are drawn to understand what we cannot comprehend. We are compelled to clarify whatever we find confusing. We sit in the movie theater, every impulse within us crying for resolution. We need a solution for the mystery, relief for the victims, a happy ending for all. Of course, as soon as we get the resolution we are craving, the story is over and we all have to go home. We feel a certain letdown at that point. Having solved the mystery doesn't seem nearly as fun as the solving, which explains some of the appeal of the pragmatic sermon.

In my house, an unfinished puzzle on a card table in the corner has a magnetic pull on the members of my family; we can't leave it alone. In the same way, a mystery-solving sermon requires the attention of the listeners. A sermon that seeks an answer to a compelling problem draws the listener. Unlike a card-table puzzle that is abandoned as soon as it is finished, however, the pragmatic sermon actually makes a difference.

Sermons are not abstract exercises in detection. Sermons are nonfiction. When we preach, we are talking about our problems, the mysteries that plague us. We are invested in the process as we try to understand God's solution for our questions. When the sermon is over, we are the ones who can live happily in the reality of the truth that has been told. Having heard from God, we are able to go out and do what he has said. It is our world that has been broken and our world that has been fixed—to some degree, at least.

Insight and Ideas | THE LISTENER'S QUESTION

The key to pragmatic preaching is the ability to understand the listener's question and to frame it in a way the listener will recognize. We want the listener to say, "Yeah, that's what I was wondering."

The problem with raising the listener's question is that our listeners often raise the wrong question. They tend to ask very human, sometimes selfish, kinds of questions that need to be redirected. Biblical preachers need to learn to help listeners by letting the Bible rephrase the question, setting it in a healthier direction that will lead to a more fruitful result.

Sometimes sermons raise more questions than they answer. That can happen when you are listening to God. The mysteries of life will not be entirely resolved this side of heaven. But God encourages us to come to him with our questions. Good preachers understand the ancient rubric: "faith seeking understanding." We trust God, but we'll do our level best to understand what he is doing. After all, that is the reason he gave us his Word.

I enjoy most mystery stories—Sherlock Holmes, Hercule Poirot, Inspector Rebus—I like them all. My favorite fictional detective, however, has to be G. K. Chesterton's crime-solving theologian, Father Brown. Father Brown understands the *inductive* nature of solving mysteries. Detectives start with an unsolved question as it exists in life and move to discover a credible explanation for the observed phenomena.

In "The Blue Cross," Chesterton describes the search for the elusive criminal Flambeau: "He remembered how Flambeau had escaped, once by a pair of nail scissors, and once by a house on fire; once by having to pay for an unstamped letter, and once by getting people to look through a telescope at a comet that might destroy the world."[1] Father Brown "thought his detective brain as good as the criminal's, which was true. But he fully realized the disadvantage. 'The criminal is the creative artist; the detective only the critic.'"[2] This is insightful. Not that God's creative actions are criminal, but detection is required to understand him.

Detectives are always playing catch-up. They don't set the agenda. They can only respond, and this is as it should be. Inductive process appreciates that we always come to God somewhat in a fog. We don't understand. How could we? God, the ultimate creative genius, sometimes makes as much sense to us in his actions as Flambeau to Father Brown. The detective can get the measure of the creative mind, however—at least to a degree—by applying his powers of detection.

These powers are invariably *cognitive*. Hercule Poirot is often offended by those who would attribute his genius to good fortune. His success, he would remind them, is due to the application of "the little gray cells." Sherlock Holmes is almost entirely without humor, such is his devotion to the pure cognitive process. While we might prefer a little spark of ingenuity, we welcome the detective's services when we need to solve a mystery.

Practical Exercise 14 | TYPES OF EVIDENCE

Physical Evidence

Material items that give insight into the mystery.

Behavioral Evidence

Clues discerned through observation of human behavior and psychology.

Testimonial Evidence

Eyewitness accounts that help unlock the truth.

How are these forms (or *are* these forms?) of evidence utilized in 1 John 1 and 1 Corinthians 15? Can you think of other biblical examples of each type of evidence?

So what does one look for in a detective? A keen sense of observation is first on the list. The detective notices the things that other people miss, like the dog that *didn't* bark in *The Hound of the Baskervilles*.[3] A detective pays attention to the details and examines every clue as evidence that could lead to a solution.

Evidence comes in a variety of forms. *Physical evidence* is the incriminating objects and fingerprints that show the culprit's trace. *Behavioral evidence* involves an understanding of the expected patterns of the human mind. The detective knows what to look for in an unguarded glance or a misdirected frown. *Testimonial evidence* is the affirmations made by third-party observers. A good detective notices everything. Not everything will be useful, but everything must be observed.

A good detective must also possess the analytical skill to interpret the clues as they present themselves. Relevant data must be separated from the irrelevant. The facts need to be set in order so that a rational analysis can be applied. The bare facts will not suggest a solution to every observer. The detective knows how to put the pieces together so that everything makes sense once we come to the last scene.

The last scene in most detective novels seems to usually happen in the parlor as all the suspects gather to hear the detective clarify the muddle. Now the truth will be known as the detective makes sense of all the data and tells his version of the crime.

Of course, for the Christian, the last scene is still in the future. Only God knows how long we will have to wait before he gathers us into his parlor and reveals who is who and what is what. Until then, we utilize our best wisdom, understanding a little at a time as he guides us by his Spirit. The preacher-detective depends very much on God's Spirit.

So how do you solve a mystery? Anyone who has ever watched an episode of *Columbo* will recognize the following steps.

1. Call for the detective. The problem with mysteries is that the victims can't help but get emotionally involved. We are too close to our own problems, so we need the wisdom of an experienced, objective observer who can come into our situation and make sense of all the facts.

Insight and Ideas | CALL FOR THE DETECTIVE

Listeners bring a variety of mysterious questions to the preacher-detective:

- How can I get ahead in my business?

- I'm so busy with family and work. How can I find time to relax?
- How can I feel better about my life?
- How can I get my husband/wife to pay more attention to me?

These questions may be pressing, but they probably have deeper implications. The mystery isn't always as it first appears.

2. Clarify the mystery. The first thing the detective will do is clarify the exact nature of the mystery. What exactly is wrong? Has someone died? Was the death of natural causes, or should foul play be suspected?

3. Identify the suspects. Usually, there are many possible culprits. Any good mystery will suggest several credible suspects with guilty consciences, which is why we call it a mystery. An effective detective will identify all the suspicious candidates, including those who don't immediately suggest themselves. Suspects are those who have a *motive* for the crime.

4. Establish all the alibis. The quickest way to narrow down the field is to determine which suspects have alibis, or which of them did not have an *opportunity* to commit the crime. Anyone who can offer a reasonable explanation as to why they could not have committed the act is eliminated from suspicion.

5. Gather all the evidence. The effective detective must follow every lead to its logical conclusion, examining each clue for the light it might shed on an ultimate conviction. A broken twig, a distinctive footprint, or best, a smoking gun can all give evidence to the identity of the criminal. No stone must be left unturned in the search for evidence, yet care must be taken to make sure that the evidence is properly interpreted. Context is critical because sometimes evidence can be read in different ways. Agatha Christie, for instance, is famous for pitting her detectives against the police, who almost always read the clues too hastily and come to a conclusion before weighing all the facts. The best detectives never draw conclusions until all the evidence has spoken and has spoken unambiguously.

Insight and Ideas | THE HERMENEUTIC OF THE MYSTERY

Robert Champigny describes mysteries as "hermeneutic tales," which is to say that while they begin in subjective experience, they move inductively toward some objective form of truth. "A narrative that attracts the reader's attention to some undetermined events but avoids determining them at the end is not a mystery story." Mysteries need to be solved, which is to say that they need the application of truth.

Robert Champigny, *What Will Have Happened: A Philosophical and Technical Essay on Mystery Stories* (Bloomington: Indiana University Press, 1977), 13.

6. Resolve the mystery. Having heard all the evidence, the detective now gathers the victims, suspects, and other interested parties into the parlor, where the solution will be revealed.

7. Apprehend the culprit. Once the mystery has been solved, the criminal must be arrested. A deep sense of satisfaction always comes from knowing that justice has been served. While condemning a murderer never brings the victim back, the loved ones can take a certain comfort in knowing that the truth has come to light.

Put like this, the steps to solving mysteries seem straightforward, and in truth, they are. The detective is the purest type of pragmatist. The steps are not complicated as long as the detective applies them ruthlessly. Sometimes patience is called for since the clues can be stubborn, unwilling to disclose their information. Yet the process is worth the effort as we seek to understand the truth.

Preaching the Pragmatic Sermon

Like a detective, the cognitive-inductive preacher is also a pragmatist. The pragmatic sermon is all about life application. The search for truth is intended to make a difference in the life of the listener. Biblical and theological knowledge is given so that we might love more, be more truthful, or act with greater humility. Knowledge is never given for its own intellectual value. Knowledge without application simply puffs the listener's ego (1 Cor. 8:1), inflating self-importance and making a person miserable. You may have noticed that some of the most ornery people in church know the most about the Bible.

The Bible was given to us to change our lives. The purpose of Scripture is to train us, rebuke us, correct us, and generally shape us for living life in the likeness of Jesus (2 Tim. 3:15–16). Sermons, then, ought to be pragmatic, which is to say that they will work to motivate a tangible change in us. Things turn out to be meaningfully different from week to week because we have gathered together and heard what God has had to say to us.

? Discussion Question 19 | HOW-TO SERMONS

Pragmatic sermons are often characterized by the words *How to* in the title: "How to Succeed as a Christian in Business" or "How to Find True Joy in Life," for example.

Do such how-to sermons create "consumer Christians?" Does catering to the listener's needs create selfish believers?

Inductive preaching, as we have seen, is pragmatic. It begins with the application and works back toward the cognitive principles that motivate the necessary change. While the purpose of the sermon is not strictly to inform the listener's mind, meaningful change will not happen until we learn to think differently. Our actions are controlled by our thoughts, so if we want to help people change, we will need to work to renew their minds (Rom. 12:2). In that sense, pragmatic preaching must be cognitive. If we want our broken computer to run properly, we call someone who has the knowledge to fix it. We will not fix life until we learn to think correctly about life.

The pragmatic preacher, then, works to change lives by changing the way listeners think. The preacher works on listeners' minds, not simply to change their minds but to change the way they live their lives. Think differently and you will live differently.

The steps to the pragmatic sermon are as follows.

1. Pray for Wisdom

Life-application preaching can be risky business. Haddon Robinson said that more heresy gets preached in application than in any other aspect of the sermon.[4] This is because we bring our own lives to the Scriptures. People are usually too close to their own problems to perceive their own prescriptions. Whenever we are stymied, we need help to find our way. We need to "call for the detective," inviting the Holy Spirit to guide us into truth. We could also profit from an objective preacher who operates by the Spirit's lead.

Insight and Ideas | TEAMING UP

If you are struggling to anticipate your listeners' thinking about your text and sermon, why not ask them? Form a team of "consultants" with whom you can discuss your sermon theme before preaching.

In some churches, this team consists of the worship leaders and production assistants. Everyone involved in creating the service gets involved in creating the sermon.

Part of our problem is our tendency to manipulate our understanding of the Scriptures. Unless we are clearly guided by the Holy Spirit, we can easily twist the intent of the Bible toward the things we decide we want. Pragmatic solutions can seem mechanical: problem A is solved by the application of solution B. One can begin to think that God is little more than a mathematical formula. But the work of God in changing lives is far more mysterious than anything that can be reduced to automatic function. The pragmatic preacher starts with prayer, knowing that spiritual change is the work of the Holy Spirit.

2. Raise the Listener's Question

The pragmatic preacher begins at the point of application and then moves back toward understanding. We must clarify the mystery. Something is malfunctioning or something is unclear. The listener is having trouble with an aspect of the Christian life and is looking for help. Sometimes the problem isn't even evident until the preacher puts her finger on it. This is often the case in evangelistic sermons, in which the listener might not be concerned about or aware of his or her need to be reconciled with God.

The pragmatic preacher looks at the lives of the people who will gather and asks what they need to hear. This implies that we are actively involved in our listeners' lives. The better we know our people, the better we will know what they need. Of course, it helps when we realize that we are listeners too. Often the most effective way to discern a problem is to look at one's own life. What are the issues you are tripping over? Are you having trouble with your family, your employers, or your money? Sorry to meddle, but your preaching will be better for it.

Sometimes an issue that needs to be addressed is seen as we read the Scriptures. The Bible comes at us like a challenge. It is countercultural, making demands on us and pushing us to places we don't necessarily want to go. The Bible compels us. It requires us to respond. Often those demands don't rest easily on us. We find ourselves reacting to the discomfort and struggling with the implications. We feel the bind, and we don't like it.

Here is where preaching can be compelling. When we directly deal with the issues that upset us, we connect with the listener at a powerful level of consciousness. We grab the listener by the arm and say, "We've got a problem here. Perhaps it's time we deal with it."

Insight and Ideas | QUESTIONING THE THEME

One way to come up with "the listener's question" is to take a proposition from Scripture and imagine its antithesis. Invert the proposition and write it as a question.

For example, perhaps you want to preach from John 3:16 on the love of God. From the perspective of your listeners, however, God may seem anything but loving. So use that. Invert your sermon theme: "For God so loved the world" becomes "God doesn't seem to love me." Phrased as a question, your theme becomes "How could God love me if I hurt so much?"

Humans question much of what the Bible says. We will always struggle with God's Word this side of heaven.

It will be helpful to express the sermon issue in the form of a question: "How can I avoid temptation in my marriage?" "If God loves me, why does he seem so far away?" Questions like these rise up from the listener's experience. Framing the problem as a question encourages the listener to get involved in the search for a solution. The more the listener recognizes the impulse leading to the question, the more engaged he or she will be in the sermon as a whole.

It is best to raise a single question rather than trying to solve a whole group of issues in a single sermon. Avoiding the word *and* and other conjunctions can help ensure that the question maintains a laser focus. Generally, the fewer words used, the better.

Finally, the question should be posed in the words of the listener. The trick is to help the listener recognize the problem as his or her own. "Am I alone in the world?" "Should I be truthful even though it might cost me my job?" Listeners will see their own experience in questions like these. Real-life experience colors the question, drawing on real emotion from actual situations in the listener's life. The listener will fill in the faces and circumstances that surround the problem posed.

3. List All of the Possibilities

A variety of possibilities may be giving rise to the listener's problem. You would do well to make a list of them, as if you were identifying all the suspects—everything that might motivate or contribute to the problem. This work is not unlike that of the doctor who seeks a diagnosis for an illness. The root issues will not always identify themselves immediately, so you must list them all and work through them one by one.

Perhaps the listener's question has to do with truth-telling: "Must I tell the truth every time?" It seems there is a price to pay for telling the truth. If my boss really knew what I was thinking, the listener thinks, I might miss the next promotion, or worse. I can't always tell the complete truth to my husband, can I, or to my children? This is a serious matter, and though we are not accustomed to thinking of ourselves as liars, on closer examination, we all find we play a little loose with the truth.

The question is, why? What are the possible reasons for our lack of truthfulness? (1) It is possible that we don't have a problem with lying because we don't believe that lying is a problem. But then, that might be a little twisted. (2) Perhaps, rather, it is a question of confidence. We feel that if others really knew what we were thinking, it could put us in a bad light. (3) It could be that we are just being pragmatic. Lying can give us a strategic advantage over others when the truth is bent judiciously. (4) Maybe we have unwittingly created a values hierarchy in which the Ten Commandments matter only for the "really big situations." (5) Perhaps it is a much more fundamental struggle with integrity. We have failed to see the importance of honesty in our relationships, and we don't really care because we have sin in our hearts, which is corrupting our judgment.

We find plenty of suspicious characters once we start snooping around our hearts and minds. We need to chase them all down. You never know where the culprit might be hiding.

Insight and Ideas | THE USE OF TEXTS AND VERSIONS

Because pragmatic preaching begins with the listener's question rather than with the biblical text, many pragmatic preachers utilize a wide variety of biblical passages to support their teaching, often using multiple versions and choosing the one that expresses the truth most helpfully in each case.

While there is nothing inherently wrong with this approach, the preacher must be sure to handle the texts with care. In fact, correctly interpreting many texts in their contexts can be a lot of work. It can also be confusing to listeners, who have to focus in several directions.

Still, when done well, the multitext approach gives people a broader and deeper appreciation for the wisdom of Scripture on their question. Even when the preacher puts the major focus of the sermon on one specific text, using parallel supportive texts is almost always a good idea.

4. Eliminate the Illogical

Pragmatic preaching is cognitive preaching. It is inherently logical. So having lined up all the suspicious possibilities, we need to apply ruthless logic to them. You will find that some of these suspects "have an alibi" and will be ruled out for being foolish or impossible when they are examined under the harsh light of logic. Why does the listener feel so alone? It couldn't be because they are alone. We are living in a world of more than six billion people, none of whom are all that different from their neighbor. There are plenty of people around, so the problem must be something deeper. Perhaps it is not that we are literally alone but that we have failed to meaningfully connect with those around us. Now, there is a more promising suspect.

When we examine our earlier question about truthfulness, we see that the only one of our five suspects that has a clear alibi is the first possibility. None of us truly believe that lying doesn't matter, because we all have seen that it truly does matter. Every one of us has been hurt by someone who has been less than truthful with us. We all understand that the foundations of society would crumble if people consistently lied to one another.

The next three suspects—the confidence problem, the pragmatic suggestion, and the values hierarchy—seem like real possibilities. None of them have an obvious alibi. On closer examination, however, we see that they all have one feature in common. The lie, in each of these cases, is offered strategically as a means of protecting ourselves or advancing our interests.

Practical Exercise 15 | MORALISM IN APPLICATION

A common problem in pragmatic preaching is moralistic application—that is, applications that call on the listener to do better or to live better without offering the appropriate theological or exegetical support.

Examine five pragmatic sermon texts (on the Internet, from books, or from your own notes). Look for examples of moralistic applications. How might they be reshaped so that they will be more faithful to the intent of the Bible?

This leaves us with the fifth and most likely suspect: sin in our hearts. We have already established that suspects two through four boil down to self-protection or self-advancement, which naturally leads us to the doorstep of suspect number five. We are selfish because we are sinners. We are willing to bend the truth because we care more about ourselves than we care about the will of God. It is a harsh verdict. The truth often is.

In the end, it comes down to theology. It always does. The messages we preach boil down to the nature and will of God and to the way that we respond to him. Theological truth will lead to meaningful changes in the listener's life.

5. Gather All of Scripture's Wisdom

Now it is time to "examine all the evidence." The preacher's casebook is the Bible, and it is this book that will provide the necessary clues.

The first form of biblical evidence the preacher looks for is *propositional*. The preacher is looking for specific instructions relating to the issue at hand. If the problem is fear, 1 John 4:18 will need to be considered: "Perfect love drives out fear." Of course, you will then need to discover what the text means by "perfect love." As in any great mystery, one clue usually leads to another. The mysteries abound, but the good detective stays on the trail, following every lead until a satisfactory solution can be found.

The second form of biblical evidence is *testimonial*. Just as the detective interviews witnesses and suspects, the preacher needs to talk to the people in the Bible to find guidance. Of course, we cannot directly question people long dead, but we can study their testimonies given in the Scriptures. The Bible offers a wealth of eyewitness testimonies, the testimonies of people who have seen with their eyes and touched with their hands the truths that God has revealed in his Word (1 John 1:1–3). How did Peter deal with pride? What were the circumstances surrounding Thomas's experience of doubt?

The narrative passages of Scripture allow us to put our questions in a human context to see what God has in mind for the application of his will. Investigating the way that greed and deceit influenced the actions of Judas can inform our own response to the same problems in our lives. Insight comes as we see the propositions of the Bible in the context of the narratives of real people in the Bible.

This kind of broad biblical search can be a lot of work. As we range around the Bible, looking for clues to understanding, we must make sure that we interpret every clue correctly. Clues are open to interpretation, and we need to make sure we understand them rightly so that we don't find ourselves chasing off in the wrong direction. As mentioned earlier, much of the tension in a detective novel builds on the differences in how people interpret the clues. The bystanders have one view, the police detectives another, but only the great Poirot is able to understand the truth.

Thus, all the normal rules of evidence must be carefully observed. In the case of biblical investigation, we are talking about the rules of exegesis, which we discussed in chapter 3. Due attention to context and definition, and a dogged insistence on the intent of the author are required.

Insight and Ideas | THE PREACHER'S PERSON

Nothing accredits or discredits the sermon as much as the character of the preacher. It is true that good preachers get out of the way of the sermon so that the Holy Spirit can speak. It is also true that the preacher's integrity is a critical factor in the listeners' ability to respond to what they hear.

Of course, none of us are perfect. We all have sinned and have fallen short of the glory of what we preach, but people need to understand that we are keeping close to God, we are accountable to others, and we are serious about practicing what we preach. We don't care about this simply because it makes us more effective. We do it because it is right. We do it because we love to obey God.

In the case of our sermon on truthfulness, there are several places we could go to gather evidence. The first place has been already mentioned; Exodus 20:16 enshrines truthfulness as one of the Ten Commandments. Proverbs 11:1 shows that honesty and accuracy flow out of the character of God: "The LORD abhors dishonest scales, but accurate weights are his delight." This principle is affirmed in the New Testament in Colossians 3:9–10, which says, "Do not lie to each other, since you have taken off your old self with its practices and have put on the new self, which is being renewed in knowledge in the image of its Creator." Truthfulness, we are told, is part of the image of God. Clearly, the propositional evidence is strong.

For testimonial evidence, we could look to the story of Achan in Joshua 7 or the story of Ananias and Sapphira in Acts 5:1–10. When they kept back some of the proceeds of the sale of their property, Peter asked why they had "lied to the Holy Spirit" (v. 3). The price for their dishonesty was death. The evidence is clear: dishonesty leads to death.

6. Answer the Listener's Question

Having examined the biblical evidence, the preacher now must "resolve the mystery." It is time to determine what God has to say about the question. The intent of the sermon needs to be stated in a clear and concise answer to the question posed. "Am I alone in the world?" "No," the preacher answers, "you are not alone. God knew you from before the foundation of the world, and he walks with you and loves you and has a purpose for your life!"

As encouraging as that is, it might benefit from a little editing. "God never leaves you alone." That is better, don't you think? A simple, unambiguous answer to the question can be stated with conviction. Of course, you can build on it as the sermon is preached, but I always like the key proposition of the sermon to have as much punch as possible.

Insight and Ideas | LOVE THEM

Preachers need to love their listeners. We might not always get it right. Things we say can be misconstrued. Sometimes we will make comments that would have been better left unsaid. Love covers a multitude of wrongs. When people are convinced the preacher really loves them, they will listen with more grace and more intention. Of course, loving listeners is another way the preacher maintains integrity with the loving message of the Bible.

"Must I tell the truth every time?" The answer to the question is, "Yes, because honesty reflects God's character." One could also say that "dishonesty leads to death." This one ultimate truth statement trumps all the other possibilities that have to do with practical selfish concerns. God is always truthful. We have been created in his image to serve his purposes according to his will. We must always tell the truth, though we might want to be merciful in the way we make it known. Any pain experienced or price paid will be cheap compared to the ultimate reward received in Christ.

Normally, many things could and perhaps should be said on a particular theme or problem that our listeners present, but ultimately, these problems find their resolution in something theological. Human loneliness is most profoundly answered by God's abiding presence. Fear is overcome by a deep awareness of the grace of God and his love for us. If that sounds overly simple, like saying the correct answer to every Sunday school question is "Jesus," I make no apologies. All preaching is intended to reconcile people to God. Understanding God and how he relates to us is at the root of every human trouble. Preaching is never so helpfully pragmatic than when it leads people to God through the mediation of his Son, Jesus Christ.

Discussion Question 20 | PLAGIARISM IN PREACHING

Plagiarism has become a significant problem in preaching, especially with our increased exposure to sermons on the Internet. Some pastors are even being fired for preaching other people's sermons without attribution. Plagiarism in preaching is a question of integrity, but the question can be complicated. It is almost impossible for a preacher to be completely original. One could question whether we even should try.

How can we profit from the work of others without stealing their ideas? Does a preacher's work need to be entirely original, or can we borrow from others?

How much is too much—an idea, a story, a complete outline? When have we crossed the line?

7. Apply the Insights Gained

Pragmatic sermons are preached to be applied. Now the sermon comes full circle. It is time to "apprehend the culprit." We began the process with a problem in the listener's life, and now comes the time to fix it. While some things will ultimately not be fixed this side of heaven, the listener can always be led to a theological understanding that can at least provide a sense of meaning that is sufficient for the present, though much mystery will remain.

All our work will be for naught if we cannot help listeners apply the sermon's insights to their lives. The listener was asking, "Am I alone in the world?" The preacher answers, "No. God never leaves you alone, and here is how to make sure you don't forget his presence." The more specific the preacher is in application, the more helpful the sermon will be in resolving issues for the listener. Concrete examples can be given: The lonely listener can be encouraged to cultivate a life of prayer so as to stay aware of God's loving presence. He can be encouraged to remain in fellowship with other believers who can embody God's love in his presence.

In our sermon on truthfulness, the application is fairly straightforward: "Tell the truth." If you are afraid to tell your husband what you are really thinking about, maybe you had better change what you are thinking about. If you are afraid that truthfulness will set you at a disadvantage in a business deal, you might want to consider whether you are willing to pay the price of your integrity or your obedience to God for the slight advantage you might gain. Of course, sometimes these things can be extremely painful. Preachers need to be sensitive in the way they challenge listeners. Grace and mercy are always welcome. Our churches need to offer the full support of our communities to those people who have to pay a price for their willingness to honor God.

Practical Exercise 16 | SERMON HANDOUT

A common practice of pragmatic preachers is to give listeners a handout for the sermon. These handouts help make the sermon interactive. People are encouraged to fill in the blanks, which engages them with more than just their ears.

Prepare a handout for your pragmatic sermon, one that is suitable for inclusion in the church bulletin. Use large margins for writing in and leave blank spots that will require people to keep active as they fill in the details.

The preacher will go through these seven steps twice, once in his or her own study and once more in the presence of the listeners. The sermon repeats in public the process that the preacher-detective experienced in private. Remember that the preacher leads the people through the same process of discovery that he or she experienced in study. The outline for the sermon will begin with the question and precisely follow through all of the steps the preacher has taken. Of course, every topic is different and will vary in direction, but the outcome will be the same: a question has been posed, and a question has been answered.

There is a sense of expectation in the air whenever people gather in the parlor, or the sanctuary, anticipating the possibility that their lives might be improved by a new understanding of their problems. Everyone present—sinners, saints, and suspects—senses the prospect of solution. God is about to speak through his Word, and we will surely benefit from the experience.

For Example: Rick Warren

The most prominent practitioner of the pragmatic sermon is Rick Warren. While not every Warren sermon begins with the words "How to," his preaching always begins with the listeners at their point of need. "We don't have to make the Bible relevant," he says. "It is. But we do have to show its relevance by applying it to today's needs."[5] Warren's preferred way of doing this is through what he calls "verse-with-verse exposition." This method, in contrast to the traditional verse-by-verse approach, begins with an idea that is relevant to the listener's life and then brings all of the Bible's wisdom to bear on the subject.

"There is no specifically biblical style of preaching," Warren says.[6] "What do Finney, Wesley, Calvin, Spurgeon, Moody, Billy Graham, Jesus, Peter, and Paul all have in common? None of them were verse-by-verse, through the book teachers. Not one of them."[7] According to Warren, it is okay to start with an idea instead of a text as long as you deal with the text appropriately.

Resource Recommendation | WARREN'S WEBSITE

Rick Warren's website is www.pastors.com. If you are willing to pay the subscription fees, you will find a storehouse of resources for pragmatic preaching.

Warren says that both Paul and Jesus always started with the needs, hurts, and interests of their audiences, and preachers today must do no different. In Warren's own practice, he uses a more traditional expository format for his midweek services, which are geared for believers predisposed to a deeper treatment of a biblical text. For his weekend seeker services, however, he utilizes a more need-oriented or problem-focused approach. "I use about fourteen to sixteen different verses," he says. "I will use different translations.... Sometimes the New American Standard says it better. Sometimes The New Living Translation says it better. Sometimes the NIV says it better, so I use that." The key is that a Warren sermon always takes the Bible seriously. "I don't care how the Bible is taught," he says, "as long as the Bible is taught."[8]

Warren describes a continuum that shows "interpretation" on one side and "personalization" on the other. Commentators, he says, tend to live in the interpretive world, while communicators tend to live in the personalized world. In the middle is "implication." "The key is always finding the implication of the text.... It's a fine line and you can fall off on either side. It is easy to be biblical without being contemporary or relevant. It is easy to be relevant without being biblical. The test is right there in the middle, walking that fine line."[9]

Sermon Example | "WHAT ON EARTH AM I HERE FOR?"

This sermon, offered as the first in Warren's much utilized Purpose Driven Life series of sermon outlines, bears many features of the pragmatic sermon.

The primary question, given in the title, is broken down into three supporting questions: (1) Why am I alive? (2) Does my life matter? and (3) What is my purpose? These questions form the outline of the sermon.

Warren offers some suspicious answers—perhaps our lives have no meaning, perhaps we were not created for any special purpose—before leading us to the biblical truth. Warren brings the Scriptures into focus, overwhelming the listener with a sense of promise and of hope. At least eleven different texts are offered, each offering an encouraging message of the hope and purpose that are found in life under God's hand.

In the end, the answer to the listener's question is made plain: We are here to know and to serve God. This purpose was established from before the foundation of the world and will remain forever.

"We actually read Scripture aloud together," Warren says. "We probably read more Scripture aloud than the average church does because I have it on an outline. I say, 'Now, let's all read this together.' I'll say, 'Circle that word, underline that, star that.' Then they can take it home with them and put it up on the refrigerator, pass it on to friends, (or) teach a Bible study on it."[10]

Warren uses the acronym CRAFT to guide his methodology. *C* stands for collect and categorize, *R* is research and reflect, *A* is apply and arrange, *F* is fashion and flavor, and *T* is to trim and tie it all together. While this method of preparation is slightly different from what has been described in this chapter, the result bears all the hallmarks of the pragmatic sermon.

Template for the Pragmatic Sermon

Preacher: ____________ **Date:** ____________ **Text:** ____________

Good titles are creative and compelling, offering listeners a reason to listen, without giving too much away.

The Listener's Question: ________________________

State the theme of the sermon in the form of a question from the listener's perspective.

Proposed Solutions:

- ________________________
- ________________________
- ________________________
- ________________________

List the various ways people could respond to the question (problem).

The Wisdom of Scripture:

- ________________________
- ________________________

• ____

• ____

Describe the scriptural evidence (propositional and testimonial) that leads to an answer to the question.

Answer to the Question: ______________________________

Write the answer to the question in a succinct declarative sentence. This is the sermon theme (the big idea).

Application:

• ____

• ____

• ____

Suggest concrete action steps the listener could take to respond obediently to God.

Example of the Pragmatic Sermon

Preacher: Rick Warren **Text:** Proverbs 4:23

Title: Myths That Make Us Miserable

The Listener's Question: What can I do about the myths that make me miserable?

Proposed Solutions:

• It doesn't matter what you believe as long as you are sincere.... Now, that sounds so good. It sounds so broad-minded, so tolerant.... The only problem is it's absurd and irrational to hold this view. (Illustration: following the wrong car.)

• Don't always believe everything you hear.... A belief doesn't have to be true for it to affect you emotionally or cause emotional turmoil.

The Wisdom of Scripture: (A few of the many texts offered.)

• John 8:32: My guess is that we expose the lies that we've been taught by our culture and apply the truth.

• Romans 3:4: When it comes down to it, you have only two options. You have either the world or the Word of God. You will build your life on either what culture says or what Christ says. The world or the Word.

• Luke 21:33: God's Word has stood the test of time. You can trust it as your guidebook, as your authority, as your basis.

• Matthew 7:24: Do you want to get it together? You need to hear and you need to practice the truth.

• Romans 12:2: Would you like to be free from emotional hang-ups that keep you from being happy? It's possible. God can transform your mind and replace the old myths with a new system of beliefs based on the truth.

Answer to the Question: The myths that make us miserable are destroyed by confrontation with the truth.

• Our beliefs have a fundamental, profound impact on our lives.

• False beliefs are often damaging.

• Truth is the key to overcoming the myths that make us miserable.

Application:

• Commit to seeking the truth.

• Commit to living the truth.

• Commit to believing the truth.

Evaluating the Pragmatic Sermon

Preacher: ________________ **Date:** ______________ **Text:** ____________

What was the primary question that the preacher was trying to answer?

____

____

To what degree could you identify with this question?

(circle one) 1 2 3 4 5

What solution did the preacher offer to this question?

____

____

To what degree did you find this answer convincing?

(circle one) 1 2 3 4 5

What kinds of responses did the preacher challenge you to make?

____

____

How likely are you to follow through and make these responses?

(circle one) 1 2 3 4 5

Describe the preacher's manner and appearance during the event.

____

____

To what degree did the preacher's manner enhance the sermon?

(circle one) 1 2 3 4 5

Offer any further comments you think might be of help.

Chapter 7 | TELL A STORY

the narrative sermon

example: Eugene Lowry

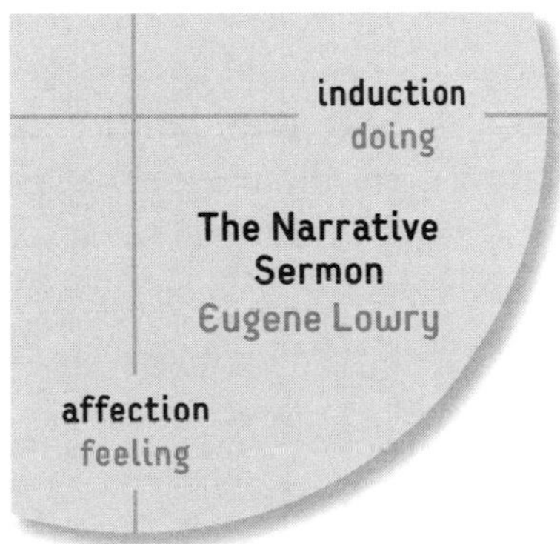

The *narrative* sermon is the preferred manner of preaching in many "mainline" and "emerging" evangelical churches. Relating somewhat to the "new homiletic" of the late 1970s and early '80s, narrative preachers offer the sermon in the form of a story.[1] Like a novelist, the narrative preacher tries to work the sermon into life-size shapes. These preacher-storytellers appeal to Kolb's doers and feelers, evoking an experience of the gospel through the unfolding of the biblical story. Such preaching is inductive in that it unfolds, creating a sense of discovery for the listener, just like any good story based on life does. It is affective in that it uses the images and experiences of life to dramatize the truths it wishes to teach.

Narrative preaching is a listener-friendly form of preaching, because everybody loves a story. I used to hear it every night as I tucked my children into bed: "Daddy, would you please tell me a story?" I always tried to make the storytelling fun, adopting silly voices for the various characters and sometimes inserting strange words in unexpected places simply for the reaction it would get. I could probably still recite *Green Eggs and Ham* without having to consult the text.

Now my children are getting older, and they don't need me to read to them at night. They are quite capable of reading for themselves and do so without encouragement. Recently my youngest daughter announced her intention to finish reading *The Fellowship of the Ring* before going to sleep that evening. Given that she was only halfway through the book at the time, her plan was ambitious. I noticed the next morning that she didn't quite make it, though she was awake early, curled up on the couch devouring the words and images of Tolkien's remarkable story.

I don't expect my children will ever lose their passion for stories. I know that I haven't. Judging by the dollars spent on the motion-picture industry, most of us haven't. Apparently, the desire for stories does not diminish with age. Robert Fulford says, "Of all the ways we communicate with one another, the story has established itself as the most comfortable, the most versatile—and perhaps also the most dangerous.... Assembling facts or incidents into tale is the only form of expression and entertainment that most of us enjoy equally at age three and age seventy-three."[2]

Preachers have always used story to some degree, but what was once a trickle has fast become a wave. Narrative is the fastest-growing category of preaching across denominational lines, perhaps because people respond so well to it.

How to Tell a Story

The model for the narrative preacher is the novelist or perhaps the screenwriter. Rather than seeing the sermon as a linear presentation of ideas, the preacher-novelist sees the presentation as a succession of scenes. The power of this approach is that truth is embedded in the context of life. Ideas are offered as images that remind listeners and readers of their personal experience. Relevance is not merely required; it is rooted in the fabric of the story. Relevance is intrinsic to the form.

Insight and Ideas | MULTISTORY SERMONS

I remember one of my mentors cautioning me against "skyscraper sermons"—sermons that simply pile one story on top of another. Yet while this is a concern, it is also true that biblical sermons need to intersect several narrative levels:

His Story

Their Story

Our Story

Their Story

The experience of the original characters and recipients of the biblical text.

Our Story

The human experience that we and our listeners bring to the sermon.

His Story

The grand story of God's redemptive work with people over time.

Storytelling is both inductive and affective. It is *inductive* in that it is set in life and unfolds in time. The "moral of the story" is usually the final piece, established only after the story has made sense of it. The truth the story teaches is earned like a piece of land gained in battle. Crisis, conflict, and tension must be resolved before the big idea can be affirmed and assimilated into life. Story allows the listener to engage in this process of discovery by getting involved intellectually and emotionally in the unfolding of the plot.

Stories work *affectively* as well because they involve listeners at the level of the heart before connecting with their minds. People connect with stories because they identify with the characters. They have lived the situations or something like them. The story becomes more than hypothetical. The listener owns the story and feels the implications as the telling rolls on.

We like stories because we live in the medium of story. Presentations that abstract and disembody principles may help me put some logic and structure to my thought, but they do not match the shape of my life. My life is plotted, not outlined. I live in time, one event after another. Sermons that are built in "time" more than in "space" have a better chance of capturing the moment and helping me meet with God. That is why a story works so well.

Insight and Ideas | TELL STORIES TO YOUR CHILDREN

If you want to learn how to tell stories, practice on your children. If you don't have any children of your own, volunteer for nursery duty. Reading children's stories is a great way of getting a feel for the way a story works. Even when speaking to adults, we could afford to be a lot more animated in our communication.

Of course, the Bible is a story—a grand story (metanarrative)—of God's offer of grace to his rebellious children. While the Bible is a story, it also contains stories, some of the best tales known to humankind. Stories like "David and Goliath" are now archetypes that play themselves out in the popular novels and movies of our time. Narrative is a staple of Scripture.

The stories in the Bible, though, are not without intention. The Bible has an agenda and so must the preachers who proclaim its truths. Stories are able to provide an environment in which a deeper sense of truth can be forged. Some of the truths in Scripture are mysterious and ambiguous. A straight telling of the deep things of God can seem difficult and obtuse. Stories (and parables) help us live with the truth of the message without necessarily locking down all of the cognitive implications.

C. S. Lewis is known for his disciplined mind and his strong articulation of apologetic logic. Yet it was this understanding of story that finally drew him to the Christian faith. Logic brought him to the place where he could believe in the existence of the creator God. Yet to believe in the premise of a substitutionary atonement seemed foolish to him. His friend J. R. R. Tolkien was able to help him see how the gospel is a story told by God himself. Like the ancient human myths, the gospel story is a means of communicating wisdom, except this time God himself is not only the storyteller but the lead character as well.[3] Lewis went on to become a master storyteller, offering the gospel narrative in the form of a delightful children's saga, The Chronicles of Narnia.[4]

Discussion Question 21 | CAN STORIES PROCLAIM?

One of the reasons people like stories so much is that they are not necessarily demanding. Stories tend to leave interpretation to the listener, which runs counter to our sense of preaching as proclamation. Is a story, then, a viable medium for proclamation? Or does story offer too much room for the listener to create his or her own version of the truth?

Of course, to speak of story is to paint with a very broad brush. Narrative takes a number of forms. Stories can take the shape of history, a factual account of past events, or a story can be a memory, vaguely recalled and fondly reminisced. Stories don't even have to be factual. Fiction is probably the most common shape of stories told today, yet fiction itself can take any number of forms. Fiction is written in novels, told as jokes, drawn as cartoons, presented on stages, and filmed for the silver screen. Sometimes stories are invented for serious purposes, for instance, when a teacher uses a case study to educate her students or when a politician uses a story as a metaphor for some great principle of public life. Other times stories are shaped as fairy tales intended to teach children about the binary experiences of human life, like good and evil, comfort and danger, love and fear. Peter Rabbit is tempted by the garden, but he fears Mr. MacGregor's wrath. Such stories will never lose their power.

Stories offer us comedy or tragedy. They take us on a journey, or they lead us on a quest. They take us from death to life, explore the justice of crime and punishment, tempt us and rescue us or leave us suffering in pain. They take us from rags to riches, from risk to reward, and from ignorance to truth.[5] Because stories so readily fit such timeless categories, we quickly find residence inside their housing. Stories work because we identify with them, and we love to rehearse the implications through retelling the story with a new and altered setting.

For all its promise, however, narrative has only recently come to be appreciated as a critical component of biblical preaching. Traditional preaching has tended to view narrative as incidental to the critical task of explaining and applying propositional truth. Narrative has been understood to be a supportive element at best and an unwelcome distraction at worst. The narrative preaching movement has sought to swing the pendulum. Noting the dominance of narrative form in Scripture, these "new homileticians"[6] have sought fresh ways to construct sermons that allow listeners to respond in a more engaging environment. These preachers have been criticized for everything from offering mere entertainment to providing a malevolent subversion. Both of these criticisms are off the mark, but only to a degree.

Entertainment is a worthy goal if the word is understood correctly. *Entertain* literally means "to hold the attention." Surely this must be a key objective of any preacher worth listening to. At the same time, if by *entertain* we mean to titillate or to merely amuse, we have not properly understood our task. Perhaps we would be more comfortable with the word *engage* instead of *entertain*. Sermons intend to do more than provide pleasure. Yet they need not always be painful. Preachers need to engage their audiences, and nothing is more engaging than a tale well told.

The idea that narrative preaching is subversive is a more important criticism. It can be shown that the "new homiletic" has roots in postmodern language theories and theologies.[7] A story is more elastic than a proposition, which leaves some who are committed to proclamation uncomfortable. Storytellers may have intentions, yet those intentions are not necessarily made explicit in the tale. The risk is that the listener can take on more responsibility for the creation of truth than what you as a preacher might desire. If the truth is not made clear, listeners could very well make of it whatever they will, which is a little frightening to those of us who see our role as ones who make God's truth known.

Discussion Question 22 | MUST PREACHING BE MONOLOGICAL?

Traditionally, preaching has been a monologue—one person speaking without interruption. Increasingly, however, preachers are exploring more interactive formats, including discussion and dialogue. Must preaching be monological, or does it depend on the size and nature of the audience? Is there something about a small group, for instance, that lends itself to a more interactive approach?

Of course, we can always make the truth overt as we come to the end of our narrative, like the fable teller who ends with "the moral of the story." Yet preachers might well be concerned. It is true that truth-telling has been set aside in recent years by those who prefer story precisely because of its ambiguity. These storytellers would rather let the listener create her or his conclusions, which runs counter to the biblical sense of preaching as proclamation.

Yet this idea that stories are completely open to the listener's appropriation is not entirely true to the nature of a story. Any consistent postmodern would admit that stories are never unencumbered by authorial intent. Stories are always shaped by their tellers. Even the most prosaic forms of history are biased by the selection and perspective of the historian. Storytellers never tell everything that could be told. Narrators choose what they will tell in order to communicate the message that they have in mind.

This is what it means to say that a story is plotted. In technical terms, narration describes a simple telling of events in sequence. To speak of a "plot" is to introduce the element of cause. Temporal succession is concerned with only the "and then" principle: this happened *and then* this other thing happened. Causality introduces the notion of "that's why" or "therefore": this happened, therefore this next thing happened.[8] Causality gives the story its sense of plot. The cause orientation of a plot invokes a sense of meaning. There are reasons for the things that happen in our stories. These reasons intend to leave a mark on the reader or listener.

Discussion Question 23 | LINEAR OR NONLINEAR?

Increasingly, television shows, books, and movies are moving away from linear presentations toward a series of nonlinear vignettes as a means of telling the story. An episode of the television drama *ER*, for instance, can feature as many as fifteen different story lines. Is this a model we could utilize in preaching? Or would a nonlinear approach confuse our listeners and do damage to the logic of our message?

This is not a problem for the preacher, who never intended to leave the listener unscathed. Preaching, particularly biblical preaching, intends to shape the hearer according to God's intention, whether or not the preaching is narrative. Storytelling is a great way to leave this kind of mark.

How does one tell a story? For most of us, storytelling comes naturally. We simply tell a story the way we experienced it. Analysis, however, helps us identify elements common to good storytelling.

1. Identify the Characters

A story is not a story without characters. This is the story's greatest strength. We are not talking in abstractions but are considering real people who live and breathe and sweat just as we do. Even when the characters in a story are animals or are inanimate, they tend to be personified (remember Peter Rabbit or the Man in the Moon) so that we can more readily identify with them.

Characterization is primarily about the "being." The "doing" simply allows the reader or listener to appreciate the character's "being." Ultimately, a good story is all about the "being." What kind of people are we talking about? Are these people kind or cruel, gentle or harsh, loving or fearful? The more clearly drawn they are, the more we can connect.

Insight and Ideas | CHARACTERIZATION

The Protagonist

The main character, around whom the events unfold.

The Antagonist

A major character in conflict with the protagonist.

The Foil

A major character who elevates the protagonist by providing a contrast or parallel.

The storyteller needs to consider the perspective from which the story will be told. Is the teller a disembodied narrator, or will the story be told from the perspective of one of the characters? If the narrator is thus embedded in the story line, will he be one of the major characters, or will he be on the periphery? Not every character bears equal weight in the story's flow. While every human is equal in the eyes of God, such is not the case in the mind of the storyteller. Shaping the story involves the selection of certain individuals for primary focus. Plot writers speak of the *protagonist*, or the main character around whom all the events unfold. The *antagonist* is another major character whose values or behavior conflicts with that of the protagonist, or hero. Another major character is the *foil*, or the person in the story who elevates the protagonist by providing a contrast or parallel.[9]

Edgar Allen Poe begins his story "The Tell-Tale Heart" with his protagonist's description of his foil: "I loved the old man. He had never wronged me. He had never given me insult. For his gold I had no desire. I think it was his eye! Yes, it was this! He had the eye of a vulture—a pale blue eye, with a film over it. Whenever it fell upon me, my blood ran cold; and so by degrees—very gradually—I made up my mind to take the life of the old man, and thus rid myself of the eye forever."[10] Through this description, we learn more about the protagonist and his madness, though the physical description is all about the foil. Poe offers us a character study that can teach us as much about ourselves as about the relatively disposable characters in the story.

2. Establish the Setting

Where and when the story happens is important if we are going to understand exactly what happens. The setting of the story establishes the time and place in which the events occur.

The place where the events occur is not primary to a story, but it is never incidental. While the setting is seldom the focus of the story, where things happen has a critical impact on how things unfold. This is another way of affirming the importance of context as an interpretive element.

Resource Recommendation | FIRST-PERSON DRAMATIC SERMONS

A popular way of preaching narrative sermons is the *first-person dramatic monologue*. In this form of sermon, the preacher takes the "Hello, my name is Paul (or Peter or Philemon)" approach. While preaching in this manner requires some dramatic flair, it can be a welcome addition to the listener's homiletic diet.

For further help, see J. Kent Edwards, *Effective First-Person Biblical Preaching: The Steps from Text to Narrative Sermon* (Zondervan, 2005).

Spending time in Europe has awakened me to the way that geography affects events. I've been startled to notice how radically the people change from place to place. In the morning, we travel from one place and its people only to encounter an entirely different people by the time we stop for lunch. From morning to afternoon, we find people radically altered in terms of culture, language, and even physical appearance. The people of Holland have been shaped by the confines of their landscape, just as their neighbors in Germany are influenced by theirs. The Gaelic speakers in the Hebrides are profoundly different from their English-speaking countrymen on the Scottish mainland. One day I was overwhelmed to encounter four different language groups and at least five different cultures in the space of an afternoon's drive.

It may be, of course, that Europe is unique, but when it comes to storytelling, the principle remains. The reader or listener will not know the characters until they know where they live and get a sense of the physical dimensions and the culture of the place. While in Amsterdam, we visited the Anne Frank House, and I have since taken the opportunity to read her famous story. In *The Diary of Anne Frank*, the house becomes a kind of character in the events as they unfold. Anne takes pains to describe the physical layout of "the secret annexe" with its close confines and its "ankle-twisting flights of stairs." "I've probably bored you with my long description of our house," Anne writes, "but I still think you should know where I have ended up."[11]

Indeed, Anne's story is defined by her physical space and the stifling sameness of its confines even as her once-familiar neighborhood is transformed by ethnic cleansing and desperate poverty. "I'm sitting here nice and cosy in the front office," she writes, "peering through a chink in the heavy curtains. It's dark but there is just enough light to write by. It's really strange watching people walk past. They all seem to be in such a hurry that they nearly trip over their own feet. Those on bicycles whiz by so fast I can't even tell who's on the bike. The people in this neighbourhood aren't particularly attractive. The children especially are so dirty you wouldn't want to touch them with a bargepole."[12]

Of course, Anne's story is as much about time as it is about place. Such is always the case. When events occur is just as important as where they occur. The beautiful canal street where Anne Frank once lived is as different a place today as Venice is from Vancouver. Events are never static; everything always changes over time.

Practical Exercise 17 | EMOTIONAL TIMELINE

Chart the impact of your sermon to get a visual sense of how your message will affect your listeners.

On the left side of your chart, draw a vertical line and mark it one to five. This line measures the level of emotional intensity given to the sermon.

Draw a horizontal line along the bottom of the chart, connecting in the bottom left corner with the vertical line. This line measures the time allotted to the sermon. Along this line, show each change of focus, or movement, in the sermon. This is your timeline.

Now graph the intended level of emotional intensity for each movement of the sermon across the timeline.

Study the chart to understand the shape and movement of the sermon. Having preached the sermon, you may want to make a second chart to compare your intention with reality.

Rick Warren describes his experience as a consultant for the movie *The Prince of Egypt*. "One day," he said, "I was in the hall at Dreamworks, and I noticed something on the wall called an 'Emotional Beat Chart.' They actually monitor the emotional highs and lows of a movie. I counted up and there were nine peaks and nine valleys in this 90 minute movie—about every ten minutes there's tension/release, tension/release. Well, you can do that in a message."

Rick Warren, "Purpose-Driven Preaching: An Interview with Rick Warren," by Michael Duduit, *Preaching* 17, no. 2 (September–October 2001): 14.

3. Order the Events

A storyteller never tells everything that happened. It simply isn't possible, nor would it be wise. A storyteller selects just those events that are necessary and orders them so as to achieve the desired impact. The classic ordering of a narrative begins with *exposition*, in which the characters and setting are established; followed by the introduction of some kind of *crisis*; which is then followed by the *climax*, or highest point of tension; and ends with the *denouement*, when everything is resolved and a renewed future is embraced. The storyteller works to build and hold tension in the listener or reader for as long as possible because that tension is what holds one's attention. Our longing for resolution keeps the story vital. The irony, of course, is that if the reader or listener had the resolution that they wanted, there would be no story and thus no reason to pay attention. A life without tension might be idyllic, peaceful, or otherwise relaxing, but wouldn't be interesting to anyone else.

A story is always told subsequent to the events in the story, which gives the narrator full control over the telling. This is not a question of truthfulness. A story is always the teller's fiction, even though the story might be "based on true events." Effective screenwriters know historical veracity stands second to the writer's need to communicate. The storyteller is allowed license over the process in order to say something to the audience. Any high school student knows that bare history is the driest dust unless the teacher can convey a sense of meaning. Storytellers shape the history to communicate meaning to their audience. If they didn't, there would be no market for their story.

Another way that narrators control meaning in their stories is by giving attention to narrative time, particularly the matters of *duration* and *pace*. Real events are measured by the clock. They take as long as they take. Storytellers, however, have time limits. Events will be expanded or compressed to fit the allotted time.

Storytellers can shape the reader's or listener's emotional or affective response by how they present the events of a story. Preachers who master the ability to identify the characters, establish the setting, and order the events will connect powerfully with their listeners.

How to Preach the Narrative Sermon

Narrative is an appropriate form for biblical preaching, if for no other reason than that it conforms to the way much of Scripture is presented. The Bible opens with the story of God's creative action and ends with a story yet to be fulfilled, when Jesus Christ returns and brings all things into accordance with his will. If the Bible can use stories to communicate God's Word, then surely so can preachers.

Stories involve listeners in a powerful inductive process of discovery, operating on an affective level to deepen the listener's capacity to respond in obedience to God. The preacher who knows how to tell stories will not fail to interest listeners. They may not always be convinced, but they will always listen if the story is well told.

Narrative preachers begin with the story that the Bible gives them. More like the declarative sermon than the pragmatic sermon in this regard, most narrative sermons that are rooted in the Scriptures will identify a particular text wherein the preacher finds his or her focus. The passage does not necessarily have to be a narrative passage. If such were the case, narrative preachers would be forced to work with a truncated Bible. But every text in Scripture offers a story because every piece of the Bible is set in real human history. The Bible is about people. It is not an abstract document. I like to remind myself that there is story even in the book of Romans because there really were Romans; they lived in Rome! Narrative preachers are skilled at delivering the propositions of Bible texts—even didactic texts—in the context of the human experience of the authors and the original audiences of the texts.

Resource Recommendation | OLD TESTAMENT NARRATIVE

Steven Mattheuson's *The Art of Preaching Old Testament Narrative* (Baker, 2002) is an excellent resource for understanding biblical narrative of any kind, but particularly that found in the Old Testament.

Remember that using stories as the formative element of the sermon is more than using illustration. Traditional illustrations are limited to the illumination or colorization of propositions. A full-bodied homiletic of story will honor the narrative as central to the text and to the sermon. Narrative does not simply serve to spice up the stuff of the sermon (the arguments). The story is the stuff, particularly in texts that present ideas in story form. Remember that a narrative sermon is plotted, not outlined. While ideas are intended, the proposition is not the narrative preacher's primary tool.

Perhaps the best way to conceive a narrative sermon or to read a narrative text in Scripture is to think the way a filmmaker would see the plot. Identifying the "shots" that make up each "scene" will allow you to more readily visualize and experience the way the plot unfolds.

In a wonderful piece called "How to Preach like John Grisham Writes," Bill Oudemolen describes his journey "from principle to plot" in his desire to involve his listeners more deeply in receiving God's Word. Contrary to what many would suspect, Oudemolen found the process harder, not easier, than the traditional principle-focused sermon he was accustomed to delivering. "Producing sermon principles is easy," he said. "Creating sermonic plot is arduous. To help me produce better plot-based sermons, I read fiction, take in movies and dramas, listen carefully to the stories of those who see me for pastoral care, and pay attention to the lyrics of country music.... But perhaps, more than anything, the disequilibrium of my own story fuels my creativity most."[13] This is good advice. Preachers looking to approach their preaching with authenticity need only look to their own lives to find substance for their sermons.

Insight and Ideas | HOW TO PREACH LIKE JOHN GRISHAM WRITES

- Start with surprise.
- Build tension.
- Wrap it up.

Here, then, are some suggested steps to the narrative sermon.

1. Pray Your Way into the Story

No less than any other form of preaching, the narrative preacher must begin with prayer. Narrative preachers know better than anyone that the sermon is not intended as abstraction. The preacher must get personally involved. There is no better way to do that than through prayer. The first step to appreciating what God is saying through a portion of his Word is to pray one's way into it.

I suggest that you engage in a specific kind of prayerful reading of the text. I'm asking you to read the text from the perspective of the various participants, seeking God's wisdom as you do. Make an investment in the text, listening closely for the Spirit as you find your own place within his Word. This will take time, but it is time well spent.

2. Involve the Listener

The greatest strength of the narrative sermon is its ability to connect listeners with Bible texts and to get them to invest in the sermon process. This will happen organically and not mechanically if the preacher tells the story well.

The text itself is the most powerful tool the preacher has for encouraging a connection, because the Bible features people. At the very least, someone wrote the text and expected someone else would read it. Who were those people, and what was going on in their experience? How does your own life experience and that of those around you mirror that of these people?

Insight and Ideas | GOD IS THE PROTAGONIST

In biblical narratives, God is always the protagonist. While it is important to note the human characters operating in the story, never forget that God is always the prime actor. Life in the Bible, like life on earth, is shaped and framed by the intent of God.

What about the people described in the passages? Can you see yourself in the shoes of each of the characters? What would it feel like to be paralyzed and lying on a mat as your friends lowered you into a crowded room (Mark 2:1–12)? If you can't relate to that, perhaps you can identify with the inventive friend who, frustrated by the crowds, came up with the idea of going through the roof. Can you imagine standing inside the house and hearing strange sounds coming from the ceiling? Imagine what Jesus was thinking, his sermon interrupted, as the debris began to fall.

Working with stories requires a sensual kind of thinking. What does the listener see? What does the text feel like—taste like—smell like? I want to feel the strain of the ropes against my fingers as I let my friend down and hear the thud when his body hits the floor too suddenly. The more I can imagine the details of the story, the more my listener is going to be able to appreciate the meaning. It will require some imagination, but as long as I don't allow my fancy to violate anything that is overtly given in the text, I will not mislead my listeners.

A key to this kind of storytelling is to work with a sense of immediacy. Stories increase in power as they increase in proximity. The most relevant stories are the ones that are offered in the present tense rather than in the distant past. Preachers ought to challenge themselves to tell their stories as if they are happening now rather than telling them as if they have already happened, sometime deep in history. Historians are fine people, and some of them can really spin a yarn, but narrative preaching intends more than a meaningful recounting of events. The power of the biblical story is not located in the distant past. We believe that the Bible is a dynamic book that speaks ancient truths from ancient places to current people in current places. God is speaking through his Word, and we must speak with an urgency that shows we know that he is speaking. Stories that adopt a present-tense experience of the story will create an immediate event in which God speaks in a moment in time.

Insight and Ideas | ONCE UPON A TIME

Beginning the narrative sermon is as easy as saying, "Once upon a time ..." All you are trying to do is to identify the characters and establish the setting. If you describe real people in real time, your listeners will find themselves able to come along and see what happens.

While the biblical story is always primary to the narrative preacher, a contemporary story can also be used to great effect. Sometimes this can be done by recasting the biblical story in a contemporary setting. In one of my sermons, I had Martha using a microwave while Jesus sat with Mary in the living room. My listeners were smart enough to know that microwave ovens are a recent invention. I'm quite certain no one was confused. I was trying to help them appreciate the events of the story in the context of their own lives today. After all, what we learn needs to be applied in our lives today.

People magazine does not sell millions of copies for nothing. Everybody is interested in other people, so that is where we will begin. Our primary objective in the opening moves of the narrative sermon is to help the listener care. We will do that by describing credible, likable characters in familiar settings to whom we find ourselves wanting to connect.

3. Create a Crisis

It seems a shame that we have to put these characters we like so much into crisis, but without tension, there is no story. If you are like me, you sit in the theater crying for the hero to be spared, only to realize that if your desire were granted, you would have no reason to be in the theater at all.

This should not surprise us, given that it is the nature of the Bible. The grand story (metanarrative) of Scripture describes humanity's problem and God's solution. The problem is that we wanted to handle life on our own terms. Unwisely, we rejected God and condemned ourselves to eternal death. Talk about a crisis!

Listeners are always going to have a problem with the Bible. The Bible always comes to us as a challenge. It runs against our grain, pushing us in directions we would really rather not have to consider. The Bible calls us to spend significant portions of our income on an investment that promises to pay only in some future spiritual dimension. The Bible asks people to give up their jobs and live in near poverty for the sake of mission overseas. The Bible asks us to risk our hard-won relationships by engaging our nonbelieving friends in conversations about religion. It is a lot to ask of us. But then that is what makes preaching what it is. Preaching without tension would not be preaching.

In the case of Jesus' healing of the paralytic (Mark 2:1 – 12), the crisis or critical moment is found in verse 5. The friends have persevered, the meeting has been interrupted, the man is lying on his litter on the floor as everyone looks to Jesus to see what he will say. A strange light from the gash in the ceiling makes the falling dust sparkle and shine. I imagine Jesus pausing and looking curiously at the unfortunate man on the ground before him. No one is prepared for what Jesus is about to do.

"Son, your sins are forgiven." He looks up as he says it, fixing the challenge of his gaze on the religious leaders at the back of the room.

The Pharisees are now the ones who are in crisis as they sense their authority slipping. Why is he talking like this? This is blasphemy. Why didn't he just heal the man and be done with it? What gives him the right ...? They are thinking it, though they haven't gotten up the courage yet to say it.

Insight and Ideas | THE RESOLUTION OF TENSION

The resolution of crisis is the "big idea" of the narrative sermon. Effective narrative sermons will offer resolution in the form of a proposition, much as a storyteller offers the "moral of the story." Of course, a sermon offers more than just a good moral thought; it offers theological truth that is *portrayed* by the characters in and out of the Bible.

You recall the story. As a narrative preacher, you want your listeners to feel the shock of Jesus' words almost as much as the original audience did. You want them to feel the uncertain surprise of the paralyzed man, the disappointment, perhaps, of the friends on the roof looking down through the hole. You want them to feel the fury of the Pharisees, who never backed down from a challenge. Everyone is on the razor's edge, including your listeners. The degree to which you can recreate this sense of crisis in the moment of your sermon might be the degree to which you can affect your listeners' souls.

4. Resolve the Tension

Once the strain has been stretched as far as possible, or as far as time allows, the preacher then moves to resolve the tension. Here is where the narrative sermon comes to a point of culmination. Following Rick Warren's "emotional beat chart," the sermon is now at its highest peak. As the "big idea" is to the declarative sermon, or the "answer to the question" is to the pragmatic sermon, the "resolution of tension" is the focus of the narrative sermon. While at its core the resolution will always hinge on a big idea, that idea is portrayed or played out by the characters within the story. It must be so. We have come to care about these characters, and they are in trouble. The listener has to know what is going to happen. We have to see them through.

Earlier I mentioned my reading of Anne Frank's diary. I found the ending of the book to be unpleasant. As I approached the book's conclusion, I had an increasing sense of dread. I knew how the story would end, and I didn't like it much. Irrationally, I found myself hoping that somehow the book would end differently from how I knew it must.

Anne's diary ends with an ordinary entry. Nothing indicates that her hiding place had been discovered and that she was days away from the concentration camp and a horrible death. It is a diary, and tragically, it just ends. There is no resolution—no denouement—and no hope. It doesn't end like stories are supposed to end. The story ends too much like life does. Of course, I am not criticizing the book. It has great value as a record of history, as the portrayal of a young woman in extraordinary circumstances, and as a cautionary tale, but it certainly isn't gospel.

Insight and Ideas | SHOTS AND SCENES

Playwrights write "scenes," while filmmakers think in terms of "shots." Scenes unfold at length in a single context. Shots move much more quickly, shifting point of view and changing context rapidly. As a narrative preacher, it will be helpful first to view your sermon as a series of scenes and then to break those scenes down into shots. This, by the way, is a helpful way to read narrative texts in Scripture.

Narrative preaching will never leave the listener wanting. In the narrative sermon we always have the opportunity to live happily ever after because in Christ there is always hope. There is always an opportunity for resolution.

The resolution is what makes the sermon gospel. Biblical preaching doesn't leave people with their despair. Preaching is always the proclamation of good news. Movies are sometimes rightly criticized for the characteristic "Hollywood ending," in which every problem is overcome, every note of discord is harmonized, and everyone lives happily ever after. Of course, life isn't like that. But who wants to pay good money to sit at the theater and see what we see all around us every day of our lives? Preachers are supposed to offer something better than anything life presents. The preacher offers a gospel of hope based on the grace of God and the sacrifice of Jesus Christ. The preacher brings good news. Narrative preaching always has a happy ending.

Jesus can read the people's minds. Not even the Pharisees appreciate the significance of what Jesus has done like Jesus himself does. Everything was intentional. He knew exactly what he was doing.

Softly he speaks to his critics. His words are a little condescending yet with a hint of encouragement. Jesus leaves no doubt as to whom he thinks he is. "Why are you thinking these things?" he asks. "Which is harder—to heal the man, or to forgive his sins? But so you know that the Son of Man has authority on earth to forgive sins ..." His words trail off as he turns to the paralytic, who had been momentarily forgotten by everyone but Jesus.

"Get up," he says, gentleness in his voice. "Take your mat and go home."

No one speaks as the man does exactly as he is told. Silently the crowd steps aside, letting him walk toward the door, a little uncertainly at first, but then with greater confidence. The man's friends, lying prone on the roof, have their heads stretched through the hole in the ceiling, their eyes wide and mouths open.

Just before exiting the door, the man pauses and looks back toward Jesus, unsure of what to say.

Jesus smiles. Nothing more is necessary.

Resource Recommendation | PREACHING TODAY

Preaching Today is a great source of some of the best sermons preached today. These sermons, available on CD or cassette, will feed your soul while stimulating your thinking about the sermons you preach. The Preaching Today website is also a great source of ideas, illustrations, and information: www.preachingtoday.com.

Sometimes the happy ending is surprising. Sometimes it brings a sense of satisfaction like you get when you fit the last piece of a puzzle. Sometimes the resolution offers us something new that we have never known or thought before. Other times it reminds us of things we have known but have mentally misplaced. Whichever it does, it satisfies.

5. Realize the Hope

Any good story has its denouement—the moment at the end of the story when we walk off into the sunset, knowing that life is good and that we will be better because we have caught a glimpse of something wonderful.

Don't you love those moments at the end of the Disney movies—or most other movies, for that matter—when the Little Mermaid marries Eric, the beast becomes a handsome prince, and the animals gather on Pride Rock to sing together one last time? It just doesn't happen that way in life, but then I guess that's why we pay our money to see these movies. The happy ending will last only about as long as the popcorn, but then what can you expect for ten dollars? When everyone lives happily ever after, you know the screenwriters have been more hopeful than they have been honest.

Yet the preacher knows no such problem with integrity. Of course, the listener will have to show a little patience, but ultimately you and I know that the day will come when we will all gather and sing that big production number at the end of the movie.

That song is a song of worship—"You are worthy, our Lord and God, to receive glory and honor and power" (Rev. 4:11)—and everyone in Christ will get a chance to sing it. We do not promise that everything will be right and good immediately, but ultimately we will have our happily ever after, and that is good news.

Insight and Ideas | HOLD SOMETHING BACK

The best storytellers know to hold something back. Don't reveal everything in the first moments of the sermon; keep a surprise in hand for later in the sermon. The moment of discovery will deepen the impact of the sermon as a whole.

It took only a moment after the paralytic left for the cheering to start. "We have never seen anything like this," people said as they turned to praising God. I imagine Jesus slipping unnoticed from the room. Perhaps he caught up with the paralytic for a little more conversation. Perhaps he went home another way. Either way, no one present would see the world the same again.

The narrative sermon concludes with the realization of hope. The listener is encouraged to move on in the realization of God's promise. A cognitive sermon concludes with a concrete application. The narrative sermon offers application, but it is described in terms of the listener's life. Now the spotlight shifts to focus squarely on the listener. We are no longer talking about the life of a third-party protagonist. Now we are telling the listener's own story, imagining the possibilities as she makes the message of the sermon meaningful in the context of her own life.

For Example: Eugene Lowry

Eugene Lowry was one of the first preachers to describe the narrative sermon. While Lowry is not well known within evangelical circles, his preaching and writing have been highly influential. I remember reading his writings twenty years ago. As a young pastor, I was tantalized by his suggestion that sermons could be plotted instead of outlined. I agreed with his observation that sometimes the flow and movement of a Bible text ought not to be restricted to three points.[14]

For Lowry, the sermon is an organic entity that exists in time rather than in space. The sermon must unfold, just like real life. "When confronted by the intricacies of real events as people actually experience them in time, our pat and precise definitions do not work. And most of us know all of this quite well in our usual rounds of ministry. But get us in the pulpit, and all of a sudden life turns simple, clear, and unambiguous!"[15]

Sermon Example | SWEPT UPSTREAM
Mark 14:1–10

This sermon, taken from Mark 14:1–10, tells the story of Mary's breaking of the jar of perfume and pouring it over Jesus' feet. It was published in Richard Eslinger's *A New Hearing* (Abingdon, 1987).

Lowry tells the biblical story in leisurely fashion, taking time to explore the implications as they play out among the people. He describes the dinner party as a somber event. The guests are aware of Jesus' impending execution — when all of a sudden "this woman bursts in." The scandal is her wasteful use of resources. Surely Jesus would rebuke her — except that he doesn't.

Lowry raises the obvious questions: Why didn't Jesus understand the logic of their objection? Why didn't they understand the nature of her gesture? Why didn't he see the waste? Why didn't they see the grace?

But, Lowry shows us, this was no time for depression; this was a time to celebrate the gracious work that Jesus was doing. This was a woman "swept upstream with gratitude," and as the listener experiences her joy, we find ourselves wanting to respond the same way.

For Lowry, plots allow a subtler treatment than the bold, bald outlines that lay out the preacher's propositions in the cold light of day. The narrative sermon, he says, is more about God's activity than about God's explanations. "Those who order ideas, virtually disregarding their theological positions, will have understanding as the bottom line.... Likewise, those who order experience ... will move toward some kind of happening."[16] This, he believes, will always offer a deeper, more profound encounter with God. "Put simply, I am asserting that when preaching turns narrative it always says more than we know (propositionally) and hence potentially opens the door for deep calling unto deep."[17]

The thing I find so interesting about Lowry's approach is that he does not limit himself to narrative texts in Scripture. His model can be applied to any text, narrative or not. Whether or not the text is given in story form, the story can inject the ideas of the Bible into the lives of the listeners.

This objective is achieved through the famous "Lowry Loop." The loop is a five-step narrative process designed to lead the listener inductively and affectively along a path from disequilibrium to resolution, guided by God's Word. "Because a sermon is an *event-in-time*—existing in time, not space—a process and not a collection of parts, it is helpful to think of sequence rather than structure."[18] Lowry's approach to plotting the narrative sermon has been given in a memorable shorthand: (1) Oops, (2) Ugh, (3) Aha, (4) Whee, and (5) Yeah.

1. Oops. Lowry's loop begins by "upsetting the equilibrium."[19] This is how he gathers the listener's interest. Lowry believes that the preacher needs to take responsibility for the listener's ability to engage the theme of the sermon. The best way to achieve this, he believes, is through intentional ambiguity. Something is missing. Something is wrong. Something needs to be completed, and the listener will not rest until things are put to right.

Insight and Ideas | THE LOWRY LOOP

Oops
upsetting the equilibrium

Ugh
analyzing the discrepancy

Aha
disclosing the clue to resolution

Whee
experiencing the gospel

Yeah
anticipating the consequences

2. Ugh. The second movement is "analyzing the discrepancy."[20] This is the most difficult aspect of the sermon, according to Lowry, and it requires the most time. The chief requirement of this analysis is a deep and careful diagnosis of the problem, which sets the stage for the Word to be proclaimed.

3. Aha. The third stage is labeled "disclosing the clue to resolution." "All problem-solving processes, whether scientific endeavors, literary plots, medical diagnoses, dime-store puzzles, or preaching on Sunday morning, look for some missing link, some explanation which accounts for the problematic issue."[21] We live in a world of cause and effect. Where there is a problem, there must be a solution. Given that we are talking about the gospel, which counters any human answer, the preacher's solution often requires a kind of reversal, or a pulling of the rug out from under the listener's feet. This is specifically true of biblical narratives and of the parables in particular. The challenge is to lead the listener to that "Aha!" moment when the gospel becomes true for him or her.

4. Whee. The fourth stage of Lowry's Loop is "experiencing the gospel."[22] Once the clue to resolution has been disclosed, listeners are ready to hear the gospel. It is the preacher's pleasure to give them what they are looking for.

5. Yeah. The final move in the homiletical plot is "anticipating the consequences."[23] Because the gospel is ultimately eschatological, the results are not necessarily felt immediately, but the way has been opened and the opportunity now exists. "In the sermonic plot, the clue to resolution does not 'solve' the issues; it only makes the solution now possible."[24]

In his more recent work, Lowry revised his program, suggesting that "experiencing the gospel" can occur at any time, though about three-quarters of the way through the sermon is usually best.[25] Regardless of whether the movement occurs in five stages or four, the unfolding nature of the sermon is its critical feature. Listeners are able to participate in the formation of the sermon as it comes across their consciousness in time instead of in space.

Template for the Narrative Sermon

Preacher: ________________ **Date:** ______________ **Text:** ____________

Title (Subtitle): ____

Good titles are creative and compelling, offering listeners a reason to listen without giving too much away.

The Setting: ____

____

Describe the place and time in which the sermon (and perhaps the text) is set.

The Protagonist: ____

____

Who is (are) the major character(s) in the story, and what is their primary need or motivation?

The Antagonist: ______________________________

____

Who is in conflict with the protagonist and why?

The Foil: ______________________________

____

Who is elevating the protagonist's conflict and how?

The Crisis: ______________________________

____

____

The crisis is the pivotal point of tension in the sermon story. Describe the issue in need of resolution.

Resolution of the Tension: ______________________________

____

____

The resolution is the theme of the narrative sermon. Describe how the crisis will be resolved.

The Hope: ______________________________

____

____

Describe the ways in which listeners will respond to the good news offered by the sermon story.

Example of the Narrative Sermon

Preacher: Eugene Lowry **Date:** 1991 **Text:** Matthew 18:22–35

Title: Down the Up Staircase

The Setting: The sermon is set in and around the chamber of the king. Lowry retains the biblical setting but describes it in fairly contemporary present-tense language to create a sense that the events are happening today. It is important to note that Jesus told this story in response to Peter's questions about forgiveness ("How many times should I forgive?").

The Protagonist: Known by gospel readers as "the unmerciful servant," the protagonist of this story is a man who is heavily in debt and who is struggling to deal with his inability to pay.

The Antagonist: The antagonist is the king, who is holding the servant to account. "Servant, it says here you owe me a lot of money. . . ."

The Foil: The foil is an unnamed man who owes the king's servant a relatively small amount of money.

The Crisis: The servant begs the king for mercy. The king obliges. The servant then encounters a man who owes him next to nothing and has him thrown into jail for his inability to pay. How is it that a man who has been forgiven "a million zillion" can have a man thrown into jail for just a few dollars?

Resolution of the Tension: Jesus is telling a joke. Ten thousand talents is a huge amount of money in a time when "the entire annual revenue into the Roman coffers all over the globe was approximately 850 thousand dollars." The man is "in a little over his head." This is the story of a man who "couldn't let himself off the hook."

"The king looks at the bottom line and says to you, 'It says right here you owe me a whole lot of money. In fact, is the figure right? It says a million/zillion that you're indebted. Is that correct?' And every last one of us in this room this morning must answer, 'That is correct, Sir. Indeed, I am heavily in debt. Even 125,000 years of effort would not suffice to repay the debt.' "

"Do you know what that king does? He takes that sheet (your name or mine) and rips it out of the book. He rips it to shreds, looks down at us, and says, 'I forgive you the debt. You are now free and clear. Go in peace.' "

The Hope: In fact, we are the King's servants. We have been forgiven extravagantly. The only question is what we will do when we get to "the bottom of the stairs" and encounter those others who are indebted to us. Those of us who have truly received this forgiveness will not need anyone to tell us what we need to do. Those who have been forgiven, grant forgiveness.

Evaluating the Narrative Sermon

Preacher: ________________ **Date:** ______________ **Text:** ____________

What was the critical point of tension in the story that the preacher told?

____

____

To what degree did you find yourself captivated by this tension?

(circle one) 1 2 3 4 5

How did the preacher resolve the tension?

____

____

To what degree did you find this resolution satisfying?

(circle one) 1 2 3 4 5

What kinds of responses did the preacher challenge you to make?

____

____

How likely are you to follow through and make these responses?

(circle one) 1 2 3 4 5

Describe the preacher's manner and appearance during the event.

____

____

To what degree did the preacher's manner enhance the sermon?

(circle one) 1 2 3 4 5

Offer any further comments you think might be of help.

____

____

____

Chapter 8 | PAINT A PICTURE

the visionary sermon

example: Rob Bell

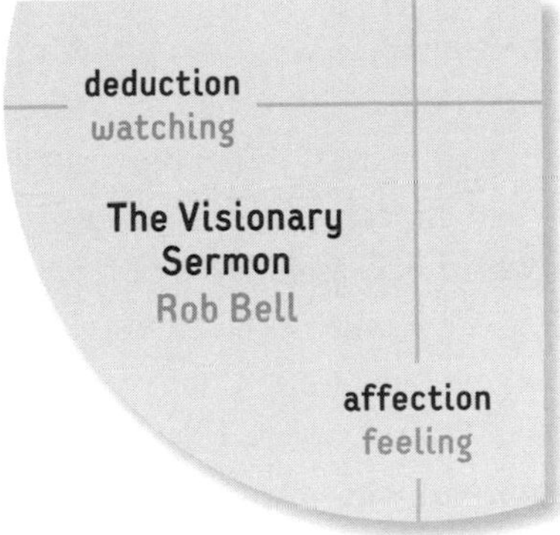

The *visionary* sermon is the dominant manner of preaching in many "emerging" churches. Younger generations of believers seem to be looking for an affective experience that doesn't sacrifice the depth and conviction of deductive preaching. Like an artist, the visionary preacher crafts the sermon into a compelling picture of truth. These preacher-artists appeal to Kolb's "watchers" and "feelers" and to others who welcome a vision of the gospel that challenges and attracts.

My wife is an artist. Among the wonderful things she has given me is an education in art appreciation. None of our vacations are complete without a visit to the gallery. I'm not sure there is a painting on public display in all of London or Vancouver that we have not seen.

All right, that is an exaggeration, though not much of one, and now she has our children involved. All three of our children can tell Monet from

Manet, Dali from Degas, Pissaro from Picasso, and Rembrandt from Renoir. Of course, it is not so difficult once one knows what one is looking for.

Currently our family is on a kind of scavenger hunt for the paintings of the Dutch master Johannes Vermeer. There are only thirty-five Vermeers in existence, a shockingly small number for someone of his stature and for the many years that he painted. We are currently up to thirteen, so we've got a ways to go, but those we have seen so far have been dazzling. I recently stood in front of Vermeer's *The Girl with a Pearl Earring*. I fixed my eye a scant six inches from the earring, looking for the artist's image, which they say can be seen in a reflection on the pearl. It took a little imagination, but I'm pretty sure I saw it.

I have been particularly impressed with Vermeer's way of expressing light and darkness through the use of tiny multicolored dots. This technique required huge amounts of time, but the result is still spectacular centuries later. The sun across the buildings in his portrait of Delft, his hometown, is convincing. From a distance of six or seven paces, one might as well be looking out a window as looking at a canvas. The colors are perfect, which is remarkable given that the artist had to make and mix his own paints out of oil and insects, minerals, plants, and whatever else came to hand.

I am fascinated by the way a great artist like Vermeer was able to take a two-dimensional piece of fabric and turn it into an image capable of displaying time and truth, majesty and mystery. Great art has a depth that defies expression through mere words.

"Mere" words, I say. One might take offense at such a cavalier treatment of the noble word. After all, didn't Jesus describe himself as the Word? Ah yes, Jesus is the Word—the Word become *flesh*, and it is this enfleshment that captivates the great artist.

Insight and Ideas | NARRATIVE VISION

Sometimes the best way to cast a vision is to tell a story. In other words, the division between the narrative sermon and the visionary sermon is not always strongly differentiated in the preaching of the emerging church. A story is often an effective way of putting the vision into context for your listeners.

Another favorite artist of ours is Caravaggio, the great Italian famous for his dramatic and lifelike portrayal of biblical scenes. Caravaggio got in trouble with the authorities for using rough street people as models for the disciples and for Jesus. Caravaggio's paintings are not iconic or idealized like those of Raphael or Michelangelo but offer an honest and truly incarnational picture of Jesus in the world.

It interests me to think about how a word is little more than an image. A word on the page is a visual symbol of an idea intended by the word. The word is a kind of picture or sign, a visual container of information or ideas. Words, in one sense, are economical in that they allow you to get to the point without delay. On the other hand, it is said that one image is worth a thousand of them. Words apparently are cheap.

Some people cannot understand unless they see and cannot see without an image. Preachers who want to help them hear from God will have to learn how to paint pictures with words, creating sermons that speak both deductively and affectively.

How to Paint a Picture

Painting is a *deductive* art in that it delivers the artist's vision as a finished product. Art enthusiasts rarely get the pleasure of observing the artist in the production of their work. Yet when finished, the painting speaks across time, diminished or altered only by the changing context of the viewer.

Painting is also *affective* in that it uses imagery to work on the right side of the listener's brain. Viewing paintings requires emotional intelligence, a bodily kind of seeing. Paintings are physical, made up of canvas, layers of paint, and heavy wooden frames. Their impact is sensual, affecting the heart of the viewer in indelible ways. Art can move people to a different way of knowing and seeing the world. Because the perception of truth is just as important as understanding truth, seeing the world and the Word rightly will always be a primary concern for the preacher.

Painting a picture does not require a great number of steps, few at least that would be universally recognized. Nevertheless, the following steps will serve our need to understand. While the process might not be complicated, the challenge is in the execution.

Resource Recommendation | PREACHING AS AN ART FORM

Calvin Miller is an artist. He is also a preacher, but in Miller's hands, preaching is an art form. He once gave me his business card. It was handmade, with an acetate painting of an eagle embedded into the card. Miller paints pictures with his hands and with his words, which is what makes his sermons so memorable. See, for example, his books *Spirit, Word, and Story* (Baker, 1996), and *Preaching: The Art of Narrative Exposition* (Baker, 2006).

1. Select the Subject

The first step is to determine the subject matter of the painting. Again, this acknowledges the deductive nature of painting. While some artists are content to paint attractive pictures that can serve to delight or to decorate, great visual artists want to communicate. The work might be pretty or technically sound, but if it doesn't articulate something of importance, it will not be of much value. Every painting needs a "big idea." Artists who have nothing to say will not find much of an audience for their work.

Painting is different from photography. Photographs tend to replicate reality, but paintings express it. In the branch of painting known as "photorealism," the artist works to create a portrayal so perfect it looks like a photograph. I saw such a painting in the Vancouver Art Gallery not long ago. I walked past the portrait twice before I realized it was a painting. Even then, I had to examine the work closely before I was sure that it was done by hand.

In the end, the piece was more of a curiosity to me than anything else. I was impressed by the artist's skill, but I found myself asking, if the goal was to make the art as detailed as a photograph, why not just take a photo? It seemed an awful lot of work for something I could accomplish with my digital camera in a matter of moments. The best paintings are not so much concerned with literally replicating reality as with somehow speaking to it and of it. Something greater is being presented in the piece.

Most paintings are impressionistic to some degree. That is to say, the portrayal will not be solely representational but will offer something personal from the artist as well. Oscar Wilde, in *The Picture of Dorian Gray*, said that "every portrait that is painted with feeling is a portrait of the artist, not of the sitter. The sitter is merely the accident, the occasion. It is not he who is revealed by the painter; it is rather the painter who, on the coloured canvas, reveals himself."[1]

Discussion Question 24 | "OVER THE TOP" PREACHING

Preachers ought to be passionate. Emotion has a legitimate place in our preaching, but can we take it too far? What are the signs that our passion has gone "over the top"? When does emotion morph into cheap manipulation?

The painter is not incidental to the painting. The painting is an expression of the artist's vision. It is her view of truth—his view of the world. The painter begins with a big idea, then seeks to use the elements of the painting to communicate the idea.

A primary means by which the painter expresses the subject matter is through the use of *ground* and *figure*. Pierre Babin explains the difference: "Figure" refers to what is the direct focus of our attention: the printed matter on the paper, the persons or action portrayed in photos or on the television screen. The "ground" in print media is the paper, the white spaces, the layout and the contrast.[2]

In terms of painting, *figure* describes the primary elements of the painting that tell the picture's story. Every picture is presented from a particular angle or point of view and placed within a context. The context is the *ground*. Babin says the ground "is usually the organization of the lines and masses. It also includes the light, the framing, the color, the texture, and even the spatial and temporal environment."[3] The figure is the thing that captures the viewer's attention, but the ground, by contrast, is what allows the figure to stand out and speak. The painter begins, then, by determining the purpose of the painting and then orders the elements accordingly.

Insight and Ideas | POSTMODERN PEOPLE ARE SEEKING GOD

According to Mark Driscoll, pastor of Mars Hill Church, an "emerging" postmodern congregation of four thousand people in Seattle, all the hype about experience-seeking might be missing the point. "Postmodern people aren't seeking experiences," he says; "they're seeking God. And the point of preaching is to unveil him."

Mark Driscoll, "When God Is Revealed, Knees Bow," *PreachingToday.com*. See also Mark Driscoll, *Confessions of a Reformission Rev.* (Zondervan, 2006).

Painting requires time and thus can be expensive. Historically, paintings were seldom painted on a whim. The expense tended to ensure that most paintings were undertaken for a purpose. Battle scenes were commissioned to commemorate a great victory, say at Trafalgar or Waterloo. Biblical scenes were intended to encourage faith among the people. Portraits of royalty and other great persons were ordered for public relations reasons. Portraits of kings and queens, for instance, feature the monarch as the dominant figure, set against a highly symbolic ground. Usually one finds the royal jewels, orbs, and scepters casually arrayed on a nearby table. Richly colored fabrics drape the portrait background. All of which is designed to declare the sovereignty of the figure on display. Such paintings were intended to motivate the viewer to the respectful submission appropriate for a subject toward a monarch. This, then, is the painting's "meaning"—the artist's intention for the work.

The meaning of a painting is the invention of the artist, who chooses what will be in the painting and who will be featured. The artist chooses what will be focused on in the foreground and what will be featured in the background. In short, the artist chooses what he or she will "say" through the work.

It must be said, however, that many recent artists and critics would argue against this insistence on meaning. This is not to say that art never has meaning but that the meaning is not assigned by the painter. Assigning meaning is the privilege of the viewer. This "reader response" approach to art allows the viewer to determine meaning in whatever is impressed on his or her consciousness when the piece is first encountered.

Andy Warhol was one of the first and foremost purveyors of this postmodern understanding of art. Attending the Warhol museum in Pittsburgh, I found the building full of boxes painted to look like Brillo and Del Monte crates, reproductions of Campbell's Soup cans, and serial silk screens of celebrities like Elvis, Marilyn, and Mao. One room offered a Warhol installation featuring several huge white pillows floating indiscriminately, kept airborne through strategically placed jets of air. The viewer was encouraged to enter the room and to play with the pillows. I have no idea what it was supposed to mean. Theoretically, it was supposed to mean whatever I wanted it to mean. I was the viewer, and it was all up to me. Yet I don't believe this was entirely honest. Most artists, if they are cornered, will grudgingly admit that they intended something meaningful in their work.

Insight and Ideas | SENSING THE TEXT

Physically sense your text. Using each of the five senses, describe, as best you can, what the text looks like, tastes like, smells like, sounds like, and feels like.

Take the Scaatchi Gallery, for instance, an expensive London storehouse of cutting-edge art. Much of what I found there was vulgar, and some of it was mean. Some pieces were genuinely interesting, but most were incomprehensible. I found it humorous to notice that the high-toned patrons tended to spend as much time reading the little white cards on the wall as they spent looking at the art. The cards gave the title and a few words of explanation. The viewers would look curiously at a piece for a moment, perhaps laugh or scratch their heads, and then rather quickly look to the card for some kind of meaning. Make no mistake, it might be obscure and it might be ridiculous, but the artist always means something by the piece. There is always a purpose. Art is never by accident.

If you want to paint a picture, this is your first task: you must decide what you want to say. What is the purpose for your investment of time and energy?

2. Compose the Scene

The second task of the painter is to put paint to canvas and compose the scene. While this task is where all the skill and effort come into play, it is considerably less significant than the selection of the subject. On the other hand, the biggest and best of ideas will languish if it cannot be communicated. The artist's execution of the painting is what allows it to be seen.

While the subject matter deals with the deductive side of painting, composition grasps the affective nature of painting. As with preaching, painting involves making a vast array of choices related to medium, texture, shape, light, and more. Each decision affects the way the piece will move on the viewer's consciousness. The artist wants the viewer to feel something that empowers them to respond in a meaningful way.

Resource Recommendation | PREACHING AND THE EMERGING CULTURE

Many books have tried to rethink preaching for contemporary times. Two of the more interesting ones are Doug Pagitt's *Preaching Re-Imagined: The Role of the Sermon in Communities of Faith* (Zondervan, 2005) and Scott Gibson, *Preaching to a Shifting Culture: Twelve Perspectives on Communicating That Connects* (Baker, 2004).

The artist's challenge is to represent the subject (the big idea) on the canvas. This representation, however, will not be as exact as a photograph but will be "affected" by the artist's interest in leading the viewer to the desired response. Painting is particularly suited to produce an affective response. A Jackson Pollock painting, with its swirling lines and hodgepodge of colors might be difficult to interpret, but it does promote response. The canvas conveys an exuberance that compels the viewer to reckon with the work.

One aspect of composition that the artist will have to consider is the matter of line and shape. *Line* describes the path left by a moving point on a page. It is the artist's means of marking the outline or edge dividing ground and figure. *Shape* describes a two-dimensional space defined by a line and filled with color or texture or both. The artist's control over these features determines the piece's direction to and impact on the viewer. Often line and shape establish how direct the artist's communication will be. Does he or she use light strokes or dark? Are the lines broad or narrow? Are they straight or flowing? Are the shapes rounded and curvy, or are they sharp and geometrical? Are the textures deep and defined, or are they shallow and sparing? Whether through intuition or intention, the artist composes the elements, selecting each element to communicate the subject.

Insight and Ideas | THE BIBLE AS SYMBOL

The Bible is a great visual symbol in the sermon. Hold your Bible in your hand while you preach. Even if you project the Scripture on the screen, you should read it from your Bible. Point to the text with your finger while you read. Make sure that everyone can see where your thoughts are coming from.

The artist's selections determine the level of *candor* with which the artist wants to speak. Will the presentation be realistic or impressionistic? Will it be idealized or humanized, subtle or direct? Dark, strong lines tend to speak more forthrightly, while soft shapes and fuzzy focus tend to be more suggestive than declarative. The former allows the artist to direct the viewer more overtly, while the latter requires more participation on the viewer's part. Sometimes both aspects will be used in the same painting, allowing the artist to focus attention directly on one aspect of the picture while offering a more open interpretive response to another segment. Again, the artist controls what is on the canvas. No choice is incidental or accidental.

A second category of choices the artist must make has to do with *color* and *light*. Will the colors be bright or muted? Will the use of light be direct or indirect? Will it cover the area or center attention on specific areas of focus? These are choices that affect the *mood* of the piece.

Through the use of color, the artist can control, to some degree, the emotional temper of the viewer. Bright colors tend to produce more exuberant emotions. Subdued colors, not surprisingly, evoke a calmer and more subdued response from the viewer. Colors can combine across the spectrum to create a sense of congruence and "rightness." Colors that clash, on the other hand, tend to produce a sense of unrest and disequilibrium. Some colors are "warmer" (orange) and some are "cooler" (blue). Some evoke a sense of freshness and growth (green), and others do just the opposite (grey). Shading provides the artist a further means of expression. Artists like van Gogh are masters at using a variety of colors that combine to create the impression of another color altogether. Some such paintings need to be observed from a distance to get the proper effect because distance blends the colors.

 **Insight and Ideas** | THE ELEMENTS OF VISUAL ART

Ground and Figure

The subject set against its context.

Line and Shape

Indicate the artist's level of candor.

Color and Light

Control the emotional temper of the viewer.

Light is a powerful artistic tool, as can be seen in the work of the hugely popular contemporary painter Thomas Kinkade. Known as the "painter of light," Kinkade is often criticized for the nostalgic and sentimental nature of his work. Whether or not one appreciates his work, one cannot question his mastery of using light as a means of achieving his effect. This effect is largely a matter of varying the degree and the placement of light in the composition. These variations of light are achieved by the use of brighter and darker shades of color and lead the viewer's eye to specific locations on the canvas and to particular points of focus.

The effect the painter realizes is calculated, created by the choices of ground and figure, line and shape, color and light. Viewers are affected by artists who can master these elements.

Preaching the Visionary Sermon

Painting is a powerful metaphor for visionary preaching. Like the painter, the visionary preacher lives at the intersection of deduction and affection. The visionary preacher comes to lay before the listener a big idea, a message that will change their lives. Unlike the declarative preacher, however, this preacher chooses to communicate his or her message by means of a powerful vision of an altered future under God. The visionary preacher paints a picture that will bring the listener-viewer to a point of reckoning. Having been exposed to the vision, the listener will have to reckon with what he or she has seen.

 **Resource Recommendation** | EMERGING CHURCH WEBSITES

In order to understand the "emerging" church, check out these weblogs:

www.emergentvillage.com

www.theooze.com

www.emergingchurch.org

www.the-next-wave.org

www.emergingchurch.info

The visionary sermon has become the preferred method of many of the younger preachers within the "emerging" church. Dan Kimball, for one, sketches an approach to preaching that is forthright and clear yet sensual and affective in its impact on the listener. Kimball admits to preaching thirty-five to forty-five minutes every week. He believes in preaching with great depth, but that depth is communicated through a wider palette than words alone allow. "What I am saying is that in communicating to emerging generations, we must not limit our mode of communicating truth merely to the use of words."[4]

Preaching in the emerging church has several hallmarks. Among them is the emphasis on a *multisensual atmosphere*. As Kimball said, these preachers are willing to use a variety of media to communicate the message, including the visual arts, human testimony, silence and reflection, sights and smells (crosses, candles), and even tactile expression. In some emerging churches, listeners will pick up a copy of a journal from a bin on the way into the service and write whatever response seems appropriate to him or her, adding it to the comments others have made in previous weeks. The journal will then be deposited back in the bin after the service for someone else to use another week. These journals, filled with drawings, poetry, and prose, offer a unique means of helping the listener reckon with what he or she is hearing. Other times listeners will be given lumps of modeling clay to play with during the sermon or will be led to stations scattered around the building where they can offer a variety of creative and immediate responses.

Visionary preaching in the emerging church is *formed in community*. Such churches believe in the power of the church—people committed to one another in a process of transformation. These churches invite people to experience the gospel within the community. Preaching is not just about laying out the arguments or doling out the facts. The facts will follow the believer whose faith emerges out of experience in the community. Preaching, then, is colored and shaped by the vision expressed in the community as a whole. The sermon is not simply the words the preacher offers but the entire experience of thinking, learning, and feeling in the context of people who have gathered for that purpose.

In the emerging church, preaching is also *integrated with worship*. These preachers understand that worship can be about the head as much as preaching can be about the heart. Worshipers can learn, just as listeners can feel. The "worshipfulness" of preaching can be seen in the expectation that people will participate in the process, if only internally. While the message is produced in a deductive, "Here's the thing" manner, the listener is expected to do business with the Word, responding to and interacting with what is presented to him or her. Sometimes the integration of preaching and worship is literal; the worship leader will intersperse the music with the message, and the preacher will interrupt the sermon with songs of praise.

Practical Exercise 18 | IMAGE STORMING

Spend at least twenty minutes "image storming." Take your sermon theme and imagine as many images, illustrations, metaphors, and stories as possible, all connected in some way to what you will be saying. Make the list as long as you can. You will use only the very best, but the longer your list, the more likely you will be to strike gold.

Visionary preaching for the emerging church focuses theologically on the *mystery of the ancient-future outlook*. There is a deductive kind of forthrightness about such preaching. Contrary to a secular postmodernism, these preachers are focused on the metanarrative of the Bible. Their theology grows out of a holistic reading of Scripture that is deep enough to respect the ancient mysteries yet relevant enough to meet contemporary needs. Their faith is rooted in the truth, once and for all delivered to the saints, but is simultaneously humble enough to respect the sense that this God is bigger than we can control or box. This is one of the reasons that the art metaphor is so valuable to such preachers. The preacher as an artist has a canvas large enough to accomodate such a breadth, a palette varied enough to work with such subtleties.

Visionary preachers in the emerging church understand their task as providing *motivation for all of life*. There is a sense that the sermon continues to live throughout the week, much like a painting lingers in the viewer's awareness. The sermon is not a static presentation that dies upon delivery. The sermon offers the Word of God, which lives and pulses with the breath of God himself (2 Tim. 3:15–16). It is the gift that keeps on giving. More than words, the ideas and the operation of God's Holy Spirit remain active long after the music has ended and the people have gone home.

Finally, visionary preaching in the emerging church understands the *humility of the fellow struggler*. The preacher knows that he is not the ultimate authority, unlike a motivational speaker who knows it all and has the DVDs for sale to prove it. The preacher, rather, is stumbling heavenward just like everybody else. In some ways, she might be a little more experienced; most often, however, that experience has only created the need for further grace. The visionary preacher, like all good preachers, understands that the authority for the sermon comes from God himself through his Word.

Insight and Ideas | AFRICAN-AMERICAN PREACHING

Much African-American preaching is visionary preaching. Building on the beauty of the biblical text, preachers like Gardner Taylor, E. V. Hill, and even Martin Luther King Jr. paint pictures for their listeners and then "make a beeline for the cross." King's famous "I Have a Dream" speech changed the world in part because the imagery of "little black boys and girls holding hands with little white boys and girls" was so evidently sensible and indelible in our memories.

Specifically, then, how does one preach the visionary sermon? The method resists a step-by-step approach, much like painting does. The paint-by-numbers approach to preaching will not produce a pleasing product. This approach to the sermon rests less on steps than it does on understanding how to use the elements. The preacher, then, will intuitively order the elements in a way that will make the desired impression.

1. Determine the Vision

Like the painter, the visionary preacher must identify his or her subject matter. What will occupy the ground, and what will be the figure? As with declarative preaching, visionary preachers need a big idea, though that idea will be expressed pictorially.

The sermonic vision is derived through hard deductive study of the Bible. Though some will feel tempted to take a shortcut, there is no easy way here. The visionary preacher must do the hard work of exegesis, struggling to determine the message of the Bible according to its intention. Such preachers may be sensitized to the affective, human element of the text, and they may be more open to the mysteries, but nevertheless, the mission and message of the Bible must be the mission and message of the preacher.

The visionary preacher chooses a text of Scripture and seeks to understand it. People who look at paintings often fail to understand the technical preparation that underlies a work of art. Painters don't just stand before the canvas and let the colors fly. The deductive work must be done so that the message is rightly measured and the mission is fulfilled. Visionary preachers do not presume upon the Bible but look to let it speak for itself. Having heard from God in his Word, the preacher can then communicate what God is saying. The preacher's task is not to create meaning but to create a means of speaking God's meaning. The preacher's job is to help people hear from God.

Insight and Ideas | ACCOUNTABILITY AND INTEGRITY

Preachers need to be accountable. The history of preaching is riddled with discarded preachers whose gifts were nullified by their personal sin. Don't ever be afraid of letting others ask you hard questions and hold you to account. Honesty before people and before God will help ensure that you preach with integrity.

The visionary preacher listens for the voice of God, but not in a detached and abstract way. The visionary preacher is looking for a picture of the truth that will result in a practical application. He or she will be concerned to bring the listener to a point of reckoning. He or she reads the Bible searching for an answer to the question, what will it look like when we hear what God is saying and actually do what he says? The preacher seeks to visualize the answer, seeing it in terms of real people and real events. The answer to that question will determine what life looks like as people hear and respond to God, which is a way of saying that visionary preachers read for application and seek to motivate listeners to action by means of a compelling picture of an altered future.

Discussion Question 25 | LEGALISM AND APPLICATION

Application has become a lot more challenging in these days of "postlegalism." How does the preacher suggest an application of the sermon without creating a legalistic requirement? Should preaching be prescriptive, or does that just create more unwelcome guilt?

To determine the vision, then, the preacher needs to distinguish ground from figure.

Ground and Figure. The preacher needs to identify the *who* or the *what* that will be at the center of the scene. Is the focal point a person, or is it an idea? Will the preacher establish the listener as the primary focus of the vision, or will the approach be more indirect, perhaps having a biblical character or a hypothetical person take the center of the scene.

The central figure of the sermon must always be seen against its environmental background. Where is the picture located? Is it a domestic scene? A biblical scene? Perhaps the vision lives in a professional environment or a relational environment, or perhaps it lives within the church itself.

What are the circumstances giving rise to the concern? Will the vision exist in a supportive environment or one set against it? Does the issue require immediate attention, or is it something less insistent? Is the vision set against a problem, or does it reinforce something wonderful and good?

What needs to be drawn into the picture to help it make some sense? Are there technical matters that require explanation? Is the environment foreign to the normal experience of the listeners, requiring visual description?

For example, let us say that you have selected to preach from Jesus' Sermon on the Mount—particularly his discussion of murder and the impediment that anger can be to worship (Matt. 5:21–23). Emerging from your exegesis, you have determined that the big idea of the text is "Contempt Kills." First, it kills one's brother. Jesus said that if you call someone "fool," you have acted in your heart just as if you had killed that person with your hands. Second, it puts you in danger of losing your life, if Jesus can be believed. The one who holds another in contempt is in danger of eternal judgment. Third, if that were not enough, it kills one's worship. If you have a relational problem—someone has something against you because you have treated him or her with ugly contempt—your worship will not get past the ceiling. You might as well immediately stop what you are doing, go make things right with the person, and then come make your sacrifice of praise.

Insight and Ideas | AN OPTIMISTIC VISION

Our vision for the congregation ought to be optimistic. Pessimism is easy. We can always find reasons to be critical of the crowd, calling them down for their sins, real or perceived. No doubt, the criticism could be warranted, but what your mother taught you is still true: you catch more flies with honey than with vinegar.

Why not look for opportunities to praise your congregation? Take time to praise them for the things they do that please God. If you reinforce the good the people do, they will be inspired to do good even more.

Your homiletic *figure* is the one who comes to worship. You may want to specify that person, describing your own experience perhaps or that of another person, real or imagined. Perhaps you will decide to impose the image directly on the listener ("When you come to worship ..."). You may have a particular instance in mind, or you may treat it hypothetically.

The *ground* is an environment of bitterness, where worship has become futile and prayer is now perfunctory. How broadly you want to draw the image depends on how wide a canvas you want to use. Your vision could be very specific and very personal, or you could choose to speak broadly, describing church- or community-wide conflict.

You may want to be deliberate in your discussion of the circumstances. Contempt, deserved or not, will always have a cause. Whether you choose to give the details in the background or simply evoke the environmental heaviness depends on your own intuitive sense.

2. Articulate the Vision

Having determined the message to be preached, the visionary preacher then moves to create a compelling word picture of the vision, composing the scene. The challenge is to put forward the big idea framed as a visual image.

It could be that the visionary sermon will comprise a series of pictures, a little like a comic strip, or perhaps even like a dual picture with a "before and after" aspect. The final focus of the visionary sermon, however, is always on the "after," always on the last picture in the strip, because preaching is about the gospel and must always give the listener hope.

Line and Shape. What kind of treatment does the text itself propose? Is this a text that requires firm handling, or does it require a softer touch? Should we approach the matter directly, or can we be more subtle in our manner? Should we draw our lines clearly, or is this the place for humility as we come face-to-face with mystery? Should the preacher speak with candor, or is a little tact in order here? It all depends on the text and the message.

What shape will we give the message? Will our descriptions be full and comprehensive, or will they be suggestive, allowing the listeners to fill in the details for themselves? Will the preacher move aggressively toward the conclusion, or would it be better to let the sermon simmer, letting it "fester" for a time, working subtly on the listener's psyche?

Color and Light. Color relates to the sermon's affective direction. Light refers to the sermon's mood. The colors on the preacher's palette include things like desire, joy, fear, hope, love, and peace. These "affections" are visions in themselves, but they also have a tone to them. The preacher needs to adopt the appropriate tone, speaking hopefully about God's promises and fearfully about his majesty.

The homiletic lighting will likewise be purposefully set, according to the intention of the subject matter. Should the preacher approach the subject positively and hopefully, or would it be better to establish a darker, more consequential mood? Perhaps both might be in order for the benefit of contrast. It all depends on the message the preacher has in mind.

Insight and Ideas | THE PAIN AND THE PRESENCE

Visionary preaching can be painful because we surface difficult memories and emotions for the listener. As you help your listeners feel the pain, make sure you always invoke the healing presence of Jesus Christ. Holding together "the pain" and "the presence" will create a safe place for exploring hard things in people's lives.

Looking again at the sermon on contempt, you may decide to offer a pair of images. The text seems to indicate a dual imagery, focusing initially on the one who finds his worship hindered by his hatred for his brother. Jesus' use of the word *therefore* in verse 23 leads toward a brighter picture, however. Preaching always must be gospel. As the text shows, the second, more hopeful image must be the focus. It will stand out more sharply, however, set against the more negative image offered by the text. Hope stands out more vividly against a backdrop of despair.

You decide, then, to place two visions side by side. The first is drawn with broad, straight lines. Jesus has already spoken judgment and so must you. It is a hard word—harder than one might think to be the case. Since childhood we have told ourselves that "sticks and stones can break my bones, but names will never hurt me." Not so, Jesus said. The evil name is just as damaging as the stick that ends one's life. This hard word must be spoken firmly.

Further, you decide that the shape of your sermon will not focus on the details, such as why the dispute arose and who might be at fault. You choose instead to shape your presentation emotionally, helping the listener to feel the consequences of an angry heart and the impossibility of communion when one treats one's brother so self-righteously.

The colors of your painting will be dark and brooding. The light will be darkened. One comes to worship in a furtive kind of way, as if one knows there is something shameful about it. The lights are low, as if to keep one's actions hidden. The atmosphere is stifling and uncomfortable. We want to leave the premises quickly lest our duplicity be revealed.

Thankfully, the text gives us the opportunity to paint a second picture. The original picture weighs so heavily on the worshiper that he or she determines to change. Getting up from the place of worship, the worshiper finds the willingness to reconcile. God's grace is sufficient, and a new hope now ensues. The second image, then, is everything the first one wasn't. The lines are lighter and more carefree. The shape is flowing upward. The emotions now are all positive, and the colors are all bright. Light floods the second scene because God's glory is now present. Worship is wonderful and so is a life at peace with all humanity. It is a powerfully appealing vision, compelling all who see it to do what is right in their relationships and before their God.

Insight and Ideas | THE PHYSICAL ENVIRONMENT

The physical space you preach in will greatly affect your impact. Set up the space so that you are comfortable and so that visual distractions are kept to a minimum (microphone and music stands). You may want to select a few objects that visually communicate the sermon themes and set them around the platform. You don't necessarily even need to refer to them overtly. One of the best uses of PowerPoint is to project visual images and works of art that portray the ideas you want to convey.

So far, we have described the images themselves, but what will the sermon actually sound like? What does the preacher actually do?

It might be easier to describe the intuitive sermon in terms of what the preacher doesn't do. Visionary preachers do not make points. They tend not to use outlines and fill-in-the-blank handouts and PowerPoint slides. They have too much confidence in the power of their pictures to be so heavy-handed.

You really are free to follow your best impulses. Painting is an intuitive medium, and the visionary preacher will likely sense the best means of presentation. The visionary sermon will usually comprise more than one scene, presented in a linear or nonlinear format. The key is to make sure people can see that what you are doing derives directly from the Scripture, taking time to explain whatever is unclear. In the end, be sure to give people some tangible means of expressing their responses. The end of the sermon should offer a vision of what life might look like now that we have seen a picture of what God wants. Now we know what we will do.

For Example: Rob Bell

A few years ago, Rob Bell planted a church in Grandville, Michigan. Wanting to start well, Bell chose to establish his ministry by preaching through a book of the Bible. He chose Leviticus. While many preachers have championed systematically preaching through books of the Bible, few have ever counseled beginning with the Pentateuch. Genesis, maybe, but never Leviticus.

Resource Recommendation | NOOMA

Rob Bell offers a variety of excellent sermon starters on video that you can use. Check it out at www.nooma.com. These video clips raise questions visually and offer ideas so that your listeners are ready to hear you when you start preaching.

See also Bell's provocative book, *Velvet Elvis: Repainting the Christian Faith* (Zondervan, 2005), an invigorating expression of Bell's artistic approach to Christian life.

Five years later, more than ten thousand people come every weekend to hear Bell preach the Bible. Apparently you can preach from the whole Bible today—even the book of Leviticus. Perhaps Bell's time spent in one of the least preached texts of Scripture (Leviticus) was balanced later on by the six weeks he spent in the most preached text in Scripture: John 3:16.

Bell is a deductive preacher. He believes in the Bible, and he longs to make it clear. According to Ed Dobson, "Rob is driven by a passion to teach the Bible, shaped by understanding the Bible in its context, then applying the Bible to where people live. At the core, he's about the Bible."[5]

Bell's preaching is also affective. It is about more than passing along information. "I believe [that preaching] is an art form," he says, "and I want to rescue it back from the scientists and analysts. I want to see the poets and the prophets and the artists grab the microphone and say great things about God and the revolution. I think a whole art form has been lost that needs to be recaptured, a grand ambition for the art of preaching."[6]

Bell achieves this kind of preaching through use of story, image, props, and an inquisitive approach to the historical background of the text. For his Leviticus series, for instance, Bell preached with a live goat on the stage. This visual image helped his listeners connect with the historical background of the text in a tangible way. For Bell, history is about real people and real places. There is not much this preacher will not do to try to collapse the distance between text and today.

Sermon Example | "EASTER STORIES" Matthew 28

This sermon, offered on Resurrection Sunday, was available on the Mars Hill Bible Church website, mhbcmi.org, where many of Rob Bell's sermons can be downloaded for free.

Bell begins by working through the opening verses of Matthew 28. The sermon develops the idea that the power of the Christian message is in Jesus' ability to conquer death. He draws on the ancient use of the phrase "He is risen; he is risen, indeed," which became a powerful political statement that was most meaningful for people when they were suffering. "I know that it appears as though there is no hope, but because Jesus has risen, death does not have the final word, and I can hope that there is something beyond this."

The sermon is visionary in that it gives the listener a sense that "this is not all there is." Bell accentuates that message by bringing a few people to the platform to tell their "Easter stories" of resurrection and the life that is found in Jesus Christ.

Bell's challenge is to create "a resurrection community" full of people honest enough to share their pain and their rebirth.

Bell loves to get the audience involved. Whether by having them repeat back a pronunciation or by giving them something to touch and do, he wants his listeners engaged. He says, "When I talked about how Ephesians says we're God's handiwork—the word is *poima*, which means artwork—I purchased a lump of modeling clay for everybody. When you walked in, you were handed a chunk of clay. I did the whole teaching around *forming*. 'You're God's art.' The title of the sermon was 'You're a Piece of Work.' "[7]

"God is a God of props," Bell says. "The whole sacrificial system is props. That's how God explains atonement, substitutionary sacrifice, reconciliation. These are abstract. So what does God say? 'Take a goat. Slit its throat. See the blood? That's your blood.' "[8]

Preachers who can help their listeners *see* a better future under God will help them realize that future.

Template for the Visionary Sermon

Preacher: ________________ **Date:** ______________ **Text:** ____________

Title (Subtitle): ____

Good titles are creative and compelling, offering listeners a reason to listen, without giving too much away.

The Subject: ____

____

Describe the sermon subject in terms of its big idea, or theme. Express it in pictorial terms.

Figure: ____

____

What or who is the focal point of the sermon — the center around which everything else finds its focus?

Ground: ____

____

What are the contextual elements against which the figure is set?

The Composition: ____

____

Articulate the vision as it is painted on the sermon canvas. Repeat for every picture the sermon offers.

Line and Shape: ____

____

Line and shape set the sermon's candor. Is the picture direct or indirect, expressive or subdued?

Color and Light: ____

____

Color and light set the sermon's mood. Is the picture dark or vivid? Is it bright or subdued?

Expected Response: ________________________________

____

What does the sermon expect from the people who listen? What does God expect from those who hear?

Example of the Visionary Sermon

Preacher: Rob Bell **Date:** 2004 **Text:** Leviticus 16

Title: The Goat Has Left the Building

The Subject: We can live in forgiveness and freedom because Jesus took away our sin.

Figure: The focal point for this sermon is the "scapegoat," the biblical image of the Son of God who would one day carry away the sins of the people. "Then the man appointed for the task would lead the goat out into the wilderness. The word for this scapegoat is *ahahzel*. *Ahahzel* carries with it the idea of 'taking away.' The Gentile appointed to the task would *ahahzel* the *ahahzel* goat, take it away. It's removed. It's no longer there."

Ground: The goat (the figure) is set against the background of the people gathered on the Day of Atonement. "Picture a couple of hundred thousand people, gathered after ten days of weeping, fasting, and denying themselves—soul searching so they can come before their God to have their sins removed."

The Composition: The people see their sins placed upon the scapegoat, who carries the sins away into the wilderness. This is a picture of the finished work of Jesus Christ, who came to make us holy forever.

Line and Shape: The image is given directly with a strong sense of consequence. "One of the messages we can take away from this is when we are reminded of our failures and of our darkness, maybe our message to the world is 'the goat has left the building.' When somebody reminds you about your past and wants to hold your failures against you, maybe you should say, 'Excuse me. I don't see a goat in the room.' When people feel loaded down and ashamed and feel religion has beaten them down, maybe our word to the world is 'I got something to tell you. The goat? It's gone.' "

Color and Light: The mood is incredibly enthusiastic and optimistic, culminating in the congregation unleashing an extended and boisterous cheer. "In a moment, the high priest is going to sit down. I think it would be appropriate for us to celebrate that the goat has left the building. Some of you are distinguished, honorable, restrained, respected members of your community.... Some of you go to sporting events, and when a man in tight pants and a helmet runs over a goal line, you hug your spouse, you high-five your kids.... What our world needs is people who understand how to celebrate the right things in the right way."

Expected Response: There are times and places where we must celebrate what deserves to be celebrated. In honor of the King of Kings and the Lord of Lords, Jesus, the ultimate scapegoat, let's have the high priest walk in silence. As he walks in silence, you relive when it first became real to you. If we're not constantly recovering and discovering and remembering those first moments, we get stale and moldy. Maybe right now you're carrying something. You had a rough day yesterday. Maybe you've got some sort of addiction. Maybe in these moments as the high priest walks in silence—before he sits down and we raise the roof—maybe you can say, 'God, here, I'm not going to carry this junk around anymore.' "

Evaluating the Visionary Sermon

Preacher: ____________________ **Date:** ________________ **Text:** ______________

Describe one or two of the pictures that the preacher "painted" for you.

____

____

____

To what degree did you find yourself compelled by these images?

(circle one) 1 2 3 4 5

What was the big idea or the key biblical message that the preacher was teaching?

___

___

To what degree did you find this message truthful and persuasive?

(circle one) 1 2 3 4 5

What kinds of responses did the preacher challenge you to make?

___

___

How likely are you to follow through and make these responses?

(circle one) 1 2 3 4 5

Describe the preacher's manner and appearance during the event.

___

___

To what degree did the preacher's manner enhance the sermon?

(circle one) 1 2 3 4 5

Offer any further comments you think might be of help.

___

___

___

___

Chapter 9 | SING A SONG

the integrative sermon

example: Kent Anderson

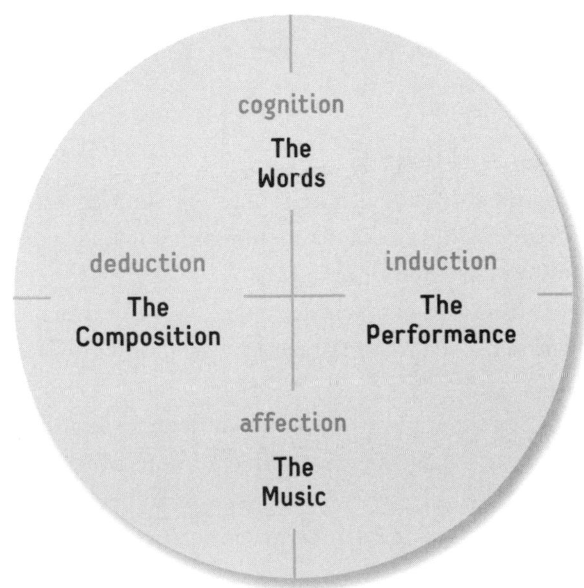

The *integrative* sermon is the natural form of preaching for those who resist limitation to one particular place on the map. Integrative preaching seeks to offer sermons that bring together all of the primary homiletic structures in order to speak to all four learning styles at once. Integrative preaching, then, is both deductive and inductive. One might say that it is "abductive." Integrative preaching is both cognitive and affective. We could say it is "behavioral" preaching. This kind of preaching is not content to focus on one group of people but hopes to offer something for every person and for every part of every person. It is a holistic form of preaching that speaks to the whole person at once. In its comprehensive structure, preaching the integrative sermon is a lot like performing music.

I love music. I love listening to it, playing it, and singing it.

It's just that I'm not great at it. I suppose I'm not terrible either. I play a little guitar, a little piano, but mostly I play my iTunes. I have sung solos and I have sung in choirs. I have even directed choirs—but all that was a long time ago. I have not done as much with music lately. Preaching has become my primary medium of expression, and there, I'd like to think, I've found my true voice.

Preaching is a kind of music, don't you think? At the very least, it is a special type of poetry. I see myself as a preacher-poet. I love the way a sermon sings—how the words roll off the tongue and drop like bombs or rose petals, depending on my purpose. On rare occasions, I've even been known to break into song while I'm preaching.

We don't hear a lot from poets anymore. The only time we hear from poets is when they set their verse to music. All the poets are musicians now—and preachers!

How to Sing a Song

Anyone can sing a song. Songs are sung at parties, at soccer games, and at church. Singing doesn't require much talent, just a tiny bit of heart. But singing well is another matter.

Singing is an abductive and behavioral practice that integrates the head and the heart, the message and the moment. Great singing attempts to bring it all together.

To this point, I have shown deduction and induction as poles on a continuum. I have suggested that in determining the message we will preach from the Bible, we can either choose to begin with the text or choose to begin with the listener. I now propose to change direction and suggest another option.

In fact, my suggestion is not so much a third option as it is the same choice elevated to another level or dimension. I suggest that deduction and induction find their point of integration in something known as *abduction.*

Abduction is described in the work of Charles Sanders Pierce. For Pierce, the relationship between deduction, induction, and abduction is hierarchical. Deduction is the lowest form of reasoning, he believed, because it adds no new information. Induction moves higher up on the ladder, but the loftiest form of reasoning, he says, is abduction, a synthetic form of reasoning that constructs hypotheses to invent new ways of seeing the world.[1]

We might well question whether abduction is a superior form of reasoning. No doubt, however, it can be a helpful way of integrating our presentation when it comes to singing songs and preaching sermons. Leonard Sweet says, "In short, the mind works less by mechanical calculations than by creative leaps and inferences. Abduction occurs when old ideas are combined in new ways; when relationships between things are reconfigured; when metaphors are mixed to yield moments of 'insight.'"[2]

Most preachers recognize the power in these "aha" moments. Even the most deductive preachers would admit, if they are honest, that some of the most powerful works God has done through their preaching were not planned, nor could they have been. The Spirit of God is actively involved in the preaching process, helping people come to concepts we could not have predicted or prescribed.

Resource Recommendation | A IS FOR ABDUCTIVE

Leonard Sweet and Brian McLaren's *A Is for Abductive* (Zondervan, 2003) is an alphabet of postmodern/emergent thought and an introduction to the idea of abductive thought.

At the same time, intending an abductive result is difficult. It may even be dangerous if by abduction we mean we will abandon logic. My suggestion is that we could learn to combine induction and deduction, and that this combination might lead to some powerful abductive results, just like it does in music. Take, for instance, the following musical elements.

1. Understand the Composition

Composition is the deductive aspect of music. When we sing a song, we generally begin with a composition delivered in the form of sheet music or perhaps learned by rote. Whether we just "picked it up" by listening to the CD over and over again or whether we have studied the music carefully, the fact is that someone wrote the song. Even when we write our own songs, we commit ourselves to patterns of notation, harmony, and pitch. This is to say that music is "composed"—it is put together by someone who intended something by the effort. You could say that a songwriter has a deductive intention and that a good singer will invest energy in learning the music well so as to represent the songwriter's intention accurately.

This is particularly important in the realm of classical music, in which replication of intent is of prime importance. I well remember the long hours of practice on my saxophone, trying to get the fingering correct for *The Marriage of Figaro*. The notes mattered, and I had to play them correctly. Technical mastery comes at the price of hard study. You need to learn the composition before you can play it, if you want to play it right.

2. Embrace the Performance

There is another element to singing songs and playing music that is a little harder to define. While music is "given" in the sense that it is composed and recorded as a score, as a performer, you have a certain amount of liberty to bring your personality to bear upon the composition.

This is to say that singing songs requires the inductive expression of the musician. I remember my old voice teacher challenging me to get beyond the notes and to find a way to "make the song my own." When you sing a song, you bring your own bag of experiences to the song. It may make you feel a little tearful, or it may fill your heart with joy. A lot depends on where you've been and what you've seen. I doubt, for instance, that I could be much good at country and western music because my wife hasn't left me, my kids still love me, and my dog died so long ago that I can hardly remember what he looked like!

Effective singers bring their personal experience to the song. Without violating the intention of the songwriter, they combine their personal expression with that of the song's composer to give the song a new level of impact for the one who has the privilege of listening.

Insight and Ideas | LEARNING TO SING

While musical talent is not essential, a preacher can profit from a few sessions with a vocal music coach. A vocal coach not only will help the preacher with her or his breathing and intonation but will help shape the preacher's feel for the nuances of the moment. A drama coach can serve much the same purpose. While preaching is not performing, it shares many of the same elements: projecting, pacing, respiration, and so on.

When one integrates the work of the composer with the work of the performer, one can arrive at an abductive presentation, best heard in the work of the jazz musician. When jazz musicians improvise, they build on a series of chords that provides the basic structure of the music. A blues tune, for instance, might be twelve bars long. The rhythm section plays the same twelve bars of music, creating a base for the soloist, who improvises melodies based on the rhythmic foundation of the chord progression. In other words, what appears to be spontaneous is disciplined by the fundamental rhythm. This discipline allows the soloist to take flight.

David Hadju, writing for the *Atlantic Monthly*, describes a surprise encounter with jazz icon Wynton Marsalis at the Village Vanguard in New York City.

> Marsalis ... performed the song in murmurs and sighs, at points nearly talking the words in notes. It was a wrenching act of creative expression. When he reached the climax, Marsalis played the final phrase, the title statement, in declarative tones, allowing each successive note to linger in the air a bit longer. "I don't stand ... a ghost ... of ... a ... chance ..." The room was silent until, at the most dramatic point, someone's cell phone went off, blaring a rapid singsong melody in electronic bleeps. People started giggling and picking up their drinks. The moment—the whole performance—unraveled. Marsalis paused for a beat, motionless, and his eyebrows arched. I scrawled on a sheet of notepaper, MAGIC, RUINED. The cell-phone offender scooted into the hall as the chatter in the room grew louder. Still frozen at the microphone, Marsalis replayed the silly cell-phone melody note for note. Then he repeated it, and began improvising variations on the tune. The audience slowly came back to him. In a few minutes he resolved the improvisation—which had changed keys once or twice and throttled down to a ballad tempo—and ended up exactly where he had left off: "with ... you ..." The ovation was tremendous.[3]

Preachers know well the annoyance of the cell phone interruption. Interruptions can make a mess of a message bound to the manuscript. Marsalis, however, was genius enough to turn the interruption into the meat of the music. He was so present in the moment that even the tinny annoyance of an electronic ring tone became fodder for his music. A performance like that could not be scripted any more than it could be invented out of nothing. Marsalis, perhaps the world's best living classical and jazz trumpeter, is famous for his iron discipline. No one knows the science or respects the history of his craft more than he. This technical background gives him the aptitude as well as permission for such spontaneity. Sublime moments grow from such a foundation.

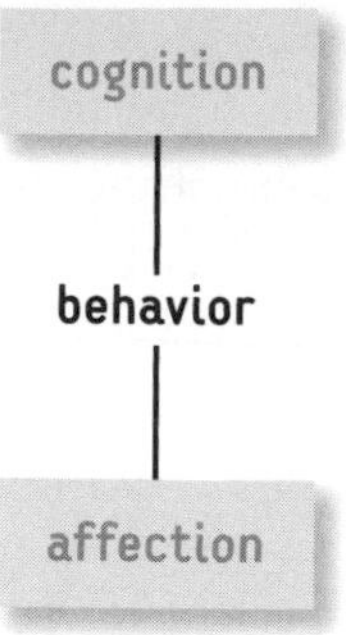

I dream of moments in preaching that are just like that—when we are moved by the Spirit in the instant. God speaks spontaneously through us when we are disciplined enough, and aware enough, to embrace what he is saying and what he is doing in the authentic expression of the moment.

Musicians also help us with another integrative art essential to the tasks of both singing and preaching. Earlier in this book, I suggested that when thinking about how to communicate the message we have heard from the Bible, we might choose between cognition and affection. I said that we could focus on the idea or on the image. But perhaps there is another level to this matter.

Cognition and affection are often seen as two legs of a three-legged stool. Cognition (the ideas we think) is placed alongside both affection (the emotions we feel) and *behavior* (the things we do). These three have an interrelationship, so that any one can lead to any of the others. While it is possible to behave one's self into a cognitive belief or an active feeling, in the practice of preaching, it usually happens the other way around. The believer's behavior is changed as we alter both the thoughts (cognition) and the feelings (affection) of the listener. When head and heart are united, behavior usually follows, and ultimately this is what we want to see happen through our preaching.

Again, singing offers a picture of what I mean. Singing is both a cognitive and an affective medium. When well presented in our preaching or our singing, they combine to produce a behavioral response.

3. Believe the Words

If you are going to sing a song, you have to know the lyrics. You can't sing a song unless you know the words, and you can't sing a song well unless you believe them. The words allow a cognitive experience of the song.

This is seen especially in some of the grand old hymns. "Immortal, Invisible" works not only because of its grand and stately orchestration; it works because the words invoke such a powerful theology of the person of God.

"Immortal, invisible, God only wise. In light inexpressible, hid from our eyes. Most splendid, most glorious, the ancient of days. Almighty, victorious, thy great name we praise."[4] The poetic theology in these hymns is food for the mind and for the soul.

Of course, your singing will always be more convincing if you actually believe what you are singing. I find it strange to hear secular choirs sing Handel's *Messiah* or other classic pieces of music and theology. One only hopes that some of the truth finds its way off the score, through the minds, and into the hearts of those who sing.

Insight and Ideas | SPREADING OUT THE PREPARATION

Preparing to preach can take a long time. Sometimes, in a busy week, we find ourselves running out of time as Sunday rapidly approaches. One thing I have done over the years is work on multiple sermons at once, spreading the preparation out over a longer duration. It doesn't cost any more minutes or hours, but it gives the ideas more time to mature.

4. Feel the Music

You have to put your heart into the music to make it really sing. Music is more than the notes, the harmonies, the tempo, and all the other elements that create the affective expression essential to any good song. A good piece of music gets inside of you. You can literally feel it flowing through your veins, which is why my mother was always nervous about letting me go to high school dances. Evangelicals have a history of suspicion about the physical impact of music. Yet God created music, and he created us. The way that music affects the human body is one of God's gifts to us. Like any gift, however, it must be used in ways that promote his glory.

Instrumental music, or music without words, can produce the same affective result, but when words and music combine, the song truly moves the soul. Truthful lyrics and powerful music can have a healthy effect on each other. The cognitive impact of the words keeps the body's physical response to the music focused and in line, just as the affective impact of the music keeps the head's contemplation of the words from being dry and antiseptic.

Insight and Ideas | REPETITION, REPETITION, REPETITION

Music is repetitive. Our appreciation of even the best music grows the more that we hear it. It is no accident that the musical hook or refrain repeats itself often. These are the elements that take root in our hearts and minds and make the piece sticky.

Preaching needs to take the same course, repeating the key elements of the sermon often to help the message adhere.

I sometimes count how often a preacher repeats the big-idea statement. I have found that it can almost never be too much. How many times did Martin Luther King Jr. repeat the words, "I have a dream"? The more we hear it, the more it sticks.

Perhaps the best example of the combined impact of words (cognition) and music (affection) on behavior is found in worship. Worship music expresses itself in behavior. Worship is a corporate (and private) expression of theological conviction. It happens when people publicly unite to express what they know to be true, by means of corporate expression in song and ultimately in deed. Worship, as we must always remind ourselves, is not only singing songs to God but also serving God through acts of obedient behavior throughout the week.

A key Greek word for worship is *proskuneo*, which means "to prostrate one's self" or to "kiss toward." The word *worship*, then, is a behavioral metaphor. Romans 12:1 calls us to "offer [our] bodies as living sacrifices." This, Paul says, is our "spiritual act of worship." Worship is laying our bodies on the altar. In worship, the truth (lyrics) converges with the will (music), to alter our behavior.

Music has a way of sticking with a person. We all know the annoyance of a commercial ditty that takes root in our minds and just won't go away. Preaching ought to stick like music as we integrate the composition and the performance, the words and music, in a way that takes us to higher levels of motivation to obedience.

Preaching the Integrative Sermon

The integrative sermon combines the primary elements of the sermon, uniting pieces often seen as polar opposites. Instead of choosing one or the other possibility, the integrative preacher will follow the model of the musician, refusing to choose but instead opting to hold all the elements together in the hope of greater impact. In music, an affective medium (music) is given deductively (composition) to express cognitive ideas (lyrics) through inductive expression (performance). The integrative sermon combines these elements to produce preaching that unites a logical argument (cognition-deduction), an underlying mystery (cognition-induction), a human story (induction-affection), and a motivating vision (affection-deduction).

1. The Logical Argument

The *logical argument* offers God's intended message (deduction) by means of intelligent argumentation (cognition). It is the intellectual content we are given from the text of Scripture. In musical terms, we are talking about how the composer's intention is expressed by means of the lyrics. The logical argument is the "meat and potatoes" of the sermon.

Biblical preaching is supposed to be deep. Preaching that feeds people will not indulge in the stories and humor of the day, or so we are told. Real preachers don't serve pabulum. They don't skim the scum off the surface. Real preachers dig down and go deep. They challenge listeners with sermons that get after the heavy and hard truths found deep in the Greek and Hebrew texts.

Insight and Ideas | THE FEAR OF MAN AND THE FEAR OF GOD

Fear is a common issue when it comes to preaching or any kind of public speaking. Much of the fear we face is motivated by our pride. We don't want to fall on our faces. We want people to like us. I suggest that when you are fearful, you try to replace the fear of man with a more healthy "fear of God." The fear of man cripples us. The fear of God empowers us.

Recently a pastor, much my senior, came to me and expressed his concern. "You are in a position of great influence for the future of the church," he told me. I assured him that I understood and that I took my responsibility seriously and with an appropriate level of humility. "You need to teach these students to go deep into the word with their sermons," he told me. "I'm concerned about the future of the church because so many preachers are feeding their people such a weak diet of homiletic kiddie food."

It was a difficult conversation for me because I respected the man. More than that, I agreed with him. I am no fan of weak preaching that holds the church captive in its infancy. As Peter well said, milk is important for children, but we need to grow. Our people need solid sermons that will allow them to develop and to prosper in their faith (1 Peter 2:2). Yet at the same time, I was uncomfortable because I knew that my conception of depth in preaching was different from what he had in mind.

I think we have too often confused complexity with depth. Some of the sermons we preach sound like a legal brief being read, and I have the suspicion that they will inspire our listeners about as much as I am inspired by reading my mortgage document. Of course, a solid sermon ought to have content more inspiring than the description of my obligations as a landholder. Yet I am afraid that even the most exciting theological truth will be lost on people who can barely read the newspaper, much less a complicated sermon. But this is exactly what many people are looking for when they challenge us to preach deeply.

An integrative sermon will make a cogent argument. The sermon will communicate the truth intended by the passage in God's Word. Sometimes, given our distance from the periods in which these texts were written, we may have to carefully explain words, ideas, and constructions that are difficult to understand. While the subject matter might be difficult, however, our explanations should not be.

Insight and Ideas | THE BENEDICTION

The benediction is an underappreciated element of the preacher's repertoire. While more a part of the overall worship experience than of the sermon itself, the benediction provides a powerful opportunity for the preacher to speak blessing on the people.

Study the benedictions of the Bible and learn several of them by heart. Write some of your own. Customize them for your audience, the time of year, and the specific message of your sermon. Don't miss this opportunity to extend the impact of the sermon.

I have put a lot of energy into trying to understand how to communicate God's Word to an emerging generation, only to discover that whenever I apply the fruits of my efforts, the older saints love it. They appreciate it anytime someone offers them the Word of God in fullness and in truth.

Given the levels of literacy we see in much of the world, we may find that listeners are not able to even hear our complicated sermons. Yet this does not mean that we can't offer depth. The simplest truths are the most profound. Integrative preachers feed their people with sermons that are profound but not complicated.

2. The Underlying Mystery

The *underlying mystery* is the place where the listener struggles (induction) to bring his or her presuppositions (cognition) into line with God's truth. The word *mystery* describes a state of being in which something is not yet known or understood. Intellectual appropriation of what is not known or believed does not come easily or without a struggle. In musical terms, we are talking about how the performer comes to own the lyrics in order to express them with integrity. It takes time.

Ideas without ownership are abstractions. Ideas that have not been appropriated have no meaning, either positively or negatively. It is as if they are weightless or inconsequential. They have no currency until one comes to take them for one's own.

I can sometimes be convinced by an abstraction, though not with much conviction. Sometimes when I hear reports on science or law or other subjects I know little about, I may find myself accepting what I hear. The more learned the speaker appears to be (the more esoteric the discussion), the more I am willing to grant the point. I won't engage the point in my own life, but I will allow the speaker the truth of what he says because I have no frame of reference to judge the truth or error of his report. The speaker may or may not know what he is talking about. Either way, it will make no imprint on my life.

Insight and Ideas | TEXT AND TODAY

Many homiletic textbooks take pains to describe the difference between "text" and "today," seeking ways to bridge the gap between the ancient text and the contemporary situation. While I appreciate the difference between the two worlds, I sometimes wonder whether we make too much of it.

For example, the *traditional sermon* might be diagrammed like this:

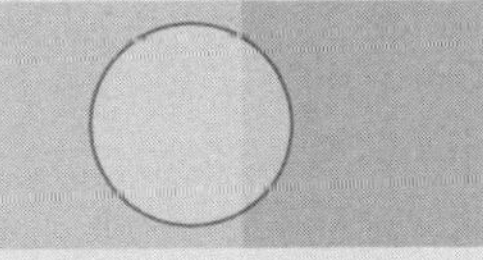

This sermon (represented by the circle) spends most of its time in the ancient text. The *contemporary sermon*, in contrast, spends most of its time in the contemporary situation:

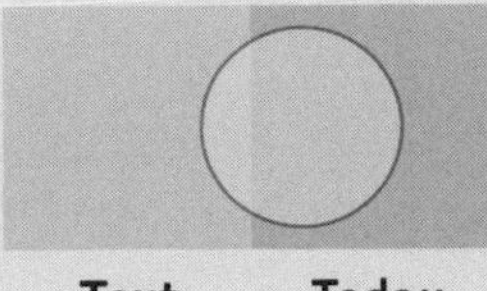

The problem could be with the paradigm. Perhaps the situation would be improved if we were to integrate text and today. The diagram would then look as follows:

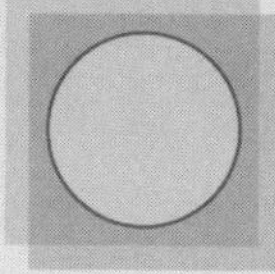

Text Is Today

This is not to make light of the historical nature of the biblical text. It is, however, to make much of the theological idea that God's Word is alive and speaking to God's people in the present.

If I am going to be persuaded by the argument in a way that changes my behavior, I am going to have to get involved. I'm going to have to invest myself in the argument. I am going to have to struggle with the mystery until I can own what I am hearing. If you are going to try to persuade me, we are both in for a fight.

The Bible always challenges us. It pushes us to deeper levels of truth and to higher standards of holiness, and we are not always comfortable with that. We will push back. Typically, preachers feel they need to suppress their own honest struggle with the text. We feel that if we show any kind of doubt at all, we risk undermining our own sermon. The truth is just the opposite. People will respond to the preacher who can own his or her struggle with the text. If we can speak with the voice of the listener, reacting and responding to the challenge of God's Word, we will invite our listeners to do the same. This kind of preaching will require a level of personal honesty not often seen among preachers. It will require that we accept and utilize our own discomfort with the Scriptures and with the ways of God. If we understand that this discomfort can be the stuff that sermons are made of, we may find ourselves less reticent to expose ourselves.

? Discussion Question 26 | PERSUASION OR MANIPULATION?

Is persuasion different from manipulation? When does our honest attempt to convince someone cross the line into a blatant exercise of power? How do we avoid unduly influencing others in our appropriate desire to convince people of the truth?

Biblical preaching ought to expose more than the text. Good exposition will expose something of the heart of the preacher. Of course, there are limitations. Preachers who bleed all over the pulpit will repulse people more than anything else. Still, I have to be real with the people. If I take the typical preacher's stance, standing above the people to drop truth on them, I will find resistance. If, on the other hand, I come to the people with the humbler persona of the fellow struggler, I will find that the audience might actually want to listen and respond to what I have to say.

I've never been much of a fisherman, but I know enough to appreciate that you don't try to reel in the fish as soon as you hook it. You've got to give the fish a little line. You have to let it run. As the fish tires, you can reel it in and bring it into the boat. Preachers who know what they are doing will do the same with their listeners. I like to give time and space in the sermon for the listener to argue for a while. I may even share some of my own arguments. As we struggle together with the implications of the text, the listener will find himself or herself drawn into the strength of the argument despite any intention to stay neutral.

Insight and Ideas | CLOCK MANAGEMENT

Athletic coaches know the importance of managing the clock. Preachers ought to learn the art as well. The preacher is allotted only so many minutes. How those minutes are used is critical. The common mistake is to be more relaxed in the opening moments of the sermon, giving inordinate attention to the first points and images. This becomes a problem when the preacher realizes that time is slipping away and is forced to rush through the concluding sections.

A better idea would be for the preacher to give thought to the amount of time necessary for each of the movements of the message. Timeline planning for the sermon is an excellent idea.

Biblical preachers have not always been willing to trust the listener with this kind of freedom of expression. We have tended to offer principles and propositions, abstracted from life and placed under glass. Yes, we eventually want to make it concrete in application, but we tend to try to leave the truth in as abstract a form as possible, for as long as possible, to keep that truth from contamination. As soon as humans get their hands on truth, they tend to mess it up. So we try to keep the truth transcendent. We like to remain "above the fray."

It is no wonder people question the relevance of our preaching. Abstract thought is never going to intimidate anybody because it never makes any demands. It is "easy-listening preaching," but who wants to listen to that? I like easy-listening preaching about as much as I like easy-listening music, which is to say, not at all. This kind of preaching is powerless to change a person in any substantial way. It doesn't require any particular response. It might be interesting. It just isn't persuasive.

Give me preaching that challenges. Let's talk about some big, mysterious ideas. Let's have it out and see who is left standing when we are done. Let the listener speak up. God's Word can stand the scrutiny. It may be intimidating, both for us and for our listeners, but we are talking about some of the biggest things in the universe, and we need people to make a commitment.

Integrative preachers will get involved in the listener's life, struggling with the questions and the underlying mysteries. We will be honest about our feelings and truthful in our speech. Our preaching will be persuasive and not abstract.

3. The Human Story

The *human story* describes the place in the sermon where we experience (affective) the lives of people who are coming to terms (induction) with God through his Word. Some of those people are in the Bible, and some of those people are in the crowd. You yourself are one of those people. Musically, we are talking about the performer expressing the music through his or her heart. The great musicians can convince you that they have "been there" and that they know where you live. Great preachers can do the same thing by means of the humanity in the Word of God.

Insight and Ideas | PEOPLE ARE PEOPLE

We need to get past the idea that biblical characters were different than we are. We tend to see them in a sepia tone, as if they were coated with a holy patina—a sheen of righteousness burnished over the years by overawed preachers. The truth is that they were people, as imperfect as those who gather to hear you preach. Some of them may have been with Jesus, and many of them deserve our respect. We can learn from them, but we'd do better to identify with them than to idolize them.

Read the Psalms and feel the heartbeats of real people who struggle to know God and to act faithfully in the fitfulness of a world given over to frustration. Or read the Epistles, for that matter. We tend to treat the Epistles as if

Paul delivered them as lectures in the hall of some university. They are letters, with a "Dear Timothy" and everything. Rather than disembodied treatises on systematic theology, these are love letters written from a father figure to those he deeply cares about. Even the book of Romans, with its rich theological presentation, ought to be read against the backdrop of the human situation that existed in Rome at the time. As I said before, there really were Romans. Read the sixteenth chapter and you will learn many of their names.

This is to say that biblical preaching is to be personal rather than sterile. Have you noticed that the sterile places on our planet are the places where life is most precarious — the laboratory, the operating room, the morgue? In the messy places, the disheveled places, life is experienced with the most vigor — the football field, the midway, the bar. Humanity is often grimy, often unkempt, and often beyond our ability to sterilize and to control. Certainly, this is true of the humanity in the Bible, with its stories of stonings and prostitutes and feasts and crucifixions. Think about the people whom Jesus met: hemorrhaging women, raving demon-possessed lunatics, and overstressed type A Pharisees. In the Bible, ears get cut off, fishnets get tangled, and at least one man falls asleep during the sermon. In fact, he falls out of a window in his slumber, which would be funny except that he dies.

The Bible is like that. It is about people — all kinds of people, including the weird ones and the messy ones. The Bible resists our every attempt to sterilize it. I would contend that preachers who take the human side of the Bible seriously are actually being more faithful to the task of biblical preaching than are those who distill the message into neat and bloodless propositions.

We need to tell people's stories, and not just those of contemporary people but of the people in the Bible as well. Personalizing the biblical text is a critical part of preaching. Integrative preaching will gain life and power as we keep it enfleshed in its inherent human environment. The Bible is personal, not sterile. It is a living document about real people and real life. So must our preaching be.

Practical Exercise 19 | INTEGRATING OTHERS

Dis-integration in preaching is often only a matter of neglect. Analyze four sermons written by other preachers. Identify which of the four major sermon elements (the argument, the problem, the story, the vision) are missing. Describe how the missing elements could be effectively added to the sermon.

4. The Motivating Vision

The *motivating vision* describes the place in the sermon where the preacher motivates (affection) people toward God's vision (deduction) for their lives. In homiletic terms, we are talking about the sermon application. In musical terms, we are talking about the composer's expectation or intention for the piece. Great composers know how to move their listeners. The Great Composer has a vision for your listeners' lives as well.

Insight and Ideas | TAGLINES

Consider using taglines to label the major movements of your sermon. Taglines are those short, punchy statements that can summarize the meaning of a whole section of your sermon. They will help you to focus your thinking and to embed the ideas in your listener's mind. For example:

1 Peter 2:19–25

- I love justice.
- Jesus just loved.

Matthew 5:13–16

- Kingdom Christians bring the zing.
- Kingdom Christians light the night.

Integrative preaching is practical and not hypothetical. I believe that the sermon is an event in God's presence. It is a unique moment in time; it can never be repeated. You cannot publish a sermon. You can publish the words that a preacher spoke, or you can record the presentation on tape, but you can never capture the essence of the moment of that sermon. That is because God cannot be captured on tape. You can only note his traces.

Nothing awakens life in a sermon like the expectation that God is going to show up. J. B. Phillips wrote a book years ago called *Your God Is Too Small.* We could probably say the same thing about the sermon. We just don't expect much from God when we set to preaching. Many preachers believe that God will speak through his Word but that it will happen in some muted sense. We don't expect our skin to tingle. We don't imagine that the hair on the backs of our necks will be raised like Isaiah's was when he met God in the temple. Perhaps our sense of God is too hypothetical. We have preached too many sermons in which nothing seemed to happen. We no longer anticipate God's powerful presence. We don't expect the ground to move or the doorposts to shake.

This is to our shame. Preachers are far too tentative far too often in our expectation of God and in our expectation that people will actually respond. Ideas are floated and propositions are posited without our ever describing a specific expected result. Or if a result of the sermon is described, it is suggested as a hypothetical possibility of what could happen someday if we ever found ourselves in the situation described by the sermon—one day, maybe, perhaps ... It is always about what we will do at some other time—at work or at school—when faced with the problem or the opportunity that the preacher has in mind. It is always about some other time and some other place.

Insight and Ideas | THE WARPED BOARD

Trying to integrate elements in a sermon can be like trying to hammer down a warped board. You get one side nailed down, and the other side pops up. But if the structure is going to stand, we must get the board straightened out. Perhaps it needs to be moistened and softened to make it more malleable. God can do that, humbling us and teaching us as we work to understand and appreciate both sides of the issue.

I keep thinking that if God were truly present, we ought to expect more and see more in the act of the sermon itself. Do we really believe that this sermon could change things? Do we really believe that God is present and will work powerfully even in the moment of the sermon? If we did, we might be a little more aggressive.

We could afford to be more aggressive in our preaching. Not in a threatening way. Listeners don't want their preacher to get in their faces and to pound on the pulpit. That's been done, and not so effectively. But listeners do want to be challenged. Listeners love the idea that something critical could happen here and now as we listen to the Word and put it into practice. Could we gain a greater vision for the preaching event? Could we push a little harder and be a little more pointed in directing our objectives?

Of course, we're talking about application, and application is nothing new. Most good textbooks on expository preaching have been talking about application for a long time. The problem is that it is dangerous. It can be easy to moralize, making a text mean whatever we think it ought to mean to further the objectives we have for our people. That is why we need to be committed to a careful reading of the given text. Integrative preachers want to get it right. When we counsel action, we want to make sure that it is driven by the Word of God and not by our own agenda, noble as it might be.

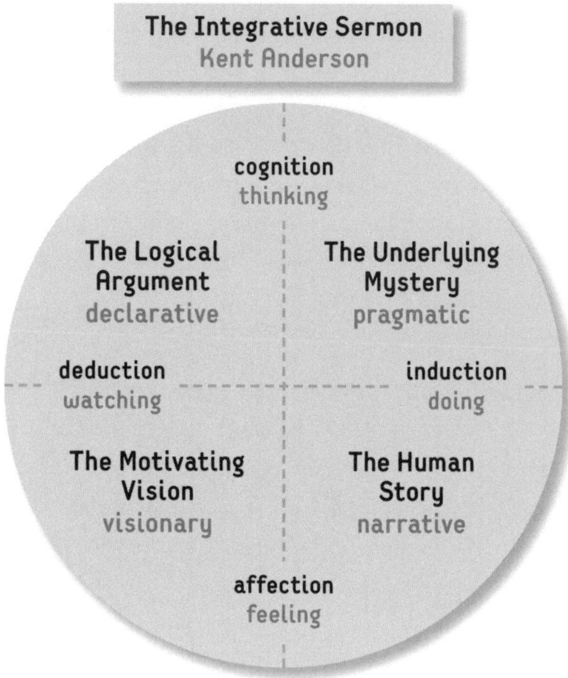

Integrative preaching will offer the listener a motivating vision and will not be shy about expecting response, right now in the moment of the sermon, or perhaps later on, but there will be a response because God is present in his Word and he will not let it return empty. Integrative preaching, then, will be practical and not hypothetical. It will make a difference in our world.

These, then, are the four elements of preaching: the logical argument, the underlying mystery, the human story, and the motivating vision. The integrative preacher will build sermons that range across all four regions.

Earlier in this book, I used the metaphor of a map to describe the four approaches to preaching that are suggested by our choices. These choices exist like territories on the map. As preachers, we need to determine where we will live or how we will move on the map.

One possible option when dealing with these cartographic options is simply to *put down roots*. We can decide that there is only one way to preach — at least for us, given our gifts and the way that we are wired. We can make our home in one of the territories and welcome everyone who is like us to come and hear. This is not a bad thing, because the truth is that there are plenty of people in every category, and as long as we have enough preachers for each territory, we will be all right.

Some of us might not be content to speak only to one group, however, preferring instead to work across the territories. Some of us, having noticed that we have people of every bent and background in our communities and our churches, might want to be more integrative in our approach.

Insight and Ideas | OPTIONS FOR PREACHING

The preacher has several choices:

Put down roots: nonintegrated

Go on a journey: consecutive integration

Tear down the borders: concurrent integration

Integrative preachers have two options. The first option is to *go on a journey*. That is to say, they could focus on *consecutive integration*. The preacher who practices consecutive integration will take the four primary elements of the sermon and offer them one at a time. The preacher might begin with the human story, follow with the logical argument, engage the underlying problem, and conclude with the motivating vision. The order is less important than the idea that every sermon will have something for everyone. If you don't like stories, just be patient; I'll have a point for you soon.

This assumes that each sermon is integrated. Another possibility, however, is to offer a variety of sermon forms over the course of several weeks. Instead of working through each element in every sermon, the preacher could offer a declarative sermon one week, followed by a pragmatic sermon the next, and so on. Over time, every listener hears a sermon that is set to his or her own frequency, and the Word of God is heard.

The second option is to *tear down the borders*—a sort of "free trade" approach to preaching in the globalized world. This kind of preaching is marked by *concurrent integration*. Concurrent integration seeks to mix the various elements of the sermon, allowing the categories to bump into one another so that the flavors blend and something new and dynamic results. This is how life works in multicultural environments, and it might be the most effective way to preach in years to come.

Peter Chang counseled a similar approach to teaching and preaching in an article titled "Steak, Potato, Peas and Chopsuey."[5] Chang argued that while linear thinking has been the dominant form of theological discourse for a long time, it might be time to consider the "chop suey" approach to thinking, in which everything is dumped into the same bowl and eaten together.

I came to this appreciation personally while teaching a course in preaching in Seoul a few years ago. Much of the preaching I had heard in Korea reminded me of the traditional North American preaching I was used to hearing when I was young. Somehow this struck me as a problem, and I began to struggle to help my students think about what an indigenous approach to preaching in Korea might look like.

The solution came to me at lunch one day. Lunch was brought in on the back of a motorcycle and arrayed on a table before us. I picked up a plate and loaded up, each food piled separately. I noticed that none of the Koreans followed my example. They all took bowls, into which they put all their food, stirring it together.

This became for me an effective picture of consecutive and concurrent integration. Both approaches contain all the necessary nutrients: grains, vegetables, dairy, meat. In eating from a plate, I tended to keep the items separate, which pictures the consecutive method of integrative preaching. The Koreans ate their foods from a bowl, a model of concurrent integration for their preaching.

Insight and Ideas | LETTING THE GENRE DETERMINE THE FORM

When considering consecutive integration, it might be worth thinking about the genre of the biblical passage. We could perhaps let the form of the sermon match the form of the text, using, for example, narrative sermons for narrative texts. This would be a natural way to integrate forms for different learning styles across time. Of course, then, the preacher needs to learn to preach several different forms of sermon.

Consecutive integration is relatively straightforward. One would string together the four preaching structures described in this book, either in the same sermon in a series of sermons. Concurrent integration is a little more challenging and requires more creativity and intuition.

Let's return to the concept of abduction. According to Sweet, abduction is an intuitive form of structuring our thinking. It is, Sweet would say, a “chaordic” form of preaching.[6] A *chaordic sermon* would have just enough chaos and just enough order to make sure that everybody stayed awake and everybody stayed on course. This is a pretty good description of how abduction works. The preacher purposefully disorders things or combines ideas and images in unexpected ways, but not so much as to create undue confusion.

The abductive preacher deliberately looks for new ways of viewing old things. Juxtaposition and contradiction are used to create insightful surprises. Sermon elements are deliberately recast—a story, for instance, is used to make a point, or a vision for the future is described in “pointed” terms. The problem is pictured, the vision is argued, the mystery is storied, and so on. All the elements are present and nothing is compromised. Like the jazz musician who uses the discipline of the rhythm and sequence to provide a framework for improvisation, the integrative preacher does not compromise the truth to engage a mystery or to offer a vision.

Insight and Ideas | HEIGHTEN THE EVENT

Train your people to expect something to happen in the sermon event. If God is speaking through his Word, we can reasonably expect that his presence will be evident. Listen for his voice. Look for evidence of his working in the people’s hearts. Give them opportunities to respond. In one church I visited, computers were set up around the perimeter of the sanctuary. People were invited to make comments or to ask questions of the preacher, even while he was in the act of preaching. Rob Bell gave his people modeling clay. Even an old-fashioned altar call can serve to give the sense that something powerful is happening.

Think also about the behavioral approach to preaching. Concurrent integration will encourage a participatory, behavioral approach to the sermon, bringing together the head and the heart in the context of community. Ideas are most persuasive when they are worked out in the context of the church. Persuasion is most powerful when it taps into the social structure of a person’s experience.[7] The integrative preacher uses the community as part of the preaching process.

There are several ways to encourage community participation in the sermon-building process. Teams can participate in the conception and creation of the sermon. Who says that a sermon must be the product of only one mind? Dialogue and feedback can be encouraged through journaling, discussion, and response. Preachers can interview people, call for personal testimony, or tell the stories of the people—with their permission, of course. Sometimes I like to address a trusted individual in the congregation. In doing so, I am able to create a line of communication with the congregation through the individual, who becomes a proxy for the people as a whole.

Behavioral responses to the sermon can be encouraged either during the sermon or when the sermon concludes. Assignments can be given, and people can be held accountable for their completion. We can be much more creative with our altar calls.

However one integrates the words and the music, the composition and the performance, preachers must remember to maintain the integrity of each element. *Integration* is, in that sense, a better word than *balance*. We could have two flat tires that are in balance with one another, but they are not going to take us very far. Balance often involves compromise. We bring one element down to compensate for a deficiency in the other. But what if we were to bring both sides up to their full potential at the same time, one hundred miles an hour down both roads at the same time? Could we not fully engage both the head and the heart? Couldn't we respect both the given Word and the one who comes to listen?

Integration means we bring together two usually separated elements in a way that does not compromise the integrity or the wholeness of either. Musicians do this all the time. I would like to think that preachers might as well.

For Example: Kent Anderson

You will have to forgive me for what might appear to be a burst of ego in offering myself as an example. I assure you, however, that my attempt to advance the practice of preaching comes only in the combination of what has already been done so well by so many in their various worlds. Of course, everyone integrates to some degree. The obvious irony in what has been written to this point is that the four previous structures are not, nor could they be, as pure and distinct as I might suggest. I have heard John MacArthur tell a pretty good story, though storytelling is not his favorite mode. Rob Bell explains points, just as Eugene Lowry explores mysteries. Rick Warren is a master of the motivating vision.

Still, I have tried to let each of them offer the primary contribution they have made to the church through their approach to preaching. All of them are God's gifts to the church. By suggesting integration, I am now offering the possibility that we might benefit from all four, utilizing all the elements of a biblical sermon in the production of our preaching.

Sermon Example | "HIS MAJESTY"
Psalm 8

In the fall of 2004, I preached this sermon taken from Psalm 8 in a small Baptist church in London. Utilizing the "majesty" imagery in the text, I worked to create a consecutive integration of the following elements in the sermon.

The Human Story: This text didn't give me a lot to work with here, but I made a lot of David's experience as king and the British experience with royalty.

The Logical Argument: Here I followed the text exactly, suggesting three points: (1) There is only one God. (2) Sorry, but you're not him. (3) We get to serve him.

The Underlying Mystery: So if God is majestic and his glory is "set above the heavens," then how "in the world" are we supposed to relate to him?

The Motivating Vision: We serve at the pleasure of his majesty (the sermon's big idea). We can be the lord of our own little lives, or we can let Jesus be our Lord, serving his pleasure and finding our own deep pleasure in the bargain.

I don't know if I am a master of the integrative sermon, but I have tried to be particularly intentional about it. I'm pretty sure I'm not done learning, but I have been deliberate about my lessons. For more than twelve years now, I have been teaching, practicing, and writing about an integrative approach to preaching, and I must say the results have been remarkable. I have experienced the favor of every type of listener, from the youngest postmodern seeker to the oldest conservative saint. In my experience, an integrative approach to preaching appeals to all generations, all cultures, and all levels of experience in life or in the faith. Best of all, it allows me to offer up the Bible without apology and with great care. I believe I have been able to help people hear from God.

Integration can be a little messy, but it works. When all four elements of the sermon sound at once, one hears a four-part harmony, a beautiful song sung by the preacher. When listeners understand what they feel and feel what they understand, when they hear the ancient truth in the context of their own experience, remarkable things happen. People hear from God himself, and who can tell what will be the result.

Template for the Integrative Sermon

Preacher: ____________ **Date:** ____________ **Text:** ____________

Title (Subtitle): ______________________________

Good titles are creative and compelling, offering listeners a reason to listen, without giving too much away.

The Big Idea: ______________________________

Describe the sermon subject in terms of its big idea or theme.

Primary Imagery: ______________________________

An integrative sermon is enhanced by the choice of a single primary image that recurs throughout.

The Human Story: ______________________________

____

____

Describe a story (biblical, contemporary, or both) that will connect the listener to the text and sermon.

The Underlying Mystery: ______________________________

____

____

What must the preacher overcome or answer to win the listener's positive response?

The Logical Argument: ______________________________

____

____

Articulate a reasonable argument for the sermon's big idea. Use multiple points if it helps.

The Motivating Vision: ______________________________________

____

____

What will it look like when we all respond obediently to what God is calling us to?

Example of the Integrative Sermon

Preacher: Kent Anderson
Date: October 18, 2003 **Text:** 2 Corinthians 2:12–17

Title: Preaching Stinks

The Big Idea: Preachers don't quit preaching just because some people think they stink.

Primary Imagery: Things that smell.

The Human Story: People are tuned to detect a preacher; they can smell us coming. When we're present, they hold their noses. When we leave, our preacher scent lingers. Paul didn't always come out smelling like a rose. There probably were times when he thought, "You know, this really stinks!"

The Underlying Mystery: If I stink, something must be wrong. All bad smells must be banished, so we invest huge amounts of our money and our time in the attempt to mask our natural odor. The problem occurs when we think we have to mask the fragrance of Christ for those who think we smell like death.

The Logical Argument: (1) We preachers carry a distinctive smell. When you know Christ, he becomes your identity, your scent. (2) How we smell depends on who is doing the smelling. To one, we are the fragrance of life. To the other, we stink like death. (3) We simply keep on preaching no matter how we smell. If some people think we stink, we'll leave it with God, knowing that he is sovereign and will lead us to eventual triumph.

The Motivating Vision: We will keep preaching, understanding that it won't smell right to everyone. Not yet anyway. Smell the cross, the sweat, the blood, the stench of death. Smell the dewy daybreak, the fragrant morning resurrection. Can you smell Jesus? Do you recognize the smell of hope? We preach Jesus, confident in the God who called us. We pour our preaching out like perfume over the feet of Jesus. To some it is the smell of death, but to others it is the fragrance of everlasting life.

Evaluating the Integrative Sermon

Preacher: ________________ **Date:** ______________ **Text:** ____________

What was the human story the preacher used to help you identify with the sermon?

____

____

To what degree did you find yourself able to identify?

(circle one) 1 2 3 4 5

How did the preacher try to help you overcome your objections or answer your questions?

____

____

Was the preacher able to "read your mind" and deal with your stuff?

(circle one) 1 2 3 4 5

What was the big idea or the key biblical message that the preacher was teaching?

____

____

To what degree did you find this message truthful and persuasive?
(circle one) 1 2 3 4 5

What kinds of responses did the preacher challenge you to make?

____

____

How likely are you to follow through and make these responses?
(circle one) 1 2 3 4 5

Describe the preacher's manner and appearance during the event.

____

____

To what degree did the preacher's manner enhance the sermon?
(circle one) 1 2 3 4 5

Offer any further comments you think might be of help.

____

____

____

____

Conclusion

a tap on the shoulder

Last month I went to hear John Stott preach at All Souls Church in London. Dr. Stott is getting a little older now, and they had to help him to the pulpit, but the man can still preach. Once again I was impressed with the power and impact of the Word of God when it is honored by the preacher.

After the service, I had the privilege of meeting Dr. Stott. I thanked him for his ministry to me and to my students over the years. He returned my thanks and asked me what I was doing in London. I told him that I was on sabbatical and that I was working on a book on preaching. "Remember," he told me, "that theology always matters more than methodology."

I agree with Dr. Stott, which is why I spent so much time at the beginning of this book trying to argue for the imperative of preaching based on the doctrine of revelation. If God does not speak, we cannot speak. But given that he does speak, we have a job to do. We must preach.

Still, one can't escape the question of methodology. If we are going to preach, we have to consider how we will preach. Clearly, one can improve one's effectiveness by paying attention to various principles and examples. Our choices make a difference in terms of the impact we will have.

Theologically, however, this idea of choosing is not without its problems. How is it that my good or bad choices make a difference in what God will or will not do? Am I dependent on God for power by the Spirit, or am I responsible before God to serve with wisdom and with courage? Do I have to make a choice?

My emphasis on integration is where the choosing ends. My best understanding of the Bible indicates that both responses are accurate and true. I depend on God for everything that is right and good. I am nothing without him, and my best preaching is empty and void without his Spirit. At the same time, and without any diminishment in either direction, I am responsible before God to do everything in my power to be effective in preaching his Word, as well as in every other area of Christian faithfulness. In short, I must trust and I must try; the one does not contradict the other. The music sounds a harmony.

Insight and Ideas | A WONDERFUL LIFE

Years ago, when I was just beginning in ministry, I attended a convention of my denomination's churches. The speaker was a respected leader, a man with many decades of ministry, from one of our leading churches. I remember his stern face as he looked down at us from the pulpit. "Don't ever step down from the pulpit," he thundered, waving a finger pointedly, "to become prime minister." I remember thinking that the preacher was naïve. Surely a Christian voice in parliament could accomplish mighty things for God. Now, with some twenty-five years of experience, I'm starting to think that he was more right than he was wrong. God is speaking. Could there be any more powerful, more meaningful, or more wonderful way of investing my life?

The truth is, as much as I have chosen to preach, I have been chosen for it. I am well aware of Jesus' statement in John 15:16: "You did not choose me, but I chose you and appointed you to go and bear fruit—fruit that will last."

My calling to preach did not come easily. I had no desire to preach, certainly not as a career, but God used a trusted mentor to stop me in my tracks. Pastor Bruce Mateika, an old friend of my father's, took me aside and asked me if I intended to be a preacher.

"No," I said. "I don't think so."

"Why not?" he asked.

"Well," I said, trying to sound spiritual, "because I haven't been called."

"Why not?" he asked.

That stumped me. "What do you mean, 'Why not'?" I responded. "If God wants to call me, that is up to him, not me," I reasoned.

"That is true," he said, "but in my experience, God's call is heard most clearly when we are actively listening."

Pastor Bruce told me that he saw in me the gifts that might indicate God had marked me as a preacher. He challenged me to make it a dedicated matter of prayer, to pursue the possibility of my calling.

I followed his advice, and very soon I had that special sense of "calling." God spoke to me during a Communion service in a way that brought tears to my eyes and a new level of conviction to my heart. I determined that I would not waste the gifts that God had given me but would invest my life in helping people hear his voice through his Word.

I wonder if you would join me.

Preaching is not complicated. Preaching happens whenever someone cares enough to pass along the name of Jesus. It happens when small groups gather in living rooms. It happens when friends gather in coffee shops. It happens in pulpits and on platforms in churches on Sundays. It is the task of men and of women. It is the task of all who have enough motivation to use their feet—"How beautiful are the feet of those who bring good news!" (Rom. 10:15).

I probably would not have written the verse this way. "How beautiful is the tongue," I might have written, "or the lips? ... How beautiful is the throat of him who brings ..."

Paul praises the feet.

Preaching is feet first, which is to say that preaching requires intent. It must be chosen. You must determine to put one foot in front of the other—to go into all the world. And as you go, you preach the gospel to every creature.

Insight and Ideas | PREACHING STILL WORKS

David Jackman writes, "I am convinced that many more quality preachers could be produced if we were to set our minds to the task. I know that the prevailing orthodoxy is that preaching is an outmoded and inefficient means of communication. I also know that boring and irrelevant pulpiteering is positively counterproductive. But churches are still being filled where the Bible is taught properly, and none of the alternatives is as cost-effective, or as successful, in growing strong disciples."

David Jackman, "Preparing the Preacher," in *When God's Voice Is Heard* (Leicester, UK: InterVarsity, 2003), 190.

I wish I could have seen Paul's feet. I imagine they were blistered and chaffed, calloused and reddened, sweaty and stinky—beautiful feet. Paul's feet took him wherever there were people who needed to hear about Jesus—a small group in Berea, a synagogue in Thessalonica, a lecture hall in Ephesus, and a city square in Athens. Paul had beautiful feet.

I like to read Romans 10 to students in my courses on preaching. I tell them there will be a final exam, but it will not be complicated. When the exam period begins, we will have the students gather in the examination hall. We will simply all take off our shoes and socks and put our feet up on the tables. Those with the beautiful feet get the A's.

I am joking, but in a sense, I wish I weren't.

I probably don't know you personally, but God does, and if you listen carefully, you just might hear his voice. Preaching happens in so many ways and in so many venues, there just might be a place for you—perhaps in a small group or maybe in a pulpit or even on a street corner.

I often wonder what would have happened to me if my mentor hadn't tapped me on the shoulder. It is not something I like to think about for very long.

> "Everyone who calls on the name of the Lord will be saved." How, then, can they call on the one they have not believed in? And how can they believe in the one of whom they have not heard? And how can they hear without someone preaching to them? And how can they preach unless they are sent?
>
> —Romans 10:13–15

Consider yourself sent.

supporting materials for *choosing to preach*

In the CD-ROM that accompanies this book, you will find the following:

- a password "key" allowing six months of free access to the resources (listed below) available to subscribers, including the online sermon-building guide
- a PowerPoint presentation suitable for teaching the content of *Choosing to Preach*
- sample audio sermons from Kent Anderson, Eugene Lowry, John MacArthur, and Rick Warren (sample sermon for Rob Bell, "The Goat Has Left the Building," can be found online using a search engine)

Please use the CD-ROM key to www.preaching.org, where you will find tools that will allow you to do the following:

- Build a sermon in any of the forms featured in this book through use of an interactive online sermon-building guide. The instrument will formulate your work into a single document suitable for printing. Post your sermon for online feedback from others.
- Read and evaluate sermons posted by others. Search texts and key words for ideas, images, and structures for your own preaching.
- Post your responses to the discussion questions listed in this book and read the responses of others. Professors and pastors can arrange their own private "classrooms," allowing students to have their own area for this kind of interaction.
- Read new feature articles by key thinkers in homiletics.
- Read Kent Anderson's blog on preaching, church, and culture. Keep up to date with Kent's current thinking on these subjects.
- Download evaluation forms, PowerPoint presentations, and audio sermons.

notes

chapter 1: first option

1. Bruskin Associates, "What Are Americans Afraid Of?" *Bruskin Report* 53 (July 1973), n.p. See also Joseph S. Tuman and Douglas M. Fraleigh, *The St. Martin's Guide to Public Speaking* (Boston: Bedford/St. Martin's, 2003), 20.
2. Anonymous webposting: http://www.dragonzleyr.net/Q/ntcprint2LS.html.
3. Dan Kimball, *The Emerging Church: Vintage Christianity for New Generations* (Grand Rapids, MI: Zondervan, 2003), 182.
4. Ibid., 175.
5. Phillips Brooks, *On Preaching* (New York: Seabury, 1964), 31–32.
6. Ibid., 5.

chapter 2: second option

1. Merrill F. Unger, *Principles of Expository Preaching* (Grand Rapids, MI: Zondervan, 1955), 24.
2. Robert L. Thomas, "The Relationship between Exegesis and Expository Preaching," *Master's Seminary Journal* 2 (Fall 1991): 181.
3. Harry Emerson Fosdick, "What Is the Matter with Preaching?" *College of the Bible Quarterly* 29 (October 1952): 8.
4. Ibid., 7.
5. Paul Scott Wilson, *The Practice of Preaching* (Nashville: Abingdon, 1995), 20.
6. Haddon W. Robinson, *Biblical Preaching: The Development and Delivery of Expository Messages*, 2nd ed. (Grand Rapids, MI: Baker, 2001), 20.
7. Hughes Oliphant Old, *The Reading and Preaching of the Scriptures in the Worship of the Christian Church*, vol. 1, *The Biblical Period* (Grand Rapids, MI: Eerdmans, 1998), 264–65.
8. Kurt Niederwimmer, *The Didache: A Commentary* (Minneapolis: Fortress, 1998), 4.1.
9. Rudolph W. Giuliani with Ken Kurson, *Leadership* (London: Time Warner, 2002), 171.
10. Charles L. Bartow, *God's Human Speech: A Practical Theology of Proclamation* (Grand Rapids, MI: Eerdmans, 1997), 9.
11. Robert E. Webber, *The Younger Evangelicals: Facing the Challenges of the New World* (Grand Rapids, MI: Baker, 2002), 192.

12. Quoted in Michael J. Quicke, *360-Degree Preaching: Hearing, Speaking, and Living the Word* (Grand Rapids, MI: Baker, 2003), 28.
13. Billy Graham, *Just as I Am: The Autobiography of Billy Graham* (San Francisco: Harper/Zondervan, 1997), 49.
14. Billy Graham, "The Christian Faith and Peace in a Nuclear Age," *Christianity Today*, June 18, 1982, 20–23.

chapter 3: third option

1. David A. Kolb, *Experiential Learning: Experience as the Source of Learning and Development* (Upper Saddle River, NJ: Prentice Hall, 1984), 68.
2. Peter Adam, *Speaking God's Words: A Practical Theology of Preaching* (Downers Grove, IL: InterVarsity Press, 1996), 24.
3. Watts Wacker, cited in Leonard Sweet, *SoulTsunami: Sink or Swim in New Millenium Culture* (Grand Rapids, MI: Zondervan, 1999), 77.
4. Walter C. Kaiser Jr., *Toward an Exegetical Theology: Biblical Exegesis for Preaching and Teaching* (Grand Rapids, MI: Baker, 1981), 19.
5. Ibid., 70.
6. Lynne Truss, *Eats, Shoots and Leaves: The Zero Tolerance Approach to Punctuation* (London: Profile, 2003).
7. Kaiser, *Toward an Exegetical Theology*, 132.
8. Greame Goldsworthy, *Preaching the Whole Bible as Christian Scripture: The Application of Biblical Theology to Expository Preaching* (Grand Rapids, MI: Eerdmans, 2000), 6.
9. Ibid.
10. Fred B. Craddock, *Preaching* (Nashville: Abingdon, 1985), 84–85.
11. Bryan Chapell, *Christ-Centered Preaching: Redeeming the Expository Sermon* (Grand Rapids, MI: Baker, 1994), 42.
12. Haddon W. Robinson, *Biblical Preaching: The Development and Delivery of Expository Messages*, 2nd ed. (Grand Rapids, MI: Baker, 2001), 47–50.
13. Chapell, *Christ-Centered Preaching*, 43.
14. Ralph Lewis writes, "One of my students, a retired army colonel, came up to talk to me after one of my seminary senior preaching classes. 'Last Sunday,' Don reported, 'a thirty-five-year-old man came to Christ when I preached an inductive sermon in my student charge. The man said he'd never heard a preacher who respected him as a person before. I guess he was saying I was the only inductive preacher he'd ever heard.'" Ralph L. Lewis with Gregg Lewis, *Inductive Preaching: Helping People Listen* (Westchester, IL: Crossway, 1983), 163.
15. Raymond E. Anderson, "Kierkegaard's Theory of Communication," *Speech Monographs* 30, no. 1 (March 1963): 1.
16. Ibid., 3.
17. Ibid., 4.
18. Ibid., 8–11.
19. Lewis suggests that inductive preaching is an effective means of blending the pastoral role with the preaching role. In its focus on the listener's need, the inductive sermon serves as a means of group pastoral counseling. Lewis, *Inductive Preaching*, 123.
20. Grant R. Osborne, *The Hermeneutical Spiral: A Comprehensive Guide to Biblical Interpretation* (Downers Grove, IL: InterVarsity Press, 1991), 267.
21. Larry Crabb, *Inside Out* (Colorado Springs: NavPress, 1988), 77.
22. Fred B. Craddock, *As One without Authority*, 2nd ed. (St. Louis: Chalice, 2001), 48–49.
23. Ibid., 48.
24. Ibid.
25. Ibid., 46.
26. Ibid., 48–49.

chapter 4: fourth option

1. Bill Bright, *The Four Spiritual Laws* (Orlando: New Life, 1965), 12.
2. Haddon W. Robinson, *Biblical Preaching: The Development and Delivery of Expository Messages*, 2nd ed. (Grand Rapids, MI: Baker, 2001), 33.
3. John A. Broadus, *On the Preparation and Delivery of Sermons*, ed. Vernon L. Stanfield, 4th ed. (San Francisco: Harper 1979), 81.
4. Ibid., 83.
5. Ibid., 83–84.
6. Ibid., 84.
7. Ibid., 88–91.
8. J. E. C. Welldon, trans., *The Rhetoric of Aristotle* (London: Macmillan, 1886), 11.
9. For a counterargument, consider the comments of Jonathan Edwards regarding the "religious affections." Jonathan Edwards, "A Treatise concerning Religious Affections," *The Works of Jonathan Edwards*, vol. 2, ed. Perry Miller (New Haven, CT: Yale University Press, 1957). I have included quotations from this source in the next section of this chapter.
10. John Piper, *The Supremacy of God in Preaching* (Grand Rapids, MI: Baker, 1990).
11. John Piper, "Battling the Unbelief of Bitterness," *Preaching Today Sermon*, vol. 249, compact disc (Carol Stream, IL: Christianity Today, 2004).
12. David A. Kolb, *Experiential Learning: Experience as the Source of Learning and Development* (Upper Saddle River, NJ: Prentice Hall, 1984), 49.
13. Ibid.
14. Jonathan Edwards, "A Treatise concerning Religious Affections," *The Works of Jonathan Edwards*, vol. 2, ed. Perry Miller (New Haven, CT: Yale University Press, 1957), 96.
15. Ibid.
16. Ibid., 99.
17. Ibid., 99–100.
18. Ibid., 100–101.
19. Charles H. Gabriel, "My Savior's Love," *Great Hymns of the Faith* (Grand Rapids, MI: Zondervan, 1977), no. 452.
20. David Buttrick, *Homiletic: Moves and Structures* (Philadelphia: Fortress, 1987), 24.
21. Ibid., 30–32.
22. Ibid., 163.
23. Ibid., 57.
24. Ibid., 333–63.
25. Grant Lovejoy, "'But I Did Such Good Exposition': Literate Preachers Confront Orality" (paper presented to the Evangelical Homiletics Society, October 2001), 6.
26. Ibid.
27. Walter J. Ong, "Literacy and Orality in Our Times," *Journal of Communication* 30 (Winter 1980): 201.
28. Clyde E. Fant, *Preaching for Today* (San Francisco: Harper & Row, 1987), 161.
29. Ibid.
30. Ibid.
31. Ibid.
32. Charles W. Koller, *Extemporaneous Preaching without Notes* (Grand Rapids, MI: Baker, 1962).
33. Kenton C. Anderson, "The Place of the Pulpit," *Preaching* 15, no.1 (July–August 1999): 23–25.
34. Fred Craddock, quoted in John R. Throop, "Pulpits: A Place to Take Your Stand," *Your Church* 44, no. 2 (March–April 1998): 48.
35. Jay E. Adams, "Sense Appeal in the Sermons of Charles Haddon Spurgeon," *Studies in Preaching*, vol. 1 (Philadelphia: Presbyterian & Reformed, 1976), 10–11.

36. C. H. Spurgeon, *Spurgeon's Sermons: The Memorial Library* (New York: Funk & Wagnalls, n.d.), 19:212, quoted in Adams, "Sense Appeal," 12.
37. Ibid., 2:144; Adams, "Sense Appeal," 13.
38. Ibid., 1:163–64; Adams, "Sense Appeal," 18–19.
39. Ibid., 19:121; Adams, "Sense Appeal," 23.
40. Zachary W. Eswine, "The 'Holy Fancy' of Charles Haddon Spurgeon: Visual Logic for Traditional Preaching in a Postmodern Ethos" (paper presented to the Evangelical Homiletics Society, Orlando, Florida, October 20, 2000).
41. Spurgeon, *Spurgeon's Sermons*, 1:102; Adams, "Sense Appeal," 53.

chapter 5: make an argument

1. "Any man who was only a man and who said the kinds of things that Jesus said would not be a 'great moral teacher.' He would either be a lunatic—on a level with the man who says he is a poached egg—or else he would be the Devil of hell. You must make your choice. Either this man was, and is, the Son of God: or else a madman or something worse. You can shut Him up for a fool, you can spit at Him and kill Him as a demon; or you can fall at His feet and call Him Lord and God. But let us not come with any patronising nonsense about His being a great human teacher. He has not left that open to us. He did not intend to." C. S. Lewis, *Mere Christianity* (Glasgow: Fount Paperbacks, 1989), 52.
2. T. K. Trelogan, "Arguments and Their Evaluation," University of Northern Colorado, http://www.unco.edu/philosophy/arg.html.
3. Jonathan Swift, *Gulliver's Travels* (New York: Random House, The Modern Library, 1931), 282.
4. C. H. Spurgeon, *Lectures to My Students* (Grand Rapids, MI: Zondervan, 1972), 89.
5. John MacArthur Jr. and The Master's Seminary Faculty, *Rediscovering Expository Preaching: Balancing the Science and Art of Biblical Exposition*, ed. Richard L. Mayhue and Robert L. Thomas (Dallas: Word, 1992), xiv.
6. Ibid.
7. Ibid., 137.
8. Ibid., 324.
9. Ibid., 342.
10. Ibid., 343.

chapter 6: solve a mystery

1. G. K. Chesteron, "The Blue Cross," in *Father Brown: Selected Stories* (London: Collector's Library, 2003), 15.
2. Ibid.
3. Arthur Conan Doyle, *The Hound of the Baskervilles* (Oxford: Oxford University Press, 1998). In this famous story, Sherlock Holmes solves the mystery by observing that there was no barking dog when logic indicated that there ought to have been.
4. Haddon W. Robinson, "The Heresy of Application," *Leadership* (Fall 1997): 21–27.
5. Rick Warren, *How to Communicate to Change Lives: Teaching and Preaching That Makes a Difference*, audio lecture and notes (Lake Forest, CA: Purpose Driven Church Resources, n.d.).
6. Ibid.
7. Rick Warren, "Purpose-Driven Preaching: An Interview with Rick Warren," by Michael Duduit, *Preaching* (September–October 2001): 14.
8. Ibid., 10.
9. Ibid., 9.
10. Ibid., 10.

chapter 7: tell a story

1. Richard L. Eslinger, *A New Hearing: Living Options in Homiletic Method* (Nashville: Abingdon, 1987).
2. Robert Fulford, *The Triumph of Narrative* (Toronto: Anansi, 1999), x.
3. Christopher Humphrey, *The Inklings: C. S. Lewis, J. R .R. Tolkien, Charles Williams and Their Friends* (London: Harper Collins, 1981), 43–45.
4. C. S. Lewis, *The Complete Chronicles of Narnia* (London: Harper Collins, 2000).
5. Steven D. Matthewson, *The Art of Preaching Old Testament Narrative* (Grand Rapids, MI: Baker, 2002), 48–50. Matthewson describes the various archetypical story forms as catalogued by Leland Ryken, Robert Alter, Simon B. Parker, and Robert C. Culley.
6. Eslinger, *A New Hearing*, 7–8.
7. Robert Stephen Reid, "Postmodernism and the Function of the New Homiletic in Post-Christendom Congregations," *Homiletic* 20 (Winter 1995): 1–13.
8. Shlomith Rimmon-Kenan, *Narrative Fiction: Contemporary Poetics*, New Accents, ed. Terrance Hawkes (London: Routledge, 1983), 17.
9. Matthewson, *Art of Preaching Old Testament Narrative*, 58.
10. Edgar Allen Poe, "The Tell-Tale Heart," in *The Complete Stories and Poems of Edgar Allen Poe* (Garden City, NY: Doubleday, 1966), 121.
11. Anne Frank, *The Diary of Anne Frank*, ed. Otto Frank and Mirjam Pressler, trans. Susan Massoty (London: Penguin, 2001), 25.
12. Ibid., 76.
13. Bill Oudemolen, "How to Preach like John Grisham Writes," *Leadership* 17, no. 4 (Fall 1996): 91.
14. Eugene L. Lowry, *The Homiletical Plot: The Sermon as Narrative Art Form* (Atlanta: John Knox Press, 1980), 13.
15. Eugene L. Lowry, *Doing Time in the Pulpit: The Relationship between Narrative and Preaching* (Nashville: Abingdon, 1985), 48.
16. Ibid., 25.
17. Ibid., 83.
18. Lowry, *Homiletical Plot*, 25.
19. Ibid., 28.
20. Ibid., 36.
21. Ibid., 47.
22. Ibid., 62.
23. Ibid., 67.
24. Ibid., 68.
25. Eugene L. Lowry, *The Sermon: Dancing the Edge of Mystery* (Nashville: Abingdon, 1997), 78.

chapter 8: paint a picture

1. Oscar Wilde, *The Picture of Dorian Gray* (Oxford: Oxford University Press, 1981), 5.
2. Pierre Babin and Mercedes Iannone, *The New Era in Religious Communication*, trans. David Smith (Minneapolis: Fortress, 1991), 8.
3. Ibid., 64.
4. Dan Kimball, *The Emerging Church: Vintage Christianity for New Generations* (Grand Rapids, MI: Zondervan, 2003), 186.
5. Rob Bell, "The Subversive Art: Interview with Rob Bell," *Leadership* 25, no. 2 (Spring 2004): 25.
6. Ibid., 27.
7. Rob Bell, "Crafting an Experience," *Preaching Today*, compact disc, no. 247.
8. Bell, "The Subversive Art," 29.

chapter 9: sing a song

1. Charles Hartshorne and Paul Weiss, eds., *Collected Papers of Charles Sanders Pierce* (Cambridge: Harvard University Press, 1960), 5:171.
2. Leonard Sweet, "And Glory Crowns the Mercy Seat: Towards an Abductive Homiletic" (paper presented to the Evangelical Homiletics Society, Deerfield, IL, October 2002).
3. David Hadju, "Wynton's Blues," *Atlantic Monthly*, March 2003, 44.
4. Walter Chalmers Smith, "Immortal, Invisible," *Great Hymns of the Faith* (Grand Rapids, MI: Zondervan, 1977), no. 34.
5. Peter Chang, "Steak, Potato, Peas and Chopsuey: Linear and Non-linear Thinking in Theological Education," *Evangelical Review of Theology* 5, no. 2 (October 1981): 279–86.
6. Leonard Sweet, *SoulTsunami: Sink or Swim in New Millenium Culture* (Grand Rapids, MI: Zondervan, 1999), 71–106.
7. J. A. C. Brown, *Techniques of Persuasion: From Propaganda to Brainwashing* (Middlesex, UK: Penguin, 1963), 297.

index

Page numbers in italics indicate figures and sidebars. Notes are indicated by the letter n.

We want to hear from you. Please send your comments about this book to us in care of zreview@zondervan.com. Thank you.

GRAND RAPIDS, MICHIGAN 49530 USA

ZONDERVAN.COM/
AUTHORTRACKER